GRUYÈRE

ROQUEFORT

PARMIGIANO

REGGIANO

MANCHEGO

NOV 1 1 2024

D1233870

Cheese
Sex
Death

Cheese Sex Death

A BIBLE *for the* CHEESE OBSESSED

by ERIKA KUBICK

*Stained glass illustrations
by Martin Hargreaves*

ABRAMS, NEW YORK

Editor: Laura Dozier
Managing Editor: Glenn Ramirez
Design Manager: Heesang Lee
Production Manager: Larry Pekarek

Book design by Jen Quinn, Indelible Editions

Library of Congress Control Number: 2021932488

ISBN: 978-1-4197-5354-1
eISBN: 978-1-64700-467-5

Text and photographs © 2021 Erika Kubick unless otherwise noted on page 345
Cover © 2021 Abrams
Cheese Sex Death® is a registered trademark of Erika Kubick

Produced by

INDELIBLE
EDITIONS

Published in 2021 by Abrams, an imprint of ABRAMS. All rights reserved.
No portion of this book may be reproduced, stored in a retrieval system, or
transmitted in any form or by any means, mechanical, electronic, photocopying,
recording, or otherwise, without written permission from the publisher.

Printed and bound in China

10 9 8 7 6 5 4 3 2 1

Abrams books are available at special discounts when purchased in quantity
for premiums and promotions as well as fundraising or educational use.
Special editions can also be created to specification. For details, contact
specialsales@abramsbooks.com or the address below.

Abrams® is a registered trademark of Harry N. Abrams, Inc.

ABRAMS The Art of Books
195 Broadway, New York, NY 10007
abramsbooks.com

Contents

For all cheese sluts, everywhere.

Introduction

THE NUMBER-ONE QUESTION PEOPLE ASK ME IS,

"Why cheese?" Of all the possible passions one could pursue, why did I devote myself to evangelizing what is essentially solidified milk in a state of controlled decay? It's a valid question. Obviously, it's delicious, which was what seduced me in the first place. But this fermented dairy product is so much more than just food.

Cheese is no less than a miracle. It's the extraordinary meeting of two worlds: human and natural. It has the power to ground us in a connection to Mother Nature, the people who create blessings from Her gifts, and the history of civilization. There is something inextricably spiritual about cheese, and fermented foods in general.

A ripe wheel of Harbison from Jasper Hill Farm in Vermont

Fermentation itself is a mysterious phenomenon wherein microbes transform a food through decay. This metamorphosis not only preserves sustenance, it breathes new life into a decomposing product, creating a reservoir of nutrients and flavors. It's resurrection through delicious rot—an acquired taste that is specific to the individual cultures that have historically relied on these fermented foods.

The first coming of Cheesus occurred roughly eight thousand years ago, though scholars argue about the exact time and place. What we do know is that for this first generation of dairy disciples, fermentation was the messiah. The process of converting liquid milk into solid cheese solved two problems. First, it created a durable product out of perishable milk, saving precious nutrients for storage through winter and famine. Second, it did away with the troublesome effects of lactose on digestion by converting it into lactic acid. Thus, by way of Cheesus, the gift of fermentation resurrected the life-giving nutrition within milk.

Cheese is the product of faith, nature, and nurture. In its raw state, milk is blessed with colonies of living microbes from the land, animals, and humans that it encounters along its journey. These microbes begin the act of fermentation, and the milk miraculously shape-shifts from liquid to solid. The young cheese is then entombed in a cool, humid cave, where it matures and transforms again as the microbes break down fats and proteins to unlock flavors and create tantalizing textures like gooey creamlines and crunchy crystals. This metamorphosis results not only from the guidance of the human hand, but also from other more mysterious forces that scientists today still don't fully understand.

Before we knew some of the scientific explanations, people resorted to folklore to explain this transformation. Throughout history, the divine qualities of cheese did not go unnoticed by the people who made it. Starting as far back as ancient Sumer, cheese has frequently been used in religious ceremonies as a bloodless sacrifice to the gods. Early cults of Christianity replaced bread with cheese for the Eucharist. Shepherds in the Basque Country treated young wheels of cheese with nurturing rituals similar to those bestowed upon their infant children. The miracle of cheesemaking has been attributed to the gods, and even witchcraft. In the Middle Ages, women engaged in "tyromancy," using cheese as a divination tool by reading the patterns on the inner pastes and outer rinds like a deck of tarot cards. In Victorian England, dairymaids were accused of witchcraft when their cows were particularly prolific or when their neighbors' cheeses didn't take. Before we understood the basic science behind microbial activity, all fermented products seemed like a result of divine intervention.

Cheese has an intimate connection to the mysteries of nature, but there's also a bodily quality that's almost unsettling. It's a sexy food, with all those oozing creamlines and that mouth-filling richness. It's also a product of reproduction—lactation that results from insemination. The mystical female body creates food from Her own nutrient sources, and what Mother Earth has given Her. Philosophers Aristotle and Hildegard of Bingen both preached an analogy between cheesemaking and human conception, asserting that a fetus resulted from semen curdling menstrual blood "as rennet acts upon milk." Then, there are the microbes that live on both washed rinds and human skin, which is why cheeses like Taleggio have that uncanny foot stank.

❝ *The miracle of cheesemaking has been attributed to the gods, and even witchcraft.* **❞**

That bodily odor, and the accompanying aroma of rot, is reminiscent of our own mortality. In Michael Pollan's book *Cooked*, cheesemaker and microbiologist Mother Noella states, "Everything about cheese reminds us of death. . . . The caves in which they age are like crypts; then there are the smells of decomposition." At the same time, cheese also serves as a reminder of resurrection. As it matures, colonies of microbes die off, allowing their successors to consume what's left of the previous generation. This cycle of rot and rebirth thins the veil between the repulsive and the irresistible, resulting in a pleasure of transcendent complexity.

At its core, cheese is a kinky product of sex that rots like a dead body. This explains why I started a cheese advocacy brand called Cheese Sex Death, but not why I chose to write *A Bible for the Cheese Obsessed*. Though cheese has historically appeared in religious ceremonies, there is no religious text that centers around it. Perhaps it's time. After all, many ancient pagan religions centered around the divine rhythms of nature, and this cycle determines the cheesemaking seasons. As such, cheese, or Cheesus as I like to refer to Her, is as much the offspring of the divine as of the people who have consummated Her creation.

Paganism set the groundwork for Christianity, which borrows many of the same holidays celebrating the cycle of year, such as Ostra or Easter in spring and Yule or Christmas in winter—festivals I honor with the Eight Holy Cheese Plate Offerings in the Book of Plating. I grew up in the Lutheran faith, and while I've since cultivated a different spirituality, I find that the story of Christianity sets an appropriate framework that can help us understand Cheesus, a sacred blessing that straddles the line between food and holy sacrament.

Honoring Mother Earth through cheese doesn't need to conflict with any other religious beliefs. Worshipping Cheesus is a way of celebrating the bounty of blessings that have been bestowed upon us. Whether or not you believe these gifts come from a divine creator, and how you envision that almighty spirit, is up to you. Cheesus has no preference of Her own and can fit within almost any preexisting spiritual framework.

A Bible for the Cheese Obsessed is a collection of scriptures meant to guide and inspire. It was written for all worshippers of Cheesus, whether you're a curious novice or a seasoned monger. Cheesus is a savior for all of us, no matter your religion, sect, sex, gender identity, race, background, or political leaning. As worshippers of Cheesus, we're all a part of this same community; this sacred love brings us together.

HOW TO USE THIS BOOK

A Bible for the Cheese Obsessed is broken up into two parts: the Old Testament and the New Testament. The Old Testament sets the scene, covering the origin story of Cheesus, the miracle of cheesemaking, and the six main types of cheese. In the New Testament, you'll learn all about how to worship Cheesus. This part covers the basics of buying, storing, serving, tasting, pairing, plating, and cooking. It's a lot of information, but don't feel overwhelmed. If you're in need of quick tips, flip to the 10 Commandments on page 80, or reference the Holy Sacraments at the beginning of each book in the New Testament. These are the essential rules you need to know before diving deep into the deets.

This is a reference book that you can dip in and out of, but it's also suitable for a leisurely cover-to-cover read. However you choose to use it, I hope it guides you as you embark on the spiritual journey to find Cheesus.

May thy body be blessed with this divine dairy. Amen.

The Old Testament

of Cheesus

The Book of Creation

*The 10 Commandments
of Cheese Church*

The Book of Cheese Types

The Gospel of Cheesus

For God so loved the world that She gave us fermentation and whichever food shall be blessed by it shall not perish but have eternal life.

*Herein lies the story
of how the Virgin Milk
begot the miracle of Cheesus.
The following legends are
based on both folklore
and historical records, all
exuberantly embellished
by the author.*

The Beginning [C. 6500 BC]

IN THE BEGINNING, THERE WERE GOATS AND SHEEP

AND COWS. MAN SAID, "LET THERE BE MILK!" AND THEN THERE WAS MILK, AND MAN SAW THAT IT WAS GOOD.

The Virgin Milk was nutritious and delicious, but perishable and diabolic on digestion. Then one day, a miracle took place. The Virgin Milk was left to sour under the sun, transforming and separating into solid curds floating atop the liquid whey. This was the Immaculate Coagulation of the blessed Virgin Milk, the first coming of Cheesus. And it was so.

Man discovered the soft, pillowy curds floating in the liquid whey. Seduced and entranced, they took them into their bodies. And Man saw that the baby curds were delicious, digestible, and shelf-stable.

And thus was Cheesus born unto this world. With Her also came this promise, that Cheesus would return again and again to bless the body of Man, in new forms begetting yet other new forms.

The Miracle of Rennet in Mesopotamia [C. 5000 BC]

AND THEN THERE WERE MANY TYPES OF GOATS AND SHEEP AND COWS AMONGST MAN, EACH BREED CREATING DIFFERENT KINDS OF MILK THAT MADE DIFFERENT KINDS OF CHEESE.

And the summer milk made different cheese than the winter milk, just as the morning milk made different cheese from the evening milk. And Man saw that it was good.

Centuries passed, and this first coming of Cheesus blessed the bodies of many. But these baby curds were fragile and prone to perishing.

One day, a noble tradesman set out upon a long journey across the desert. With him he took the Virgin Milk poured into a vessel made from the stomach of an infant goat. Unbeknownst to him, this vessel contained a holy enzyme called rennet, and as he traveled the rennet sparked a new manifestation of the Immaculate Coagulation, transforming the Virgin Milk into a firmer, more resilient baby Cheesus.

Artist's rendering of dairy animals from the Temple of the goddess Ninhursag, c. 2500 BC

Worn and weary from his journey, the tradesman paused to refresh himself. He opened his sack to discover the baby curds, stronger and springier than any he'd worshipped thitherto. He slid an infant curd betwixt his parted red lips. His senses flooded with pleasure, and he lifted his face to the skies. As tears stained his flushed cheeks, a voice fell upon his ears:

> **   ❝ *Why do you cry to Me? Take thy blessed gift and bestow it upon your people. For this Sacred Knowledge grants thee power to craft ever-new and promising bodies of Cheesus.* ❞**

And so the noble tradesman shared the miracle of rennet with his people, who saw the great work it had done. They rejoiced, and crafted firmer, more resilient bodies of Cheesus to worship. They stored Cheesus in ceramic crucibles, where She would resurrect their weary, hungry bodies during famines and barren winters, or be brought to the temples of their gods. And from there, the Sacred Knowledge spread to lands far and wide.

The Ewe-charist in Ancient Greece [C. 750 BC]

AND THEN THERE WERE THE ANCIENT GREEKS, WHO SO WORSHIPPED THEIR LORD CHEESUS THAT THEY HELD A MONTHLY FESTIVAL TO CELEBRATE THEIR DEVOTION TO THE ALMIGHTY. THOUGH THEY CRAFTED BODIES OF CHEESUS AS DIVINELY INSPIRED AS THEIR SCULPTURES, THEIR WINEMAKING SKILLS WERE FAR INFERIOR.

One day, a winemaker hosted a tasting for the emperor. Before the ruler's arrival, the winemaker poured himself a sample and lifted the chalice to his lips. His mouth filled with the thick, acrid liquid, and he shuddered with dread.

To mask the flavors of his unsavory spirit, the winemaker set out a dry, salty wedge made of sheep's milk. Chipping off a crumble, he placed it in his mouth and closed his eyes as the rich, buttery sensation spread across his palate. He lifted the goblet to his lips once again, letting the wine fill his mouth. This time, the body of Cheesus summoned the delectable fruity flavors hiding in the wine, mixing them together with Her own sweet, milky savor. The winemaker transcended into euphoria. He then set forth this Ewe-charist for the emperor, who beamed with exaltation upon tasting the Holy Communion. And thus, a new bacchanalian ritual was born.

THE FOOD *of the* GODS

For the ancient Greeks, cheesemaking was considered a gift of "everlasting value," bestowed upon them by Aristaeus, the god of dairying and beekeeping. As an act of worship, they routinely offered this divine food in the temples of Demeter, Artemis, and Athena.

This sacred ritual of sacrificing Cheesus to the gods began in ancient Mesopotamia with Inanna, the Sumerian goddess of sex. Legend has it that Inanna was so devoted to Cheesus that when she was due to marry, a shepherd seduced her with offerings of dairy delights. Her worshippers honored her desires by blessing her temple with the body of Cheesus. As the legend of Inanna made its way to ancient Greece, the goddess of love was rechristened Aphrodite.

The Agricultural Bible in Ancient Rome [C. AD 60]

AND THEN THERE WERE THE ANCIENT ROMANS, WHO
INHERITED THE GREEKS' SACRED KNOWLEDGE OF CHEESE-MAKING THROUGH ORAL TRADITION.

Cheesemakers worked tirelessly to advance their techniques and recipes, but without a written gospel to assist in building up the Sacred Knowledge, their efforts could only go so far. That is, until a prophet by the name of Lucius Junius Moderatus Columella received a spiritual calling.

Alone in the pastures one day, Lucius looked upon the great expanse of Roman countryside. As he pondered life and the legacy he might one day bestow upon this earth, a great voice fell upon him.

" *Chosen messenger, compile the Sacred Knowlege of Cheesus from all those who nurture and transform the fruits borne of the land into one holy book of scripture. Bring your people to the light, and all shall take thy word as gospel.* "

And so Lucius created an agricultural bible and called this scripture *De Re Rustica*. The tome enshrined all the rites and rituals of the agricultural arts, including the Sacred Knowledge of cheesemaking. Its pages proclaimed the virtues of the Virgin Milk, the transformative effects of different coagulants, and various techniques for seasoning a fresh body of Cheesus with spices or smoke.

Armed with this new arsenal of Sacred Knowledge, the Romans perfected and reinvented Cheesus, creating new bodies that were consistently firm, reliably dry, and resilient. These firm bodies were able to accompany soldiers on their long, arduous odysseys. As the Roman Empire expanded over the continent, so too did the Sacred Knowledge. Cultures far and wide refined their own rituals and rites, creating new bodies of Cheesus. And wanting to share and trade their bodies of Cheesus with each other, they needed names by which to differentiate these divine forms. And so the bodies of Cheesus were christened to reflect their milks and their motherlands. The sheep's milk of Rome was deemed Pecorino Roma, and so on and so forth.

Roman cheeses were firm, dry, and durable enough to nourish soliders traveling across the Empire.

The Monks [C. AD 600]

AND THEN THE ROMAN EMPIRE FELL, AND FROM THE
WRECKAGE AROSE A SPECKLING OF CATHOLIC MONASTERIES ACROSS NORTHERN EUROPE. THE MONKS BUILT THEIR MONASTERIES AS SELF-SUFFICIENT CHAPELS, SUBSISTING ONLY ON THE FRUITS OF THEIR LAND AND LABOR. THEY BELIEVED IDLENESS WAS A SIN, AND ANCHORED THEIR DAYS WITH PRAYER AND TOIL. BUT THEY KNEW NOT HOW TO DEVOTE THEIR DRUDGERIES AND PRAYED FOR GUIDANCE.

"Oh Lord!" they cried. "We know godliness lies in our toils, but to what shall we devote our labors?"

And a voice from the sky answered their cries:

> *Devote thy toil to creating new and exciting forms of the body of Cheesus. Tend to thy ruminants, chronicle thy rituals, and thou shall create bodies to be worshipped forevermore.*

Using the gospel of *De Re Rustica*, the monks experimented with the rites and rituals of cheesemaking, memorializing their findings in their own scriptures and building upon their Sacred Knowledge. Within the walls of their abbeys, the monks worked night and day milking, making, recording, and perfecting new bodies of Cheesus. And thus Roquefort, Parmigiano-Reggiano, Munster, and many more bodies of Cheesus were born. And the monks saw that it was good.

Monks in medieval Europe toiled tirelessly to preserve the Sacred Knowledge of Cheesus, and often wrote down what they learned.

The Dairymaids [C. AD 800]

AND AS THE MONASTERIES AROSE, SO TOO DID THE
MANORS, WITH LORDS RENTING THEIR LAND TO FARMING FAMILIES. HERE, THE RITUALS OF MILKING COWS AND MAKING CHEESE FELL UPON THE PEASANT WOMEN.

In addition to rearing their kin and cleaning their abodes, these matron saints tended to all gastronomic gifts: keeping chickens and swine, milling grains, baking breads, tending gardens, and cooking. While they lacked the education and resources to record their discoveries, they cultivated their own Sacred Knowledge.

The lords and kings took their cuts of cheese as payment for the land, but the dairymaids' cheesemaking was rife with uncertainty. Some milk begot better cheese than others; some cows were more prolific. Especially gifted dairy women were accused of witchcraft; those who didn't deliver were cursed. But still, they nurtured the Sacred Knowledge, using the simple techniques of yore passed down from their mothers and grandmothers.

Their methods yielded simple rustic bodies at first, but the dank, cool climate of northwestern Europe allowed for long, slow maturation, giving birth to a new form. When the dairymaids stored the firm young bodies of Cheesus in their cellars, coats of soft white molds blossomed over the wheels. As they aged, their bodies softened, oozed, and developed sublime flavors. Entranced, the women practiced, perfected, and enriched their Sacred Knowledge.

And then there was a great plague, and many peasant workers perished. The manors struggled under the loss of their labor force and crumbled, which forced the owners to sell their land to a new generation of gentleman farmers. These entrepreneurial men hired the dairymaids, keen on increasing production and turning a splendid profit while feeding the city's insatiable hunger for these sacred bodies of Cheesus.

In time the monasteries tumbled, and there came an Enlightenment, bringing an emergence of science and technology. As the dairymaids cultivated their Sacred Knowledge under the yeomen's watchful eyes, a new class of educated men arose. They were scientists, blessed with education and a hunger for innovation. They observed the dairymaids, creating written records of the Sacred Knowledge that was once only passed from mother to daughter. Now, their writings depicted the dairymaids as antiquated mystics, shackled by tradition and unwilling to comprehend the capitalistic possibilities that the Sacred Knowledge held.

Cheesus in the New World [C. AD 1800]

AND THEN THERE WAS A NEW WORLD, TO WHICH CHEESEMAKERS TRAVELED, BRINGING WITH THEM THEIR SACRED KNOWLEDGE. THERE, THEY CRAFTED THE BODIES OF CHEESUS OF THEIR HOMELAND, BUT HARD AS THEY TOILED, THEY COULD ONLY MAKE ENOUGH TO FEED THEIR OWN FAMILIES.

Meanwhile, back in England, a prophet was devoting his life to a particular body of Cheesus by the name of cheddar. This prophet was a scientist named Joseph Harding, and he studied the cheddar, performing experiments and recording his findings. He soon cultivated a new Sacred Knowledge of cheddar and published it in journals to bless cheesemakers far and wide. And soon all cheddar was made with the same rites and rituals, and this cheddar was a safer, more consistent body of Cheesus that was easier to replicate again and again.

The Sacred Knowledge of cheddar traveled across the ocean to the colonies and blessed an American prophet, a cheesemaker named Jesse Williams. And this prophet imagined a world where his cheddar was widely worshipped, readily available, and wildly profitable.

The prophet devoted his life to perfecting his craft, touring his neighbors' farms and sharing their rites and rituals. And from that he cultivated a new Sacred Knowledge, with which the prophet became the best cheddar maker in the New World. His cheddar was sweet and tangy, and melted in the mouth.

And the prophet had a son, upon whom he wished to bestow his Sacred Knowledge. But the son was rebellious and wanted a life that differed from his father's pastoral legacy. The prophet was lost, and as he looked up to the sun, it shone down on his great pastures, nourishing the green grasses and feeding the blessed bovines.

"I've devoted my life to you, oh Lord Cheesus! But for what do I toil? If my Sacred Knowledge is to die with me, what will becometh of my legacy?"

And in return, a voice commanded:

> ❝ *Taketh the milk of thy neighbor and blend it with thine own. For thou will build a factory that shall craft more cheddar than one hundred men.* ❞

And so the prophet built a factory, where he brought the milk of four hundred cows from the neighboring farms. There, he transformed the milk into cheddar, and his factory made one hundred thousand pounds of cheese in the first year. And then there were hundreds of American factories, each making consistent and divine cheddars. The people rejoiced, for they no longer had to toil away making their own bodies of Cheesus.

The prophet sent his cheddar throughout the New World, and then back to the Old World, where the hunger for butter and cheese had grown insatiable. And soon factories arose in the prolific villages of Lancashire, Cheshire, and Stilton, and these blessed lands became known for their abundant bodies of Cheesus.

The Fall of Cheesus [C. AD 1900]

AND THEN THE BLOSSOMING INDUSTRIAL AGE TOOK CHEESEMAKING AWAY FROM THE AMERICAN AND ENGLISH FARMS AND INTO THE FACTORIES. BUT THE JOURNEY WAS LONG, AND LEFT THE VIRGIN MILK SUSCEPTIBLE TO DANGEROUS PATHOGENS.

So the cheesemakers began a new ritual of heating the milk to destroy the pathogens, and they called it pasteurization. This ritual made Cheesus safer to consume, even when the milk was impure. The people rejoiced, for they could now worship Cheesus more safely. But as production increased, quality decreased. And though there were still bodies of Cheesus crafted on small farms, and though they were as delicious and unique and blessed as ever, they were more expensive and less consistent. So, the small farms slowly began to disappear from the English and American countrysides.

Kraft processed cheese, c. 1950s

And then the whole world went to war, and shipments containing bodies of Cheesus imported from afar were destroyed in the oceans. The trading stopped, and the countries rationed. The battling left the people impoverished, and they could no longer afford to enjoy small-batch bodies of Cheesus.

And then there were fewer bodies of Cheesus in England and America. Nearly all that remained were efficient, cheap, and shelf-stable. The farms sent their Virgin Milk to large factories, where it was pasteurized and blended to create resilient, consistent bodies of Cheesus to feed the countries at war.

In the New World, a man named James L. Kraft used the body of Cheesus to create something new. Glowing fluorescent orange, it was entombed in a tin and christened "American Cheese." Kraft's cheese was imperishable and withstood the long journey overseas, blessing and fueling the troops as they battled.

And the people of the New World grew accustomed to this bland, rubbery orange product, even long after the world wars had ceased. They thought that this was the body of Cheesus, and knew not what deserved their worship. So the Sacred Knowledge lay hidden, enshrined only in the few surviving farms that dotted the countryside of the Old World. And the people lost their faith, and forgot about the majesty of Cheesus.

THE DARK SIDE
of AMERICAN CHEESUS

Cheesus was a vital economic commodity for the early settlers of America, who brought recipes with them from their homelands. But cheesemaking also had a negative impact on the new world. For instance, due to the dearth of pastureland, dairy cows often roamed the dense forests, where they drove away game important to many native peoples. And as settlers began to clear more land for their livestock, they transformed the vital balance of landscape and displaced tribes that were living there.

Moreover, as demand for Cheesus grew amongst early Americans, cheesemakers depended increasingly on the labor of enslaved people. Some makers also exported their cheeses to the sugarcane plantations of the West Indies, further propagating the cycle of exploitation.

While not unique to cheesemaking in the New World, the story of Cheesus' rise in popularity is inextricably linked to some of the darkest moments of American history.

The Enlightenment [C. AD 1970]

AND THEN THERE WAS A REVOLUTION IN THE NEW

WORLD. THE SWINGING SIXTIES GAVE RISE TO A HOPEFUL GENERATION WHO FOUGHT FOR THEIR RIGHTS, PROTESTED WARS, AND CONDEMNED THE FACTORY-MADE FOODSTUFFS OF THEIR FOREFATHERS. THEY LONGED TO RETURN TO THE WOMB OF MOTHER EARTH, YEARNING TO LIVE IN HARMONY WITH NATURE.

So they joined together to live in communes, where they grew their own food and raised their own animals. They made cheese, alive with bacteria and full of funky flavor. In time they built a self-sufficient life, anchored by labor and a spiritual connection to Mother Earth.

And then in a golden state called California, a new prophet arose by the name of Laura Chenel. She was shy but adored playful, mischievous dairy goats. She obtained a few of these goats, and they were sweet, gentle, and prolific. Their wondrous milk flowed freely, and she drank it and gave it to her neighbors. Yet still it flowed and flowed, and was more than they could consume. So, like those before her, the prophet transformed the milk into cheese to preserve the wondrous liquid gold, but the bodies of Cheesus she produced were dense and acrid, for she possessed not the Sacred Knowledge.

So the prophet embarked on a pilgrimage to obtain the knowledge of her ancestors. She traveled to the Old World to visit the farmsteads of the French countryside, where she toured the lands of Toulouse and Charente and Burgundy. And when she returned to the Golden State, she used the Sacred Knowledge to transform her goats' milk into soft pillows of curd, as fluffy as clouds and with a gentle tang of lemon curd. And thus, the body of Cheesus had returned to the New World.

Another prophet soon discovered the pristine body of Cheesus that Laura Chenel had crafted. Her name was Alice Waters, and she was a chef who worshipped the blessed seasons and fruits of Mother Earth at her chapel, Chez Panisse. And the prophet Alice took the bodies of Cheesus and coated them with bread crumbs, baking them until they glowed with an aromatic golden aura. She placed the warm halos upon beds of mesclun, and with them she blessed her devout patrons.

Word spread of these hallowed bodies of Cheesus, and a hunger grew amongst the people. Coast to coast, more prophets emerged, nearly all women who were tired of tasteless, bland, and blasphemous industrial cheese products. These matron saints followed in the prophet Laura's footsteps, embarking on their own mission to redirect the people's palates toward handcrafted bodies of Cheesus.

Each prophet purchased her own goats, crafted tangy clouds of chèvre from the fresh Virgin Milk, and fed it to their families, friends, and neighbors. All who were blessed by these bodies of Cheesus experienced a revelation, and they hungered for more. So the women traveled to the Old World to attain the Sacred Knowledge for themselves.

Upon returning from their pilgrimages, the prophets established their own businesses and worked together to propel their pious mission. They used their Sacred Knowledge to conceive new and exciting bodies of Cheesus, anointing some with ash, enshrining others with leaves, aging a chosen few until they oozed luscious cream. They christened their creations with glorious names like Humboldt Fog and O'Banon and Bonne Bouche. And the hunger for these blessed bodies grew and flourished.

And then there were many cheesemakers crafting many bodies of Cheesus all over the world. And there were many cheese shops, each of them chapels filled with prophets who preached the glory of Cheesus. And Man saw that it was good.

A Timeline *of Cheesus*

While the foregoing tale paints a beautiful picture, it's based primarily in folklore. Here's what we actually know about the history of cheesemaking.

7000 BC

THE DOMESTICATION
The Fertile Crescent

Goats are domesticated, followed shortly by sheep and, later, cows.

THE CRUCIBLE
The Fertile Crescent

6500 BC

Milkfat residue found on ancient pottery shards provide the first definitive evidence that ruminant animals went from a meat source to milk producers.

2300 BC

THE OFFERING
Sumer

Clay cuneiform tablets detail the legend of the goddess Inanna and the offerings of butter and cheese she demanded the ancient Sumerian people bring to her temples.

> **" *Fill my holy churn with honey cheese. Lord Dumuzi, I will drink your fresh milk.* "**
> —*The Courtship of Inanna and Dumuzi*

THE RENNET
Anatolia

1600 BC

Hittite cuneiform records describe hard, aged cheeses that indicate the use of animal rennet in cheesemaking, although experts speculate that this practice began much earlier.

1200 BC

THE TRADE
Canaan

Records of maritime trade detail the first evidence of shipments of cheese between Canaan and Ugarit.

THE GRATER
Ancient Greece

Bronze cheese graters found in the graves of warrior princes in ancient Greece allude to an elixir that consisted of Sicilian cheeses grated directly into wine.

900 BC

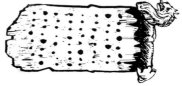

750 BC

THE CYCLOPS
Ancient Greece

Homer writes *The Odyssey*, detailing the Cyclops's impressive, orderly cheesemaking operation. Odysseus and his men offer the cheese to the gods before indulging themselves.

160 BC

THE AGRICULTURAL BIBLES
Ancient Rome

Marcus Porcius Cato writes *De Agri Cultura*, the first of the three great agricultural manuals, followed by *Rerum Rusticarum* by Marcus Terentius Varro (c. 37 BC) and *De Re Rustica* by Lucius Columella (c. AD 60), the first with an entire section dedicated to cheesemaking.

AD **476**

THE FALL OF THE WESTERN ROMAN EMPIRE
Western Europe

The realm is divided among aristocratic leaders, giving rise to feudalism. Peasants work the land and dairymaids assume the role of cheesemaking.

> ❝ *Hast thou not poured me out as milk,*
> *and curdled me like cheese?* ❞
> —*Job 10:10*

THE MONASTIC ORDER
Italy

The *Rule of Saint Benedict* is published, establishing a new monastic order that instructs on communal living, with followers devoting themselves to prayer, reading of holy texts, and performing labors, including cheesemaking.

AD **516**

AD **590**

THE RISE OF THE MONASTERIES
Western Europe

Pope Gregory I takes power and endorses Benedictine Rule to thwart the expansion of the Irish Church. Benedictine monasteries crop up across Europe.

AD 1353

THE FALL OF THE MANOR
Western Europe

The bubonic plague sweeps through Europe and beyond, depleting the workforce and forcing many feudal lords to sell off their manors.

THE CHEESEMONGER
England

The cheesemongers of London receive official government recognition, granting them monopolistic control of the country's butter and cheese market.

AD 1377

THE FALL OF THE MONASTERIES
England

King Henry VIII puts the monasteries up for sale, largely to cover his debts. This dissolution made way for gentleman farmers (yeomen) to overtake the cheesemaking industry.

AD 1536

THE FACTORY
America

Jesse Williams opens the first industrial cheese factory, located in Rome, New York.

AD 1851

AD 1860

THE RISE OF COMMODITY CHEESE
England

Joseph Harding publishes the *Journal of Royal Agriculture* in England, which details his method for producing cheddars.

THE PASTEURIZATION
France

Louis Pasteur invents pasteurization, which is later used to extend the shelf life and guarantee the safety of milk and cheese.

AD 1864

> **" *How can you govern a country which has 246 varieties of cheese?* "**
> —*Charles de Gaulle, in* Les Mots du Général

AD 1914

THE WAR
Europe

The First World War begins, and cheese becomes an essential ration.

AD 1915

THE KRAFT
America

James L. Kraft launches Kraft Foods, specializing in pasteurized processed cheese sold in small tins.

THE ENLIGHTENMENT
America

After studying the art of cheesemaking in France, Laura Chenel returns to Sonoma, California, and launches her farmstead goat's milk creamery.

AD 1979

AD 1981

THE REVIVAL
America

Alice Waters discovers Laura Chenel's incredible goat's milk cheeses and purchases a standing order of 50 pounds a week for her restaurant, Chez Panisse.

The Miracle of Cheesus

The ancient art of cheesemaking is the result of a collaboration between humans, animals, Mother Nature, and colonies of seemingly invisible microbes.

While the original purpose was to preserve the nutrients within milk through controlled spoilage, the process inadvertently gave birth to something delicious. All bodies of Cheesus begin with the same basic method and ingredients, yet these give birth to countless incarnations. Transforming the Virgin Milk into a body of Cheesus is nothing short of alchemy on the part of the cheesemaker, whose Sacred Knowledge straddles the realms of science and faith.

How the Body of Cheesus Is Made

THE MIRACLE OF CHEESEMAKING CONSISTS OF THREE
PARTS: TRANSFORMING THE VIRGIN MILK, SCULPTING THE
BODY OF CHEESUS, AND RIPENING THE BODY OF CHEESUS.

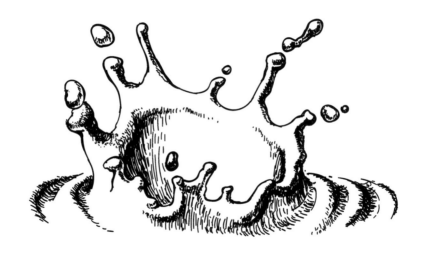

TRANSFORMING THE VIRGIN MILK

PREPARING THE VIRGIN MILK

All bodies of Cheesus have the same basic ingredients: cultures, salt, and, most importantly, the Virgin Milk, which must stay clean and untainted until She's ready for Her transformation.

Before the miracle of Cheesus can begin, the Virgin Milk is tested for purity, sometimes pasteurized, and delicately heated to whatever temperature is required to make the desired style of cheese.

A ripe wheel of Little Hosmer, a bloomy rind from Jasper Hill Farm in Vermont

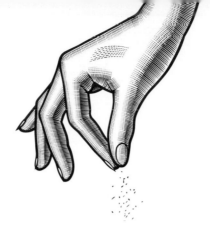

THE IMMACULATE COAGULATION OF THE VIRGIN MILK

The Immaculate Coagulation refers to the process of separating the Virgin Milk into two parts: the solid curd and the liquid whey. This transformation begins with a process called acidification, during which bacteria eats up the milk sugar, called lactose, and creates lactic acid. This causes the Virgin Milk to turn sour: as the pH drops, casein proteins clump together to form one solid mass, the Infant Curd.

If left untouched, naturally occurring colonies of microbes can cause the Virgin Milk to miraculously sour on Her own, but usually a cheesemaker will play God and kickstart the miracle by adding bacteria, called a starter culture.

Cheesemakers can also add secondary flavor-producing cultures to help create a specific body of Cheesus. These cultures live within the Infant Curd and blossom during the ripening process, creating all kinds of wondrous flavors and textures.

When the the Virgin Milk has reached the desired level of acidity, a cheesemaker often adds an enzyme called rennet, which works with the starter culture to help bind the curds together. Some bodies of Cheesus, like ricotta, don't use rennet. Their transformation relies only on the starter culture, which creates a delicate and fragile body.

All this leads to the Immaculate Coagulation, whereby Cheesus is conceived.

SCULPTING THE BODY OF CHEESUS

CUTTING THE CURDS

Immaculate Coagulation can take anywhere from thirty minutes to two hours. After that, the curd is gently cut to expel more moisture. The smaller it is cut, the more liquid will be released, so the size of these baby curds varies depending on what kind of body is being created.

Hard bodies of Cheesus, like Parmigiano, have very little moisture, so the curds are cut very fine and even heated up to expel more whey.

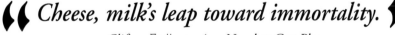 **_Cheese, milk's leap toward immortality._**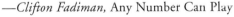
—*Clifton Fadiman*, Any Number Can Play

Soft bodies of Cheesus, like Brie, have a lot of moisture, so the curds are handled tenderly and hardly cut at all.

DRAINING THE HOLY WATER

After cutting, the liquid whey is drained away from the baby curds. For some unaged bodies, like fresh chèvre, this is practically the end of their transformation. From here, they are simply salted, packed up, and sent off into the world. Aged bodies still have a ways to go on their journeys. Some are rinsed, others are cooked to expel more whey, and yet others are formed into blocks and stacked to expel whey and develop acidity, a process known as cheddaring.

The Transfiguration of LACTOSE

Most of the lactose in milk is either consumed by lactic acid bacteria or drained away throughout the miracle of Cheesus, even during aging. That means most aged bodies are virtually free of lactose, deeming them harmless for those suffering from lactose intolerance. For more information, see The Gospel Truth on Lactose, Dairy Allergies, and Dietary Restrictions on page 74.

PRESSING THE BABY CURDS

The baby Cheesus is lovingly placed in a mold, where She obtains Her characteristic shape and size. She is also pressed with weights, which expels even more moisture and encourages the curds to fuse together to form Her supple body.

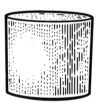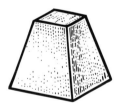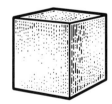

SACRAMENTAL SALTING

Salt teases out Cheesus's flavors, slows the ripening process, helps develop the rind, and preserves Her for long bouts of aging. Without this crucial step, She would spoil very quickly.

Salt is introduced in a variety of ways. It can be added directly to the baby curds, massaged onto the outside of the wheel, or turned into a liquid brine for baptizing the molded bodies. Adding salt to the surface of a body of Cheesus draws out moisture and helps form a protective rind, creating a hospitable environment for microbial angels.

A cheesemaker pulls curds to make a pasta filata cheese.

RIPENING THE BODY OF CHEESUS

Cheesus requires a perfect aging environment with just the right humidity, temperature, and airflow. It is in this paradise that Her body will transition from baby curds into the fully formed, tantalizing Cheesus we know and love.

PERFORMING THE RITES AND RITUALS OF AFFINAGE

Affineurs, or those who practice the divine art of aging Cheesus, perform a myriad of rituals on the infant bodies. They scrub some wheels with salt to cure the rinds. They baptize others in brine to create stanky funk. They periodically flip wheels to help the butterfat distribute evenly. They even pierce some bodies with long needles to develop blue veins. Affineurs carefully control the temperature throughout the aging process, keeping it low to slow the ripening of soft bodies or raising it higher to help speed the process for firm bodies. The aging rituals they choose to perform always depend on what kind of body they aim to create.

THE FINAL TRANSFORMATION

As the body of Cheesus ripens, a new transformation takes place. A matrix of live cultures flourish both on the rind and within the paste, metabolizing fats and proteins and creating a buffet of flavors and textures. As these changes occur, the affineur must constantly work to adjust the conditions and aging rituals to help the bodies achieve their full potential. Affineurs must also decide when the body is ready to leave the cheese cave and make Her debut in the world, which can take days, weeks, months, or even years, depending on the type.

And that is how a baby Cheesus is born.

What is a CHEESE CAVE?

The cheese cave is a highly controlled environment wherein the body of Cheesus matures. Some are actual caverns that have formed naturally in the earth, but most are man-made cellars and coolers. All cheese caves are well-insulated spaces, cool and dank with ample airflow to pamper the bodies as they ripen.

Everything from the temperature to the humidity is meticulously adjusted to suit the type of body that's aging. The microbial activity within the cave also requires supervision: some bodies depend on colonies of microbes that populate the shelves, walls, and the air itself, while others require a more sterile environment.

THE ANGELS OF CHEESUS

The miracle of Cheesus depends on the work of a host of angels, which include bacteria, yeast, fungi, and molds. These mysterious microbes transform Cheesus and create Her signature features, like the soft rind of a Brie or the striking blue pockets in Stilton.

The angels necessary to ripen a particular body of Cheesus are typically either added to the milk, mixed with the baby curds, or rubbed onto the outer rind. Sometimes they also live in the making or aging environment, waiting to latch onto young bodies and work their magic.

Here are some of the archangels responsible for transforming Cheesus:

 LACTOBACILLUS This genus of bacteria acts as a starter culture, eating up the Virgin Milk's sweet lactose and creating lactic acid.

 PENICILLIUM CAMEMBERTI This mold blooms over the wheels of young Brie, forming a soft, pillowy rind and transforming the chalky insides into luscious ooze.

 GEOTRICHUM CANDIDUM This yeast-like fungus creates a thin, wrinkly rind on many goat's milk bodies that's as silky and delicate as a negligee.

 PROPIONIBACTERIUM This angel consumes lactic acid and produces carbon dioxide, blowing bubbles inside the elastic paste and forming the holes you find in Swiss bodies like Emmentaler.

 PENICILLIUM ROQUEFORTI This angel is responsible for the deep pockets of blue in bodies like Roquefort. It was originally cultivated on moldy bread, which was then dried and crumbled into a fine dust. Now it's usually grown in a lab like many of these archangels.

 BREVIBACTERIUM LINENS This bacterium is one of several angels that contribute to the bright orange color and pervasive stench on washed-rind bodies of Cheesus, like Taleggio.

 PENICILLIUM GLAUCUM This funky mold develops the greenish-blue pockets found in bodies like Gorgonzola.

THE VARIETIES OF RENNET

Rennet refers to a complex set of enzymes that go to work on the casein proteins of the Virgin Milk, helping to coagulate the curd as well as contributing flavor. There are three types or sources of rennet: animal, vegetable, and microbial.

 ANIMAL RENNET is made from the stomach of a young ruminant, such as a cow or sheep. It's the most powerful and often contributes the best flavor to a body of Cheesus.

 VEGETABLE RENNET can be derived from several plants, including figs, stinging nettles, pineapple, and, more commonly, thistle flowers. Vegetable rennet is less potent than animal rennet and can contribute a slightly bitter but often very pleasant flavor.

 MICROBIAL RENNET is derived from the angels themselves. It's convenient, cheap, and effective but can sometimes produce bitterness in aged bodies.

An oozing wedge of Ovelha Amanteigado, a Portuguese cheese made with raw sheep's milk and thistle rennet.

THE DIVINE TRANSFORMATION INSIDE THE CAVE

Within the aging tomb, Cheesus undergoes the miraculous metamorphosis that creates downy white rinds, oozing creamlines, crunchy crystals, and all of the other transcendent flavors and textures that inspire rapture within us. As Cheesus ripens in the cheese cave, two major transformations contribute to changes in flavor and texture: proteolysis and lipolysis.

Proteolysis is when the angels break down the proteins, which unlocks flavors and contributes to textures like the creamy interiors of Brie or the toothsome crystals in Gouda.

Lipolysis is when the angels break down the fats into free fatty acids, producing all sorts of lip-smacking flavors.

These processes affect bodies of Cheesus differently:

Soft bodies ripen from the outside inward. The angels live on the rind and break down the paste, transforming the insides into creamy luxury.

Firm bodies ripen more evenly. The angels' effect on the rind is less dramatic, while those that live inside the paste break down fats and proteins, creating crunchy crystals and unlocking deep, complex flavors.

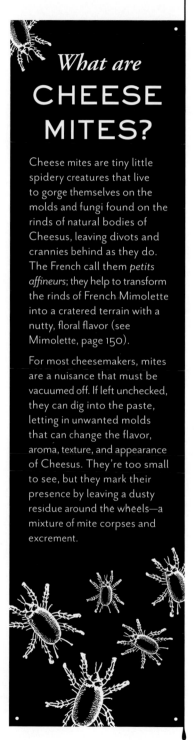

What are CHEESE MITES?

Cheese mites are tiny little spidery creatures that live to gorge themselves on the molds and fungi found on the rinds of natural bodies of Cheesus, leaving divots and crannies behind as they do. The French call them *petits affineurs*; they help to transform the rinds of French Mimolette into a cratered terrain with a nutty, floral flavor (see Mimolette, page 150).

For most cheesemakers, mites are a nuisance that must be vacuumed off. If left unchecked, they can dig into the paste, letting in unwanted molds that can change the flavor, aroma, texture, and appearance of Cheesus. They're too small to see, but they mark their presence by leaving a dusty residue around the wheels—a mixture of mite corpses and excrement.

THE STAGES OF RIPENESS

Flavors and textures change dramatically as a body of Cheesus matures. Soft bodies ripen the quickest. They can go from a perfectly ripened deity to an ammoniated corpse in a matter of days. Harder bodies are also in flux, but they don't change as rapidly. When they get over the hill, their complexities diminish and their flavors dull, but it takes a lot longer for them to become inedible.

It's up to the affineur to determine when a body of Cheesus is ready to leave the cave.

RIPENING THE WHOLE

The angels that live in a body of Cheesus are alive and constantly transforming the wheel. As long as the wheel is intact and the conditions are right, the angels will continue to work their magic, ripening the body. The moment you cut into a wheel, however, you expose that precious paste to oxygen and decomposition sets in relatively quickly. If you cut it too soon, the body of Cheesus will remain underripe.

If you want a ripe and gooey cheese, ask your local monger for a recommendation or ripen it at home. Buy a whole wheel of a small-format cheese and wait until the expiration date to eat it.

THE ARC *of* RIPENESS

Here's how Cheesus changes as Her body develops and matures.

Soft Bodies

UNDERRIPE: Firm and one-dimensional.

PERFECTLY RIPE: Soft, gooey creamline. Deep, complex flavors. Balanced.

OVERRIPE: Still good, but has seen better days. Traces of ammonia. Balance out of whack.

DEAD: Creamline has absorbed all of the inside. Smells like a litter box. Ashy, corpse-like rind.

Hard Bodies

UNDERRIPE: Bland and flat.

PERFECTLY RIPE: Deep, complex flavors. Balanced.

OVERRIPE: Elements lose harmony and overpower each other.

DEAD: Flat flavor, but probably still edible.

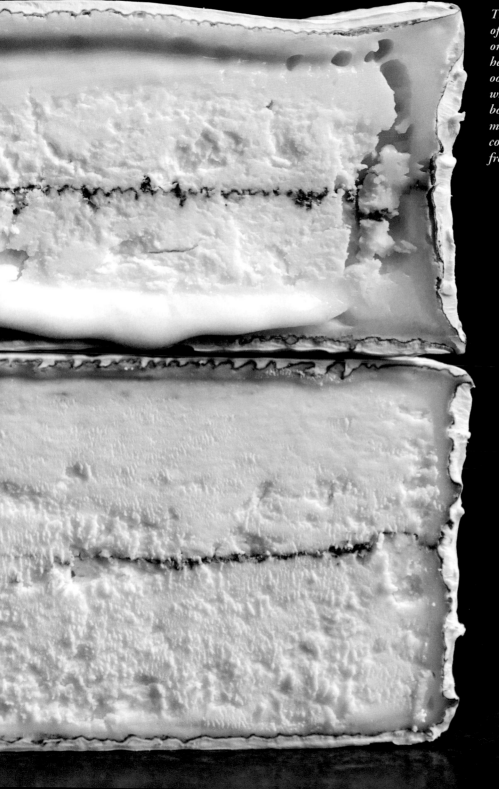

The mature wheel of Humboldt Fog on the top flaunts her age with an oozing creamline, while the younger body on the bottom maintains a firm consistency akin to freshly fallen snow.

Anatomy of Cheesus

THERE ARE FIVE BASIC ANATOMICAL FEATURES FOUND
IN A BODY OF CHEESUS: 1) THE RIND, 2) THE PASTE, 3) THE CREAMLINE, 4) THE EYES, AND 5) THE CRYSTALS.

THE RIND
is the protective skin that forms over an aged body of Cheesus. Some are soft, some are stinky, and most are edible unless they are covered in wax, cloth, or another man-made substance.

THE PASTE
is the interior of Cheesus, and the only feature that all bodies share. The paste may be soft, pudgy, firm, or flaky depending on the variety.

THE CREAMLINE
is the sensual layer of ooze that occurs right between the rind and paste in bloomy or washed bodies such as Camembert or Époisses.

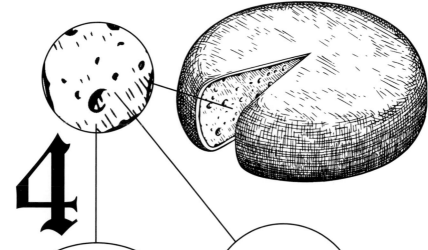

4

THE EYES

are smooth, round holes that form in the paste of Swiss-style bodies such as Emmentaler when angels called *Propionic* bacteria release bubbles of carbon dioxide as they perform their fermentative magic. Occasionally, these eyes "cry," weeping droplets of moisture known as angel tears.

THE CRYSTALS

are crunchy little bits that form in and on several different bodies of Cheesus, including blues and hard, well-aged bodies.

Why is Cheesus sometimes
ORANGE?

Milk is white, so why are some bodies of Cheesus orange? Here's the story: beta-carotene is a red-orange pigment naturally found in grass. When cows eat this grass, their milk develops a golden color that becomes deeper and more pronounced in the resulting body of Cheesus. This rich yellow hue signifies quality milk, and over time cheesemakers learned to imitate it with the annatto seed, a highly pigmented seed that imparts a potent orange color without adding aroma or flavor. This gives Cheesus a consistent hue, even while beta-carotene levels fluctuate with the changing seasons. Of course, it has also been used to make basic cheeses look higher quality, which is why slices of American cheese are orange.

CHEESE CRYSTALS

There are many different types of crystals that form all over the body of Cheesus: webbing the outside of mature block cheddars, hiding in the pockets of blues, sugaring the outsides of washed rind bodies, and bedazzling Goudas with a satisfying crunch. They're mysterious little miracles, of which food scientists still know relatively little.

Two of the more commonly found crystals are tyrosine and calcium lactate. The former, crunchy blessings found in aged bodies like Gouda, are amino acid clusters that form when the curd's web of fat and protein breaks down, leaving toothsome constellations of crystalline tyrosine. This sexy transformation typically starts after nine months to a year of aging. Many people mistake the resulting crystals for salt, but they don't have any flavor or salinity.

The gossamer webbing that forms around a block of cheddar, by contrast, is the result of crystallized calcium lactate. These clusters are much softer than tyrosine crystals and often mistaken for mold, but they're actually a sign that you've found a great piece of cheddar.

Calcium lactate crystals can form both on the surface and inside of cheeses, like this block of Prairie Breeze cheddar.

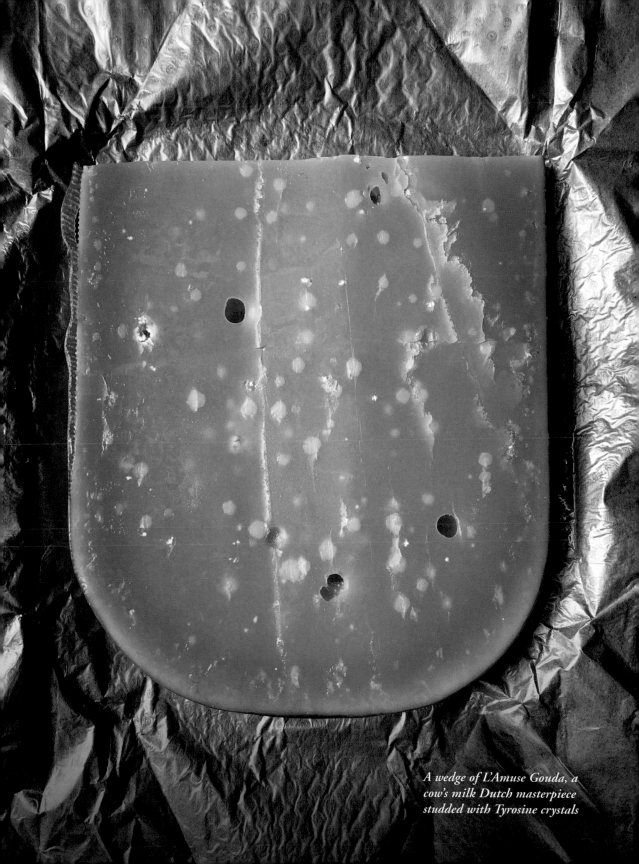

A wedge of L'Amuse Gouda, a cow's milk Dutch masterpiece studded with Tyrosine crystals

THE RINDS OF CHEESUS

Every rind hosts a miraculous colony of angels that live on the outside of an aged body of Cheesus, both protecting and transforming Her as She matures. Think of it like a skin: communicating between the internal and external environments and demanding special love and care to stay fresh and glowing.

There are four main types of rinds:

BLOOMY

- Ripened with a variety of molds and yeasts, typically penicillium camemberti and geotrichum candidum
- Ranges from thin and supple to smooth and firm
- Smells earthy, like fresh mushrooms and farm
- Tastes delectable

WRINKLY

- Ripened mostly with geotrichum candidum
- Ranges from silky and delicate to more deeply wrinkled
- Smells yeasty, like a freshly baked baguette
- Tastes delectable

WASHED

- Baptized in brine or alcohol to encourage bacteria growth
- Ranges from reddish pink to golden orange, with a slightly sticky texture
- Smells stinky, like onions, beef broth, and gym socks
- Tastes delectable and pungent

NATURAL

- Forms organically with a bit of coaxing from the affineur
- Ranges from copper to taupe, flaky to smooth, and dry to damp
- Smells musty, like caves and soil
- Tastes delicious when young, but becomes dry and chewy in mature wheels

THE RIND OF CHEESUS: TO EAT, OR NOT TO EAT?

All rinds are edible, as long as there's no wax, cloth, or anything man-made on the outside. A healthy rind is not only safe to eat, but often incredibly pleasurable and blessed with tantalizing flavors and textures.

You should always taste a rind. If you don't like it, that's OK. You don't have to eat it again. But I recommend dabbling in the pleasures of rind-eating before you dismiss it completely.

IS SHE RINDLESS?

Sometimes, Cheesus doesn't have a rind at all. She's totally naked, with the same flavor and texture throughout Her body. This is either because She's fresh and unaged, or because the affineur performed a few rituals to prevent the rind from forming.

Some bodies are cloaked in wax, plastic, or foil to prevent the angels from creating a rind. Other cheeses are baptized in a salty brine to form a thin rind and then waxed to further protect the body as it ages. If you peel the wax away, the rind beneath is still edible and often quite tasty due to the extra salt.

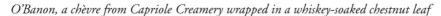

O'Banon, a chèvre from Capriole Creamery wrapped in a whiskey-soaked chestnut leaf

Farmer, Earth, and the Virgin Milk

AS THE FAMOUS FRENCH CHEESE PROPHET PIERRE ANDROUËT ONCE SAID, "CHEESE IS THE SOUL OF THE SOIL. IT IS THE PUREST AND MOST ROMANTIC LINK BETWEEN HUMANS AND THE EARTH."

I like to think of Cheesus as the holy daughter of Mother Nature and the prophets who transform Her gifts into divine dairy blessings. It all starts with the dairy farmer and how they tend to and collaborate with the land and animals—and that's really hard work.

You can't make good cheese from bad milk, so it's up to the farmer to ensure their practices result in a quality product. Dairy farmers work pretty much 24 hours a day, 365 days a year, tilling the soil, fertilizing the pastures, managing the forage, cleaning the stalls, and milking the herd. They don't take a lot of breaks. Even on holidays and birthdays, they still have to manage their land and tend to their herds. It's a life of incessant, grueling work with long hours and endless tasks that only restart the next day.

In addition to all that, dairy farmers must work within the natural rhythms of nature. As the seasons change, so too does the composition of the Virgin Milk. The breed of animal, time of day, lactation cycle, climate, geography, and especially the seasons all affect Her makeup and how She will transform into a body of Cheesus. Fresh spring grasses produce bright, herbaceous flavors in fresh goat cheeses; the rich bouquet of a summer pasture manifests in the golden pastes of Alpine cheeses; and the fatty milk of autumn creates the custardy richness of cheeses such as Vacherin Mont d'Or.

MILK TYPES

The species and breed of animal have a profound effect on the Virgin Milk and the body of Cheesus, affecting everything, including appearance, flavor, texture, and even digestibility.

THE HOLY COW 🐄

Cow (EN), *Vache* (FR), *Vaca* (IT), *Vaca* (SP)

The bovine is the most well-known and popular milk-producing animal. They have long lactation cycles, and because they're bigger than sheep or goats, they produce more milk by volume. Cows are beautiful but high-maintenance and expensive, demanding ample feed and cushy quarters.

ANATOMY OF COW'S MILK

Appearance: golden yellow due to the beta-carotene in grass, which travels through the cow's bloodstream into the milk

Texture: buttery and smooth

Flavors: fruity, earthy, and creamy

Examples: Brie, cheddar, Stilton

EXAMPLES OF COW BREEDS

Jersey: Named for the island in the English Channel off the coast of Normandy, these chestnut-colored ladies produce rich milk with large fat globules, perfect for making butter and soft cheeses.

Brown Swiss: Originating in the Swiss Alps, these silvery-brown cows are favored for their full-flavored milk that's perfect for making hardy aged cheeses.

Opposite page: Jersey girls at pasture

Montbéliarde: An elegant breed from the French Alps splattered with reddish spots. Their milk is used for many famous French cheeses, including Comté, Morbier, and Cantal.

THE EWE-CHARIST 🐑

Sheep (EN), *Brebis* (FR), *Pecora* (IT), *Oveja* (SP)

Though less popular than cows, sheep are heartier, less demanding, and adapt better to rockier, more barren terrain. They're less prolific than cows, but their milk contains more protein and nearly twice as much fat as cow's milk.

ANATOMY OF SHEEP'S MILK

Appearance: pale and ivory

Texture: unctuous and rich

Flavors: nutty and sweet with gentle wooly notes from the lanolin oil on sheep's skin

Examples: Manchego, Pecorino, Roquefort

East Friesian sheep

EXAMPLES OF SHEEP BREEDS

East Friesian: Originating in the Netherlands, these docile sheep are white and fluffy with long ears and skinny tails. They produce more milk, but it has less fat and protein compared to other breeds.

Lacaune: These noble Frenchies are elegant and sassy with short, fine coats and pink noses. Their milk is used for the famous French blue Roquefort.

Sarda: With elegant faces and long coats of crimped wool, these Italian queens are beloved for their ability to withstand rugged terrains while still producing delicious milk.

THE GLORIOUS GOAT

Goat (EN), *Chèvre* (FR), *Capra* (IT), *Cabra* (SP)

Goats are the most common choice for small producers because they're relatively low maintenance and have playful, pet-like personalities. Despite their reputation as scavengers, most dairy goats can be really picky eaters.

Think you HATE GOAT CHEESE?

It's much more likely that you just haven't met the right goat's milk body of Cheesus. Great chèvre is fluffy and clean, not stiff and gamey. That intense goaty flavor develops when the momma goats are living too close to the famously stanky daddy goats. Their animal musk is so intense that the Virgin Milk soaks it right up. If you're looking for some great beginner goat's milk bodies of Cheesus, try Bûcheron or Midnight Moon, a goat's milk Gouda from Cypress Grove.

ANATOMY OF GOAT'S MILK

Appearance: bright white, because the goat's body fully converts the beta-carotene in grass

Texture: fragile and crumbly, due to the smaller fats and proteins and the way they clump together

Flavors: tangy, herbaceous, clean, and bright

Examples: Fresh chèvre, Humboldt Fog, Garrotxa

Baby Nigerian Dwarf goats

EXAMPLES OF GOAT BREEDS

Nubian: One of the most popular breeds in America, these mischievous goats have long, floppy ears and playful, cat-like personalities.

Lamancha: Distinguished by their short pixie ears, these adorable goats have loveable, gentle demeanors and produce rich, fatty milk.

Nigerian Dwarf: Undeniably the cutest breed, these stout and sturdy goats are sweet natured, low maintenance, and prolific, producing full-bodied, dense milk.

THE BLESSED WATER BUFFALO 🐃

Buffalo (EN), *Buffle* (FR), *Bufala* (IT), *Buffalo* (SP)

While uncommon in the United States, water buffalo are used as dairy animals throughout the world, including in parts of southern Asia, northern Africa, along the Mediterranean, and in Latin America. When domesticated, they're docile creatures that produce rich milk, with twice the fat and half the cholesterol of cow's milk.

ANATOMY OF WATER BUFFALO'S MILK

Appearance: bright white

Texture: rich and luscious

Flavor: clean, creamy, and tangy

Examples: Mozzarella di Bufala, Camembert di Bufala, Quadrello di Bufala

EXAMPLES OF WATER BUFFALO BREEDS

Italian Mediterranean: Strong, sturdy, and coated with shiny black fur, their rich milk is famously used for Mozzarella di Bufala DOP.

Bhadawari: Hailing from India, these ladies sport dark, coppery coats and are prized for their ability to produce extremely rich milk in sparse conditions.

Murrah: Jet black with short, tightly curled horns, these famed dairy queens originated in India but are now found all over the world, including in Egypt, the Philippines, and Brazil.

SACRED BREEDS

Just like how grape varietals determine the resulting wine, different animal breeds produce unique traits in the body of Cheesus. Once upon a time there were many heritage breeds, but a lot of those ancient bloodlines have since disappeared. During the industrial age, heritage breeds like the beautiful tan spotted Guernsey began to disappear in favor of black-and-white, high-output Holsteins. Favored for their rich, complex milk, heritage breeds are now making a comeback among artisan producers.

HUMANE TREATMENT

The modern cheese industry has gotten a bad reputation for inhumane treatment of dairy animals. For industrial commodity cheeses, the reputation is deserved. But an artisanal body of Cheesus requires the highest quality of milk, and there's no shortcut to that. The animals must be treated with respect and love in order to produce pristine, flavorful milk, so humane treatment is in the maker's best interest. It's another reason to get to know your cheese-makers and understand their practices. If you're particularly interested in the wellbeing of the animals, look for the "Certified Humane" label (see Anatomy of a Cheese Label on page 194).

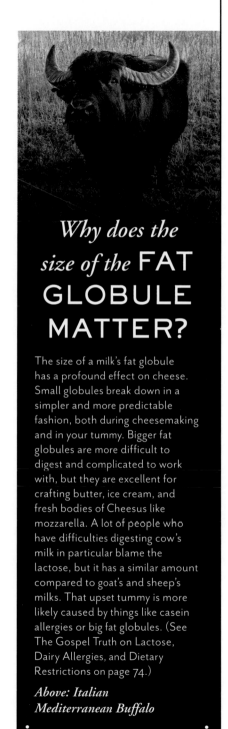

Why does the size of the FAT GLOBULE MATTER?

The size of a milk's fat globule has a profound effect on cheese. Small globules break down in a simpler and more predictable fashion, both during cheesemaking and in your tummy. Bigger fat globules are more difficult to digest and complicated to work with, but they are excellent for crafting butter, ice cream, and fresh bodies of Cheesus like mozzarella. A lot of people who have difficulties digesting cow's milk in particular blame the lactose, but it has a similar amount compared to goat's and sheep's milks. That upset tummy is more likely caused by things like casein allergies or big fat globules. (See The Gospel Truth on Lactose, Dairy Allergies, and Dietary Restrictions on page 74.)

Above: Italian Mediterranean Buffalo

THE VIRTUES OF RAW MILK BODIES OF CHEESUS

WHAT IS RAW MILK?

Raw milk is milk straight from the udder: untouched, pure, and alive with vibrant organisms. It's never heated above the animal's body temperature, preserving the natural flora that reflect the character of the land—producing what the French call *terroir,* or what the raw milk prophets at Jasper Hill Farm call the "taste of place."

Bodies of Cheesus made with raw milk often taste more flavorful than their pasteurized sisters. They have more diverse colonies of microbial angels that reflect the entire terroir: the land, the animals, the people, the equipment, and even the environments where the body of Cheesus is made and aged. But these microbes are also unpredictable, perishable, and prone to contamination if mishandled.

WHAT IS PASTEURIZATION?

Pasteurization is the process of heating milk to a specific temperature for a certain amount of time in order to kill bacteria prior to cheesemaking. There are different types of pasteurization: low and slow, which prevents any cooked flavors, and high and fast, which has a bigger impact on flavor and texture.

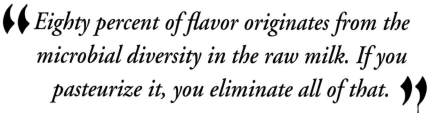

❝ *Eighty percent of flavor originates from the microbial diversity in the raw milk. If you pasteurize it, you eliminate all of that.* ❞

—*Mateo Kehler of Jasper Hill Farm*

WHAT DOES THAT MEAN FOR CHEESUS?

Pasteurization destroys potential pathogens, but it also kills all the good bacteria. It essentially scrubs the milk of character, creating a plain, neutral flavor. Don't get me wrong—there are many sacred, holy pasteurized cheeses out there, but they're always missing that deep complexity from the naturally occurring microbes.

Cheesemakers of today have access to many lab-cultivated cultures, allowing them to play God and create the same body of Cheesus consistently. They have more control over the process, like creating a designer baby with the desired eye color, hair texture, and personality traits.

IS RAW MILK CHEESE SAFE?

When handled responsibly, raw milk cheeses are not only safe to worship, they're often more delicious, complex, and sometimes even healthier due to the various bacteria at work within the body of Cheesus. Cheesemakers working with raw milk must be extremely meticulous about cleanliness—everywhere from the animals to the cheesemaking equipment to the aging environment. At the end of the day, you're probably more likely to get sick from lettuce than a raw milk cheese.

THE SIXTY-DAY RULE

Due to FDA regulations, all bodies of Cheesus that are made with raw milk must be aged for sixty days or more. This eliminates all raw milk fresh and soft bodies of Cheesus, which are past their prime by the time they reach their sixtieth day. This isn't the norm worldwide: Australians are even more chaste, allowing only a handful of raw milk imports, while Europeans famously take a free-love approach, allowing the sale of raw milk butter, Brie, and other delicacies that aren't even aged for a full day.

RAW VS. UNPASTEURIZED VS. THERMIZED MILK

In the US, there is no legal definition for raw milk. Milk that's labeled "unpasteurized" may have been heated above body temperature, but not to the specifications designated by pasteurization laws. In Europe, they call such cheeses "thermized" because their governments are more concerned about correctly categorizing the bodies of Cheesus compared to America.

St. LOUIS PASTEUR

Louis Pasteur was a French scientist whose work helped to curb the spread of infectious disease and advance microbiological studies of fermentation. In 1864, he invented pasteurization as a way to increase the consistency and shelf life of wine.

Many connoisseurs tend to look down on pasteurization, but we should all be very grateful for Saint Louis's invention, a miracle that has saved many dairy disciples. As people moved from farm to city during the industrial revolution, food had to be transported along with them. This was a problem for milk. Trapped in poor storage for days, milk found itself condemned to spoilage and forced to harbor dangerous pathogens as a result. Pasteurization killed these pathogens and made milk safe again.

Years later, pasteurization was used as a shortcut, allowing for low-quality milk to be used in cheesemaking. This not only leads to bland, lifeless cheese, but it can be a dangerous fallacy. Pasteurization is neither a magical cure-all nor a guarantee. If handled incorrectly, milk and cheese can be contaminated even after pasteurization.

THE GOSPEL TRUTH ON LACTOSE, DAIRY ALLERGIES, AND DIETARY RESTRICTIONS

Many people believe that if you're cursed with lactose intolerance, you are damned to a life without Cheesus. But that is blasphemy. Most bodies of Cheesus are virtually lactose-free.

Lactose is the sugar that lives in the Virgin Milk, and lactose intolerance is the inability to digest this milk sugar. When Cheesus is made, bacteria digest much of this milk sugar for you, turning lactose into lactic acid. Any uneaten lactose stays in the liquid whey, which drains from the solid curd throughout the making and aging processes. The longer the cheese ages, the more lactose is converted and drained, which means that firm bodies can safely bless those afflicted by lactose intolerance.

If you are cursed with lactose intolerance, let yourself indulge in firm, aged wedges, and avoid young, high-moisture bodies as well as processed cheeses, which are emulsified with whey.

Avoid: ricotta, cream cheese, mozzarella, American cheese
Favor: Gouda, Alpine styles, Manchego, Parmigiano-Reggiano

LACTOSE INTOLERANCE

Digesting lactose requires an enzyme called lactase. We're all born with lactase so that we can digest our mother's milk, but it starts to disappear as we're weaned and age. Over time, most people become somewhat lactose intolerant, but there is always Saint Lactaid to bless our bodies with enough lactase to enjoy creamy foods.

DIGESTION DIFFICULTIES AND ALLERGIES

Many people who think they're lactose intolerant or have a dairy allergy actually just have a problem digesting cow's milk. Some say that sheep's and goat's milks have a lot less lactose than cow's milk, but the levels of lactose are actually quite comparable. Sheep's and goat's milks can, however, be easier to digest because they have smaller fat globules than cow's milk.

If you have difficulty digesting Cheesus, try goat's and sheep's milk bodies or anything that's aged a year or more, like Parmigiano-Reggiano. If you have an actual dairy allergy, then all forms of dairy milk can trigger inflammatory reactions and there isn't much you can do.

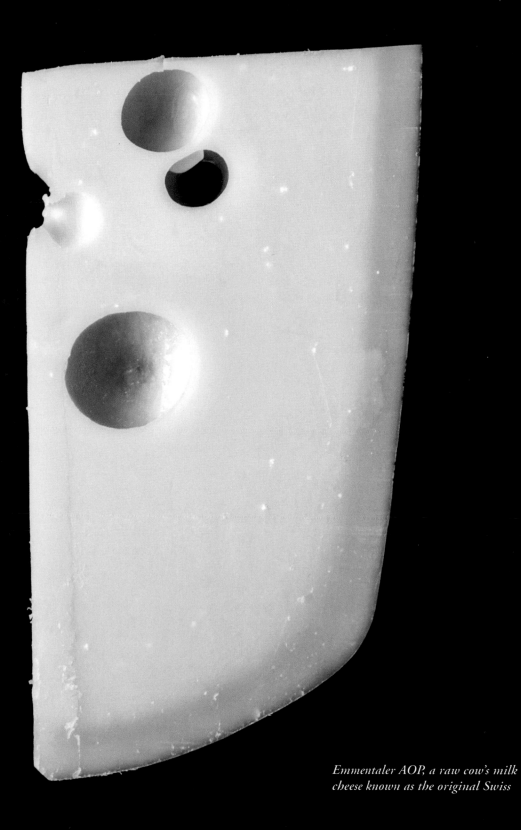

Emmentaler AOP, a raw cow's milk cheese known as the original Swiss

WORSHIPPING CHEESUS WHILE PREGNANT

Let me start out by saying that I am a cheese preacher, not a doctor, and am not licensed to give out any medical advice. I can, however, provide some insight on this subject. Pregnant women are instructed to avoid all raw milk cheeses, but I personally disagree with that. Even when pasteurized, high-moisture, soft cheeses like Camembert are more suited to harboring harmful bacteria than low-moisture, aged bodies of Cheesus, which are extremely inhospitable to pathogens.

In my opinion, it's not a bad idea for anyone who is pregnant to avoid all bodies of Cheesus with a soft, creamy texture. Instead, read up on Firm Bodies (page 138) and spend the next nine months exploring this category with abandon. This is the largest category of cheese, and there is so much to discover even for an experienced worshipper. After that baby pops out, go ahead and re-indulge in Brie, ricotta, and everything in between.

IS CHEESUS VEGETARIAN?

While many vegetarians still regularly enjoy dairy blessings, some bodies of Cheesus aren't technnically vegetarian. These bodies, like Parmigiano, are made using animal rennet, a powerful coagulating enzyme sourced from the stomach of a young dairy animal. While bodies made with animal rennet are not vegetarian, there are a lot of bodies made from alternative rennets that are. Check the ingredients on the label or ask your cheesemonger if a body of Cheesus is made with animal rennet, and see page 56 for more information about rennet types.

Some argue that dairy is never vegetarian. Cheesus begins with the Virgin Milk from a lactating animal. In order for that animal to produce milk, it needs to give birth first. That means that dairying results in a lot of baby dairy animals. While some go on to become milking animals or lucky studs, most end up as food. Luckily, vegan nut-based cheese products have improved immensely over the past few years, so if traditional cheese contradicts your dietary choices, explore those options.

CAN CATS AND DOGS WORSHIP CHEESUS?

Dogs and cats love worshipping Cheesus, and can generally do so safely. Just like people, some pets may have dairy allergies or may even be lactose intolerant, so start gently with an aged, low-lactose body like cheddar or something with small, digestible fat globules like fresh chèvre. If they get sick or don't like it, save Cheesus for yourself. If they like it, enjoy the bonding ritual of worshipping with your loving companion. Keep in mind that a lot of pets don't have as sophisticated palates as people do, so they may not appreciate the subtle nuances of the most sacred bodies of Cheesus. Be careful of moldy rinds and blues, as some strains of mold can be toxic to pets. That being said, I am a cheese preacher and not a veterinarian, so take my advice with a grain of salt.

My cat, Chandler, has a very
sophisticated palate, which always
dismisses overripe bodies of Cheesus.
His favorites are cheddar and
triple-cream Brie.

CHEESUS IS A DELICIOUS *AND* NUTRITIOUS BLESSING FOR YOUR BODY

Cheesus has a bad reputation for being unhealthy and fattening, but that is blasphemy. She's a near-perfect food: an exceptional source of protein, calcium, omega-3 fats, and vitamins D, E, and B12. The only essential nutrients She lacks are vitamin C and fiber, both of which are easily sourced from the many fruits and vegetables that pair so well with Her (see page 255 for more on accompaniments).

Research shows that worshipping regularly can improve your heart health, lower your blood pressure and cholesterol, and boost your immune system. Blessing your daily diet with Cheesus is also linked to a faster metabolism and longer lifespan. The key is portion control, which is hard to do when Cheesus is so damn tasty. But think of it this way: by eating a comfortable amount, you can worship Her more often. (See Serving Size, page 211).

IS CHEESE ADDICTIVE?

We've all seen those viral articles claiming that Cheesus is as addictive as a certain illicit substance. While these claims are misleading, there's a reason for the analogy. Truth be told, Cheesus has a miraculous ability to activate our reward centers by releasing dopamine.

Dopamine is a neurotransmitter released during pleasurable activities, like having sex or indulging in salty, fatty, or carb-rich foods like pizza. Unlike with dairy-free indulgences, our bodies get an added rush of dopamine when we digest the casein proteins found in a body of Cheesus. These proteins break down into peptides, which bind to the same opioid receptors as narcotics.

While Cheesus elicits pleasurable sensations that leave us smiling and satisfied, that doesn't mean She's addictive. We don't experience withdrawal after worship. We simply crave more because our body recognizes Cheesus as the sacred source of nutrients and pleasure that She is. So go forth and worship!

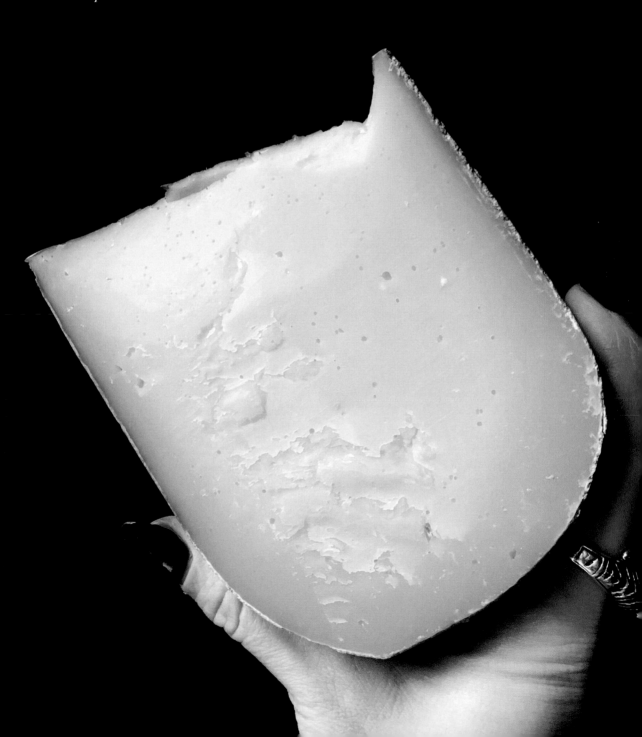

Pleasant Ridge Reserve, a raw cow's milk cheese from Uplands Cheese in Wisconsin

The 10 Commandments of Cheese Church

The following tenets will guide you in your journey toward Cheesus. They will guarantee the most pleasure as you worship, without disrespecting our Lord with acts of blasphemy.

1. **THOU SHALT BUY CHEESUS OFTEN:** As soon as She's cut from the wheel, Cheesus starts to deteriorate. The smaller the piece, the quicker She loses Her foxy flavor power. Only buy as much as you can eat in a few days, consume it quickly, then go buy more.

2. **THOU SHALT LOVE THY MONGER:** Cheesemongers are our prophets and preachers, so seek their guidance in your journey toward Cheesus. Visit them often and ask them what they are excited about. They always know which bodies are at their best and are often eager to offer a sample or pairing advice.

3. **THOU SHALT ENJOY CHEESUS AT ROOM TEMPERATURE:** Refrigeration dulls the sexy flavors in a body of Cheesus. It also makes the texture more brittle and less gooey and giving. Let your softies sit out for at least twenty minutes and your firmies for forty. This goes for cooking with Cheesus, too.

4. **THOU SHALT CUT CHEESUS WITH RESPECT:** When cutting soft bodies like Brie, aim for an equal rind ratio. Instead of cubing firm bodies, slice them thinly to maximize flavor. If She's crumbly, don't fight it; keep Her in a larger piece and chip off a few snackable chunks.

5. **THOU SHALT TRY THE RIND:** All rinds are edible, unless they're coated in wax, cloth, or plastic. Some of them are delicious and can add all sorts of kinky flavors and textures to your cheese experience. Try them all at least once. If you don't like it, that's OK. You don't have to eat it again.

6. **THOU SHALT NOT WRAP CHEESUS IN PLASTIC:** Cheesus is alive and needs oxygen to breathe and stay healthy. Wrapping Her in plastic suffocates and eventually kills Her, ruining Her flavor and even making Her slimy. I recommend using professional cheese paper, or wrapping Her tightly in wax paper and storing Her in a loose resealable bag.

7. **THOU SHALT FRESHLY GRATE THE BODY OF CHEESUS:** Freshly grated Cheesus has a better flavor and smoother texture than pre-shredded varieties, which often include preservatives and declumping agents that diminish flavor and meltability.

8. **THOU SHALT USE ONE KNIFE PER BODY:** Always use a different knife for each body, otherwise everything will start to taste the same. The unique, complex flavors of each Cheesus are special and deserve their moment in the spotlight. You don't want to funk up a delicate chèvre with a boisterous blue.

9. **THOU SHALT SAVOR WITH ALL THY SENSES:** Enjoying Cheesus is a full sensory experience, so give Her your entire body, mind, and soul. Take in Her beauty, touch Her body, and breathe in Her scent. Then, taste Her naked, savoring the flavors before adding accompaniments. When tasting multiple bodies, begin with the mildest and end with the strongest.

10. **THOU SHALT EXPERIMENT:** Eat Cheesus often and try new bodies, too. It's the only way to learn what you like and discover new lovers. Once you fall for a particular body, then get a little kinky with pairings. Discover what excites you, then test your boundaries.

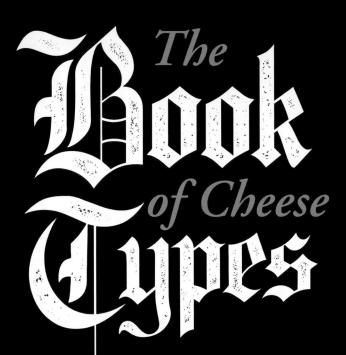

The Book of Cheese Types

Cheesus takes thousands of different forms, each uniquely seductive and divine in Her own way. While it's nearly impossible to perfectly categorize Her many beautiful body types, a bit of organization can help you navigate the sexy, exotic world of Cheesus.

I've broken down Her body types into five simple categories: fresh, bloomy, washed, firm, and blue. There is an astounding amount of variation within these groups, but familiarizing yourself with them will help you accurately describe and identify almost any cheese. You'll also have some idea of how She'll taste and what you should pair with Her.

Clockwise from top left:
Aphrodite Feta, Green Hill,
Firefly's Spruce Reserve,
L'Amuse Gouda, Roquefort AOC ,
Alpha Tolman, and Willoughby

Fresh Bodies

Holy infants so tender and mild, fresh bodies of Cheesus are unaged, plump with moisture, and meant to be worshipped soon after they are released into the world. Too young to form rinds, their bodies are supple, naked curd all the way through.

The Sultry Wheys of Fresh Cheesus

FRESHIES ARE MADE ALL OVER THE WORLD: FROMAGE BLANC IN FRANCE, QUARK IN GERMANY, MOZZARELLA IN ITALY, PANEER IN INDIA, FETA IN GREECE, ACKAWI IN THE MIDDLE EAST, AREESH IN EGYPT, AND SQUEAKY CURDS IN WISCONSIN, TO NAME JUST A FEW.

Relatively cheap and easy to produce, they make enticing prey for industrial labels, but an exquisite fresh body will always make Herself known. Untouched by the transformative effects of aging, there's very little to hide behind. A quality fresh body of Cheesus is a blessed gift that reflects the glory of pristine milk and expert craftsmanship.

GRASS RESURRECTED

A truly sacred fresh body of Cheesus is the purest manifestation of milk—a celebration of sunshine and the vivacious vegetation that nourished the animal. The best freshies reflect the quality of the grasses, herbs, and flowers, so the season heavily influences the milk. The juicy, nutrient-dense first blades of spring grass create some of the most dazzling fresh bodies of Cheesus. Imagine the flavor of a peak-season strawberry, bursting with sweet, sticky nectar, and you'll get an idea of how lush spring pastures taste to a grazing dairy animal.

A GENTLE HAND

To keep their bodies plump with moisture, freshies are made with large, delicate curds that require the utmost tender loving care. It's like making pancakes: if you're aggressive and overmix the batter, you'll get a dense, tough cake. If you gently fold the ingredients together, the delicate batter will yield fluffy cakes as light as the featherbeds of angels. There's nothing like that gentle human touch, which is why it's important to seek handcrafted freshies when possible.

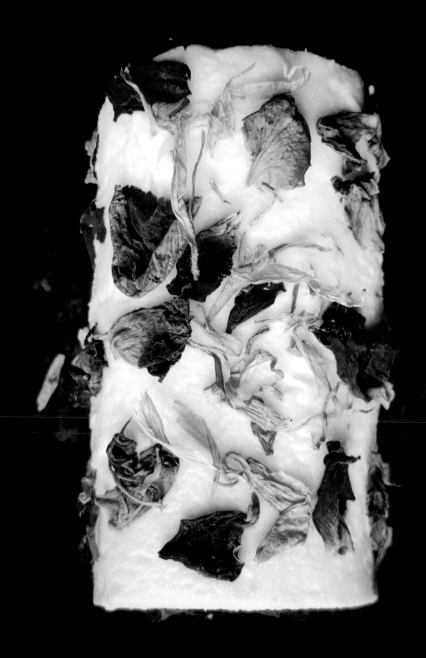

Fresh chèvre with edible flowers

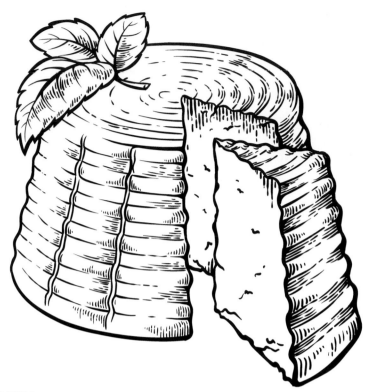

EAT IT NOW

The high moisture content that makes freshies so luscious also welcomes spoilage. While a vacuum seal or brine will extend their lifespans, the moment you break the seal or lift their bodies from their salty baptismal waters, the clock starts ticking. Traditionally, fresh bodies of Cheesus were purchased just before eating and meant for immediate consumption. It's not always possible to get a cheese that's so fresh, but we can honor the tradition by buying local and devouring promptly.

WORSHIPPING FRESH CHEESUS

WHAT TO LOOK FOR: local, handmade cheeses, thoroughly white or ivory with fresh, milky sweet flavors and smooth textures

WHAT TO AVOID: industrial cheeses with grainy textures, splotches of color, and sour, funky flavors

SHELF LIFE: 1–5 days

STORAGE: airtight bags or tubs with lids; if She comes stored in brine, keep Her in there until She's gone

Types of Fresh Bodies

FRESH BODIES OF CHEESUS ARE UNAGED AND RINDLESS, RANGING FROM SOFT AND SPREADABLE TO BOUNCY AND SPRINGY.

 **SPREADABLE, LIKE MASCARPONE** These cheeses have lots of moisture, which keeps them smooth, creamy, and even dippable. They soften when baked and loosen into saucy richness when tossed with hot pasta.

 **PASTA FILATA, LIKE MOZZARELLA** These cheeses are formed by baptizing baby curds in hot water, then pulling and stretching them into a smooth, shiny mass. Aged versions of this cheese type include provolone and scamorza.

 **BRINED, LIKE FETA** These fresh bodies are pickled for weeks or months in a salted solution that keeps them moist and preserved. While this extends their shelf life, once they leave the safety of their brines, their lifespans reduce to a couple of days.

 **PRESSED, LIKE PANEER** These spongy, springy bodies are lightly pressed to expel moisture and help knit the curds together. Some varieties, such as Halloumi, are also gently cooked in hot whey.

What do PDO/DOP/AOC mean?

These markers stand for "protected denomination of origin" and designate a cheese that's made in a specific region with special practices. For more information, see Protected Origin Designations on page 195.

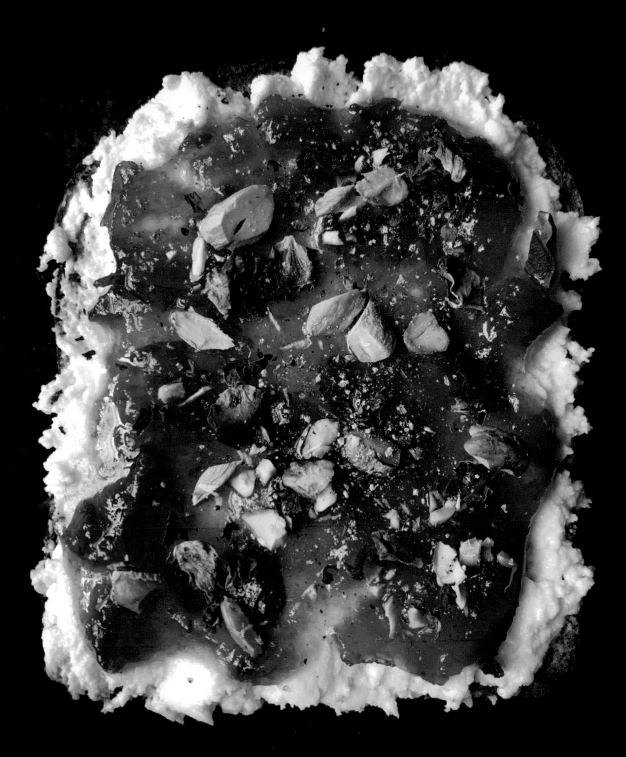

Ricotta with plum preserves, pistachios, and rose petals

FAMOUS VARIETIES

RICOTTA *Italy*

Traditional ricotta isn't actually cheese, because She's made with leftover whey. Her name is Italian for "recooked," because she's made by heating whey until the remaining bits of protein clump together, spawning a mildly sweet, nutty curd that tastes faintly of candied pecans. She's like a miraculous secret, hiding in the whey of all milk types. Most American ricottas are made with a mixture of fresh cow's milk and whey, but it's worth seeking versions made with sheep's or water buffalo's milk. Supermarkets are often stocked with factory versions preserved with gums and stabilizers, but a high-quality ricotta is sweetly satisfying and as fluffy as cotton candy.

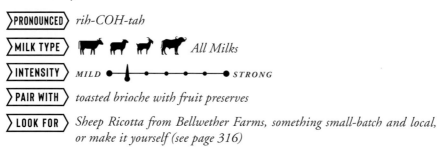

> **PRONOUNCED** *rih-COH-tah*

> **MILK TYPE** *All Milks*

> **INTENSITY** *MILD* ●—|—●—●—●—● *STRONG*

> **PAIR WITH** *toasted brioche with fruit preserves*

> **LOOK FOR** *Sheep Ricotta from Bellwether Farms, something small-batch and local, or make it yourself (see page 316)*

MOZZARELLA DI BUFALA CAMPANIA PDO *Italy*

True, authentic mozzarella is made with buffalo's milk in the Campania region of southern Italy, where cow's milk versions are called *fior di latte* (flower of milk). These sacred orbs are sweet and grassy with a briny spray and shiny shell that houses a fork-tender flesh that peels like the juicy interior of a fried chicken breast. Delicate and highly perishable, they're difficult to export, but luckily there are many wonderful cow's milk versions that are vastly superior to the rubbery factory imitations.

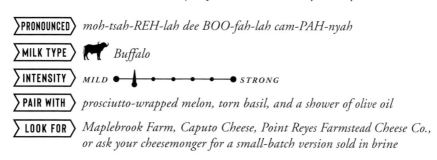

> **PRONOUNCED** *moh-tsah-REH-lah dee BOO-fah-lah cam-PAH-nyah*

> **MILK TYPE** *Buffalo*

> **INTENSITY** *MILD* ●—|—●—●—●—● *STRONG*

> **PAIR WITH** *prosciutto-wrapped melon, torn basil, and a shower of olive oil*

> **LOOK FOR** *Maplebrook Farm, Caputo Cheese, Point Reyes Farmstead Cheese Co., or ask your cheesemonger for a small-batch version sold in brine*

Fresh vs. Low-Moisture
MOZZARELLA

There are two kinds of mozzarella: low-moisture and fresh. Low-moisture mozzarella is the flexible enchantress that blesses pizza with that mesmerizing cheese pull. She's more of a firm body than a freshie, created using rituals that reduce Her water weight to increase both shelf life and melting potential. Unfortunately, this also sacrifices the sweet beckoning flavors of fresh mozzarella.

Cooking with fresh mozzarella can be tricky. Plump with moisture, She'll readily drip Her wetness onto any bed of baked carbohydrates, rendering them flaccid and soggy. Many sacred recipes depend on Her delicate milky flavor, like Margherita pizza. Replacing Her with another body of Cheesus would be sacrilege, so you must proceed with caution.

HERE'S HOW TO PREP FRESH MOZZARELLA TO AVOID SOG WHILE COOKING:

- Lightly blot sliced discs with paper towels
- Drain shredded mozzarella in a sieve for 10 minutes
- Refrain from seasoning with salt until just before serving

BURRATA *Italy*

Bulging bosoms bouncing in brine, burrata is mozzarella's more decadent and promiscuous cousin. The seductress started off as a byproduct of mozzarella, made by forming the leftover bits into shells and stuffing them with shredded scraps soaked in fresh cream (a delicacy called stracciatella). Her beauty is thoroughly dependent on Her delicate youth, so consume Her immediately and do not disrespect Cheesus by letting any leftovers linger. Slice open a sphere, watch the creamy center spill out, and arouse Her with a sprinkle of flaky salt.

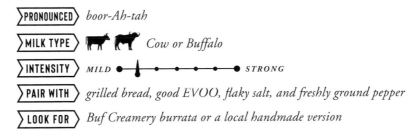

> PRONOUNCED *boor-Ah-tah*

> MILK TYPE *Cow or Buffalo*

> INTENSITY *MILD* ●━┿━●━━●━━●━━━● *STRONG*

> PAIR WITH *grilled bread, good EVOO, flaky salt, and freshly ground pepper*

> LOOK FOR *Buf Creamery burrata or a local handmade version*

*Burrata with EVOO, ramp
salt, and freshly ground pepper*

Mascarpone with maple syrup and smoked salt

MASCARPONE *Italy*

Sinfully silky with a meringue-like fluffiness, mascarpone is the richer, more sophisticated cousin to cream cheese. Originating in Lombardy, rumors suggest that Her name arose from *mas que bueno,* meaning "better than good" in Spanish, during the era when Spain ruled the region. Milky sweet and nearly as voluminous as whipped cream, mascarpone is often found blessing desserts like tiramisu with Her satiny richness. She loves a sweet canvas, but she's also happy to show off in a savory context. Spread Her over grilled toast and top with salty anchovies, sliced radish, and a spritz of lemon (see Seven Blessed Toasts on page 318).

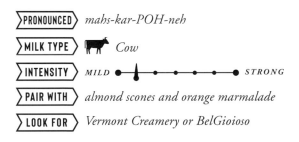

PRONOUNCED ⟩ *mahs-kar-POH-neh*

MILK TYPE ⟩ *Cow*

INTENSITY ⟩ *MILD* ●——╀——●——●——●——● *STRONG*

PAIR WITH ⟩ *almond scones and orange marmalade*

LOOK FOR ⟩ *Vermont Creamery or BelGioioso*

QUESO FRESCO *Mexico*

Spanish for "fresh cheese," queso fresco can include a vast variety of unaged cheeses made in Latin America. The version you are most likely to encounter is a salty, wet loaf of tender, springy crumbles, similar to ricotta or a soft, mild feta. She's simple and milky-sweet with a charming lactic tang that begs to coddle the syrupy juices of ripe fruits, such as melons, citrus, and guava.

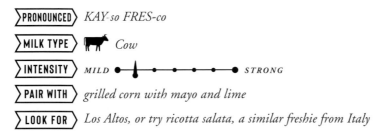

> **PRONOUNCED** *KAY-so FRES-co*

> **MILK TYPE** 🐄 *Cow*

> **INTENSITY** *MILD* ●—┃—●——●——●——————● *STRONG*

> **PAIR WITH** *grilled corn with mayo and lime*

> **LOOK FOR** *Los Altos, or try ricotta salata, a similar freshie from Italy*

PANEER *India*

Paneer is beloved for Her ability to absorb flavors in hot stews without losing Her firm, bouncy body. Traditionally made with cow's or water buffalo's milk, She's often found blessing Pakistani and northern Indian dishes. Here in the United States, it's hard to find a great paneer, but She's relatively easy to make at home. Her gifts and talents are best worshipped in the kitchen, where She's as versatile as tofu. Brown or fry cubed paneer and serve Her with chutneys, or drop Her into a flavorful stew for bites of milky luxury.

Fried paneer with pistachios, honey, and pepper

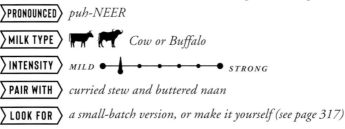

> **PRONOUNCED** *puh-NEER*

> **MILK TYPE** 🐄 🐃 *Cow or Buffalo*

> **INTENSITY** *MILD* ●—┃—●——●——●——————● *STRONG*

> **PAIR WITH** *curried stew and buttered naan*

> **LOOK FOR** *a small-batch version, or make it yourself (see page 317)*

HALLOUMI PDO *Cyprus*

Firm and bouncy like a new mattress, Halloumi is a Cypriot cheese traditionally made by hand using a mixture of sheep's and goat's milk. The baby curds are shaped into discs, folded into half-moons, and flavored with mint. A lot of versions are also made with cow's milk and shaped into blocks about the size and shape of a wallet. Regardless of the silhouette, all Halloumi has a tight protein structure that resists melting, rendering Her perfect for browning over a grill or crisping in a pan. She's also delightful when served unheated, especially when tossed with olive oil, fresh herbs, and crunchy salt.

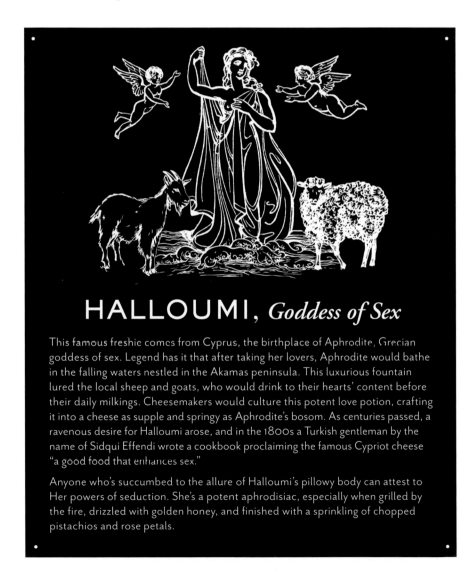

HALLOUMI, *Goddess of Sex*

This famous freshie comes from Cyprus, the birthplace of Aphrodite, Grecian goddess of sex. Legend has it that after taking her lovers, Aphrodite would bathe in the falling waters nestled in the Akamas peninsula. This luxurious fountain lured the local sheep and goats, who would drink to their hearts' content before their daily milkings. Cheesemakers would culture this potent love potion, crafting it into a cheese as supple and springy as Aphrodite's bosom. As centuries passed, a ravenous desire for Halloumi arose, and in the 1800s a Turkish gentleman by the name of Sidqui Effendi wrote a cookbook proclaiming the famous Cypriot cheese "a good food that enhances sex."

Anyone who's succumbed to the allure of Halloumi's pillowy body can attest to Her powers of seduction. She's a potent aphrodisiac, especially when grilled by the fire, drizzled with golden honey, and finished with a sprinkling of chopped pistachios and rose petals.

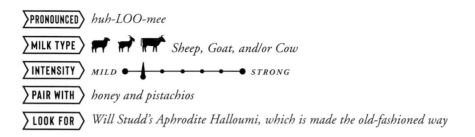

> PRONOUNCED › *huh-LOO-mee*

> MILK TYPE › 🐑 🐐 🐄 *Sheep, Goat, and/or Cow*

> INTENSITY › *MILD* ●—|—●—●—●—● *STRONG*

> PAIR WITH › *honey and pistachios*

> LOOK FOR › *Will Studd's Aphrodite Halloumi, which is made the old-fashioned way*

CURDS *Wisconsin (and other cheddar capitals)*

Cheese curds are the building blocks for all incarnations of Cheesus, but these adorable nuggets sold by the bag are baby versions of what would have become cheddar. They're like the chips of the cheese world: snackable alone and perfect for building with flavors and seasonings. They squeak when they're fresh because their protein network is so tight that they audibly snap and break against your teeth. The network loosens after a day or two, and they'll lose their squeak but become stretchier when fried.

> PRONOUNCED › *kerds*

> MILK TYPE › 🐄 *Cow*

> INTENSITY › *MILD* ●—|—●—●—●—● *STRONG*

> PAIR WITH › *a deep fryer and ranch dressing*

> LOOK FOR › *something local, or order from an artisan producer in a cheddar capital like Vermont or Wisconsin*

Cheese curds

These pudgy cubes from Australia are mild and creamy, ideal for soaking up the flavorful marinade

FETA PDO *Greece*

Wet, salty, and refreshingly tangy, feta is a summer siren and flirtatious kitchen playmate. Dry-salted and pickled in brine, this Greek goddess is another unfortunate victim of industrial cheesemaking. The name is unprotected outside the European Union, so you'll find imposters made with cow's milk or even ones that have been tragically pre-crumbled and preserved with chemical stabilizers. The real thing is far superior—made in Greece using varying ratios of sheep's and goat's milk and sometimes even aged in wooden barrels. Unlike other freshies, feta has a long shelf life thanks to Her high levels of salt and acid. The best feta is sold in brine, where She stays fresh, tender, and as bright as a summer afternoon. Cube and lube with olive oil or crumble briny blessings onto juicy fruits and fresh salads.

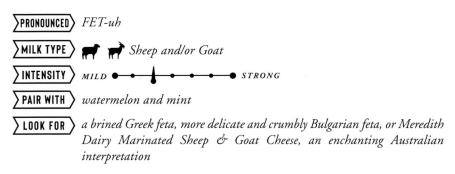

〉PRONOUNCED〉 *FET-uh*

〉MILK TYPE〉 *Sheep and/or Goat*

〉INTENSITY〉 MILD ●——●——|——●——●——● STRONG

〉PAIR WITH〉 *watermelon and mint*

〉LOOK FOR〉 *a brined Greek feta, more delicate and crumbly Bulgarian feta, or Meredith Dairy Marinated Sheep & Goat Cheese, an enchanting Australian interpretation*

FRESH CHÈVRE *Everywhere*

Fresh goat cheese is made all over the world, but it's known as chèvre because it's the French who made it so popular. The sexy, whispery name means "goat," and can refer to a variety of goat's milk bodies of Cheesus. Many people think they dislike fresh chèvre because they've only had gritty, gummy, and gamey versions. When well-crafted, She's bright and cloud-like with a pleasant tartness that never encroaches on sour. Fluffy and almost spreadable at room temperature, chèvre will loosen when heated but doesn't melt the way many firm bodies do. The best chèvre is made in the springtime, when dairy animals feast on lush new pastures and give birth to their babies, kickstarting their milk-giving cycle. The resulting cheeses glow with the vibrancy of spring, as frisky and playful as the animal that creates it.

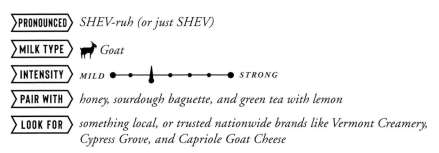

〉PRONOUNCED〉 *SHEV-ruh (or just SHEV)*

〉MILK TYPE〉 *Goat*

〉INTENSITY〉 MILD ●——●——|——●——●——● STRONG

〉PAIR WITH〉 *honey, sourdough baguette, and green tea with lemon*

〉LOOK FOR〉 *something local, or trusted nationwide brands like Vermont Creamery, Cypress Grove, and Capriole Goat Cheese*

Accompaniments and Pairings

MELLOW AND EASYGOING LIKE A SUMMER DAY, THE MILD, SIMPLE FLAVOR PROFILES AND TENDER TEXTURES OF FRESHIES MAKE THEM THE PERFECT BASE FOR SPICES AND HERBS. FAVOR REFRESHING FLAVORS FROM WARM-CLIMATE REGIONS, LIKE MEDITERRANEAN OLIVE OIL AND TROPICAL FRUITS. AVOID HEAVY PAIRINGS AND RICH BEVERAGES, WHICH WILL DOMINATE THEIR DELICATE BODIES.

SWEET
HONEYS · BALSAMIC VINEGAR · FIGS · PRESERVES · MARMALADES

CRUNCHY
CUCUMBERS · RADISHES · NUTS · SHORTBREAD · TOAST · CRACKERS

JUICY
BERRIES · OLIVES · CITRUS · SWEET CORN · STONE FRUIT · MELON · CAVIAR · TOMATOES

DRINKS
ROSÉ · BUBBLY COCKTAILS · WHITE TEA · SPARKLING WINE · WHEAT BEER

A SAVIOR *for the* SAVORY

Mild, milky fresh bodies bring balance to bold flavors.
Take a walk on the salty side with a savory accompaniment:

**PROSCIUTTO • TAPENADE • PESTO • CURED FISH • HERBED OIL • ROASTED
VEGETABLES • MARINATED CHILES • CURRY SAUCES • ZA'ATAR**

Above: Fresh chèvre with olive oil, olives, rosemary, and charcoal bread

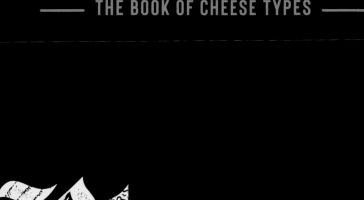

Of all the various forms of Cheesus, there is none that evokes such carnal desire as the creamy, runny, drip-down-your-arm vixens of the bloomy family. This category includes all those luxurious ladies with delicate, pale rinds and soft, sensual interiors.

Buxom Bloomies

THESE YOUTHFUL COQUETTES ARE AGED FOR WEEKS,

WITH VOLUPTUOUS BODIES THAT RANGE FROM FIRM AND CHALKY TO SPREADABLE LIKE WHIPPED BUTTER. THEY'RE ALSO DELICATE DAMSELS, RICH WITH MOISTURE AND CURSED WITH SHORT LIFESPANS. THEY'RE VERY SENSITIVE AND REQUIRE LOTS OF CODDLING WHEN THEY'RE MADE, AGED, HANDLED, AND EVEN STORED AT HOME. BUT TREAT THEM RIGHT, AND THEY'LL INDULGE ALL YOUR NAUGHTIEST FROMAGE FANTASIES.

THE MIRACULOUS TRANSFORMATION

Cheeses in this category have three distinct layers: a firm inner paste, a softer creamline, and a rind bustling with a living colony of microbial angels that bloom like white flowers in a meadow.

These microbes are either added to the milk or latch on in the cheese caves, and they work their magic on the inner paste as the cheese ages. They digest fats and proteins, transforming stiff curds into luscious, oozing cream. This process creates a soft, gooey layer under the rind called the "creamline." As the cheese ages, the creamline expands and eventually consumes the firm inside completely, at which point the wheel is likely overripe and no longer palatable.

DISCLAIMER: BLOOMY RINDS VS. BRAINY RINDS

For serious curd nerds, the term "bloomy rind" specifically refers to the thick, pillowy rinds on bodies like Brie and Humboldt Fog. This particular type of rind has a dominant presence of the angel known as *Penicillium camemberti*. This mold blossoms into a fluffy-looking coat that the cheesemaker continually pats down to form the thick rind. These rinds differ from the more delicate, wrinkly rinds as seen on Frenchies like Chabichou and American interpretations like Coupole from Vermont Creamery, which are dominated by the angel *Geotrichum candidum*. Cheese experts often categorize these bodies as "geos," "brainies," or more generally as surface-ripened cheeses. I think their similarities outweigh their differences, so I encapsulate both under the bloomy umbrella.

Geotrichum candidum helps create the wrinkly rind on this wheel of La Tur.

BUTTERFAT

The butterfat is the total fat content of a body of Cheesus. It's measured according to the dry matter, meaning without the water weight. Because Cheesus can lose a lot of moisture while She ages, measuring the fat in dry matter is the most consistent and accurate method of measuring fat content across all the various incarnations of Cheesus. However, the measurement can be misleading. For example, a triple-cream Brie that is 75 percent butterfat probably has closer to 40 percent total fat, after accounting for Her water content. By comparison, butter has about 80 percent total fat, which is far more than even the richest triple creams.

WORSHIPPING BLOOMY CHEESUS

WHAT TO LOOK FOR: voluptuous and full cheeses with an even-colored paste and soft, fresh-faced rind that smells faintly erotic

WHAT TO AVOID: bloated or squashed cheeses with a splotchy paste, cracked or bruised rind, or a stench of ammonia

SHELF LIFE: 7–10 days

STORAGE: cheese paper

What's the Difference Between
BRIE AND CAMEMBERT?

Though Americans often use the names interchangeably,
there are a few notable differences between the two cheeses.

BRIE	CAMEMBERT
· Made in Île-de-France	· Made in Normandy
· 14-inch diameter	· 4-inch diameter
· Dates back to the 700s	· Invented in the 1700s
· Cream enriched	· Not cream enriched
· Generally milder	· Generally stinkier

Types of Bloomy Bodies

SOFT-RIPENED CHEESES RANGE FROM PUDDING-SOFT
AND SPOONABLE TO FIRM AND CHALKY LIKE FRESH SNOW.

CLASSIC BLOOMY, LIKE BRIE With soft, quilt-like rinds and luxurious interiors, these cheeses are often the subject of everyone's "first time" with a fancy cheese. They're not all equal, however. Some are classy courtesans, complex and nuanced. Others are cheap lays, with bland, sticky pastes and thick, faintly medicinal rinds.

DOUBLE AND TRIPLE CREAM, LIKE FROMAGER D'AFFINOIS These sumptuous vamps are enriched with added cream to create a paste that's shamelessly spreadable. Mild and pleasing, they indulge that wistful, childlike urge to lick a stick of butter.

ROBIOLA, LIKE ROBIOLA BOSINA These young Italians are made across the northern provinces of Piedmont and Lombardy, and can vary from pudgy and playful to fresh and unaged. Robiolas that are available in America are usually petite, soft, and doughy.

ASH-RIPENED, LIKE HUMBOLDT FOG Often mistaken for blue mold, the shadowy gray hue is actually a vegetable-based ash. While the ash is tasteless and odorless, it makes for a more hospitable environment for the angels to do their ripening work. Like many other goat cheesemaking techniques, the use of vegetable ash was invented in the Loire Valley of France.

GEOTRICHUM, LIKE LA TUR These tender, plush bodies are characterized by the dominant presence of *Geotrichum candidum*. Their veiled, wrinkly rinds are as delicate and whimsical as lingerie, and they are even referred to as a *jolie robe*, or "pretty dress." Their ivory skins smell of a freshly baked baguette and occasionally sprout harmless gem-like spots of blue or green molds. Some of these bodies are lactic-set, meaning they're made without rennet. This results in a looser-set, more delicate curd.

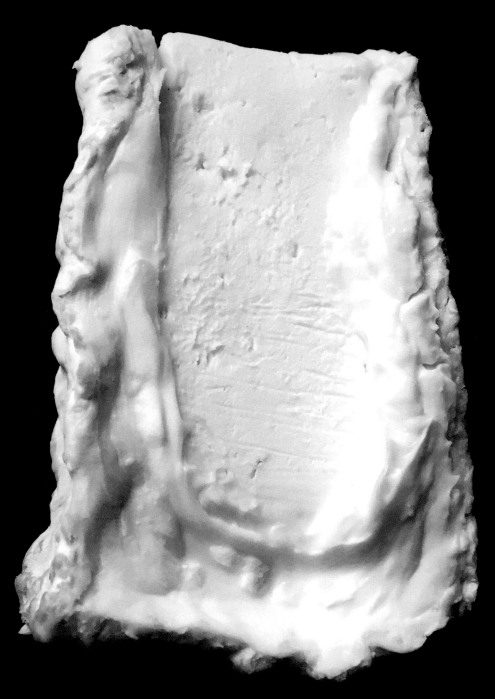

Delice de Bourgogne, a triple-cream Brie style from France that tastes like whipped butter

FAMOUS VARIETIES

DELICE DE BOURGOGNE *France*

French for "the delight of Burgundy," this classic triple-cream Brie-style cheese made by Lincet is famous for its silky, mouth-filling paste. Young wheels are as firm as chilled butter and smell of fresh mushrooms. With age, the insides transform into salty whipped luxury as indulgent as a down comforter. Watch for soft, fresh-faced rinds—anything slimy or ashy has been suffocated and likely tastes soapy.

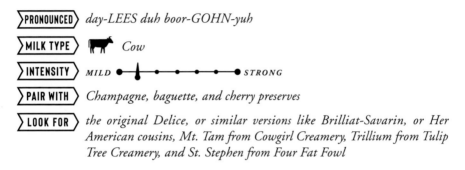

> **PRONOUNCED** 〉 *day-LEES duh boor-GOHN-yuh*

> **MILK TYPE** 〉 *Cow*

> **INTENSITY** 〉 *MILD* ●——|—●——●——●——●● *STRONG*

> **PAIR WITH** 〉 *Champagne, baguette, and cherry preserves*

> **LOOK FOR** 〉 *the original Delice, or similar versions like Brilliat-Savarin, or Her American cousins, Mt. Tam from Cowgirl Creamery, Trillium from Tulip Tree Creamery, and St. Stephen from Four Fat Fowl*

BÛCHERON *France*

Bûcheron is an approachable, eager-to-please chèvre that looks like a snow-covered Yule log. Her rind is thick, peppery, and slightly wrinkled, with a soft, oozing halo that surrounds the dense and chalky interior. At peak ripeness, She resembles a meringue pie, with a firm crust, luscious creamline, and tangy center as dense and fresh as packed snow. Her bright, lemony flavors make Her an ideal goat cheese to seduce even the most adamant of chèvre cynics.

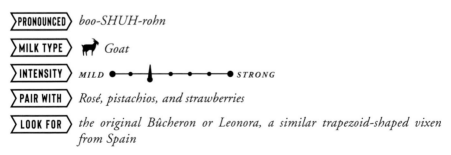

> **PRONOUNCED** 〉 *boo-SHUH-rohn*

> **MILK TYPE** 〉 *Goat*

> **INTENSITY** 〉 *MILD* ●——●——|——●——●——●● *STRONG*

> **PAIR WITH** 〉 *Rosé, pistachios, and strawberries*

> **LOOK FOR** 〉 *the original Bûcheron or Leonora, a similar trapezoid-shaped vixen from Spain*

LA TUR *Italy*

This adorable little cupcake from Caseificio dell'Alta Langa reveals the glory of all three milks: grassy goat, buttery cow, and nutty sheep. She's equal parts silky, fluffy, and oozing, with a sweet milky tang and a wrinkled rind that smells of freshly baked bread. Each luxurious wheel comes in a tiny box, like a personal palanquin, designed to contain Her fragile body. As spoonable and indulgent as pot de crème, La Tur is well suited for solo celebrations. Go ahead, eat the whole wheel with pride.

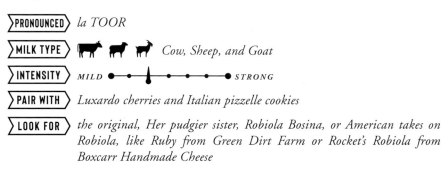

PRONOUNCED > *la TOOR*

MILK TYPE > *Cow, Sheep, and Goat*

INTENSITY > *MILD* ● STRONG

PAIR WITH > *Luxardo cherries and Italian pizzelle cookies*

LOOK FOR > *the original, Her pudgier sister, Robiola Bosina, or American takes on Robiola, like Ruby from Green Dirt Farm or Rocket's Robiola from Boxcarr Handmade Cheese*

HUMBOLDT FOG *California*

One of the most iconic cheeses on the market, Humboldt Fog was conceived in a dream by Mary Keehn, founder of Cypress Grove. An early pioneer of artisan American cheeses, Mary was flying back from a fromage tour of France when she fell into a slumber. She dreamt of a snow-white body of Cheesus, with a shadowy layer of ash cutting right through the center. She soon actualized the dazzling chèvre and named it after the fog that rolls over the white surf in her native Humboldt County. The rind is as piquant as pink peppercorns; the creamline evokes buttermilk frosting; and the dense, crumbly interior whispers with sweet lemony nothings. Humboldt Fog is such a stunning showstopper, She even moonlights as a wedding cake. Cypress Grove now makes a mini one-pound version, but I always prefer a wedge of the original five-pound wheel, which looks just as glamorous as a slice of layer cake.

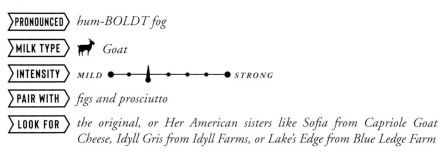

PRONOUNCED > *hum-BOLDT fog*

MILK TYPE > *Goat*

INTENSITY > *MILD* ● STRONG

PAIR WITH > *figs and prosciutto*

LOOK FOR > *the original, or Her American sisters like Sofia from Capriole Goat Cheese, Idyll Gris from Idyll Farms, or Lake's Edge from Blue Ledge Farm*

Humboldt Fog, an iconic goat's milk seductress from Cypress Grove in California

Valençay PDO, a pyramid-shaped, ash-ripened chèvre

The Legend of
KING CHARLEMAGNE,
Patron Saint of Bloomies

One day while on a long and arduous journey, Charlemagne, the legendary king of the Franks, found himself at the Abbaye Notre Dame de Jouarre in present-day France. The king was exhausted and famished, but his religious rites prohibited him from indulging in the flesh of bird or beast that day. As he begged for refreshment, the bishop set before him a ripe wedge of Brie.

Hungry and intrigued, the king took his knife and sliced off the downy white rind. The bishop gasped, "My Lord! Why must thou commit such treachery? For thou art smiting the very best part of our Holy Cheesus."

Charlemagne couldn't imagine that a man of God would mislead him, so he took the cheese—rind and paste all—and slid it between his eager lips. A moan of pleasure emerged from whence the Brie disappeared. Entranced, Charlemagne requested two crates of the cheese be delivered to his home in Aix-en-Provence immediately.

"But my Lord! Though I may procure the cheese, I can't promise that every wheel be perfectly ripened to your standards," said the bishop. "Then select the wheels you deem blessed," retorted Charlemagne, "and procure them in thy cellar, until the day arrives that the consecrated wheels are ready for my palace."

And with that, the miracle of Brie was brought to the public eye and became desired by the cultured elite. Its popularity gave birth to a plethora of other similar cheeses from all over the country made with all the different milks.

VALENÇAY PDO *France*

This ash-ripened coquette has a playful story for how She gained Her iconic shape. Legend has it that after an embarrassing defeat in Egypt, Napoleon Bonaparte returned home to an offering of Valençay. At the time, this body of Cheesus was shaped like a pyramid, which reminded the emperor of his humiliating loss. In a rage of fury, he chopped off the pointed top. Out of respect for their leader, the cheesemakers changed the shape forever, and the decapitated pyramid has remained ever since. The French original is made with raw milk and is much more nuanced than the shy pasteurized wheels found in America. Either way, this body of Cheesus is truly sacred and best enjoyed all by Herself, naked and unadulterated.

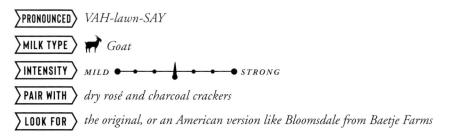

> **PRONOUNCED** *VAH-lawn-SAY*

> **MILK TYPE** 🐐 *Goat*

> **INTENSITY** *MILD* ●—●—●—|—●—●—● *STRONG*

> **PAIR WITH** *dry rosé and charcoal crackers*

> **LOOK FOR** *the original, or an American version like Bloomsdale from Baetje Farms*

HARBISON *Vermont*

The cheese equivalent to a porn that starts in a jacuzzi, Harbison from Jasper Hill Farm will captivate anyone who catches sight of Her fluid eroticism. She's a petite nine-ounce wheel with a thick, downy rind and a kinky belt of spruce bark harvested from Jasper Hill's own woodlands. She's as soft as buttercream frosting when ripe and best served whole, with Her top rind gently removed. Her custardy interior is nuanced and vegetal, buzzing with hints of forest, mushrooms, bacon, and mustard. Even the most dignified epicurean will fall victim to Her sweet siren call, charmed into sliding a slick finger straight into her quivering flesh. She's a star, ready to captivate all on Her own, yet equally eager to serve as a dipping sauce for French fries. Look for wheels nearing their expiration date, which will reward you with the gooiest interiors.

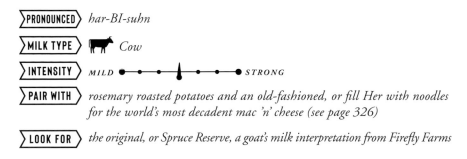

> **PRONOUNCED** *har-BI-suhn*

> **MILK TYPE** 🐄 *Cow*

> **INTENSITY** *MILD* ●—●—●—|—●—●—● *STRONG*

> **PAIR WITH** *rosemary roasted potatoes and an old-fashioned, or fill Her with noodles for the world's most decadent mac 'n' cheese (see page 326)*

> **LOOK FOR** *the original, or Spruce Reserve, a goat's milk interpretation from Firefly Farms*

A perfectly ripe wheel of Harbison from Jasper Hill Farm in Vermont

Hidden Falls Brie from Shepherd's Way Farms in Minnesota

BRIE *France*

Matron saint of bloomies, hallowed Brie thy name! Often imitated but never duplicated, true Brie cheese is made with raw cow's milk in Île-de-France, the region encompassing Paris. Raw milk Bries are nothing like their pasteurized imitators: remarkably savory with a delectable, mushroomy rind that tends to crumble away into the plump, golden paste. One taste will whisk you away with waves of garlic, sweet hay, and even fresh, juicy cheeseburgers. There are currently only two name-protected Bries: Brie de Melun and Her better known but milder sister, Brie de Meaux, which is available both raw and pasteurized. American producers have created some wonderful pasteurized versions, but nothing stands up to the unadulterated pleasure of an authentic raw milk Brie.

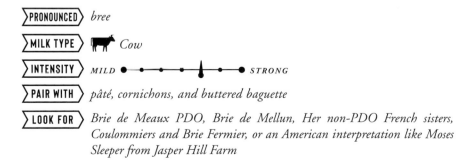

PRONOUNCED › *bree*

MILK TYPE › *Cow*

INTENSITY › *MILD* ●——•——•——•——|——•——● *STRONG*

PAIR WITH › *pâté, cornichons, and buttered baguette*

LOOK FOR › *Brie de Meaux PDO, Brie de Mellun, Her non-PDO French sisters, Coulommiers and Brie Fermier, or an American interpretation like Moses Sleeper from Jasper Hill Farm*

Camembert de Normandy PDO from Isigny Ste-Mère

CAMEMBERT DE NORMANDY PDO *France*

Camembert is the smaller, funkier, and more contemporary version of Brie, invented nearly a thousand years later. During the French Revolution, a priest named Charles-Jean Bonvoust fled Paris to escape religious persecution, bringing the recipe for Brie with him. He ultimately found himself in Normandy, a lush promised land by the sea, where he met a young cheesemaker named Marie Hamel. He blessed her with the sacred recipe, which she adapted to create a petite version of the classic, made extra savory by the sea-kissed Normandy pastures. Originally, Camembert de Normandy PDO strictly required the use of raw milk, but the rules recently changed to allow pasteurized versions as well. When ripe, Camembert is springy and plush, with a juicy creamline and zealous notes of black truffle, buttered radish greens, and boiled broccoli, as well as an assertive barnyard funk.

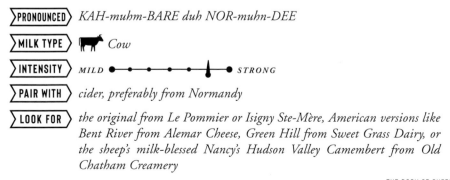

PRONOUNCED *KAH-muhm-BARE duh NOR-muhn-DEE*

MILK TYPE *Cow*

INTENSITY *MILD* ●—●—●—●—|—● *STRONG*

PAIR WITH *cider, preferably from Normandy*

LOOK FOR *the original from Le Pommier or Isigny Ste-Mère, American versions like Bent River from Alemar Cheese, Green Hill from Sweet Grass Dairy, or the sheep's milk-blessed Nancy's Hudson Valley Camembert from Old Chatham Creamery*

Accompaniments and Pairings

BLOOMY BODIES PLAY EASILY WITH AN ARRAY OF ACCOMPANIMENTS. I USUALLY PAIR SWEET FRUIT PRESERVES WITH QUIET, BUTTERY TYPES AND SAVORY PICKLES WITH FUNKIER VARIETIES.

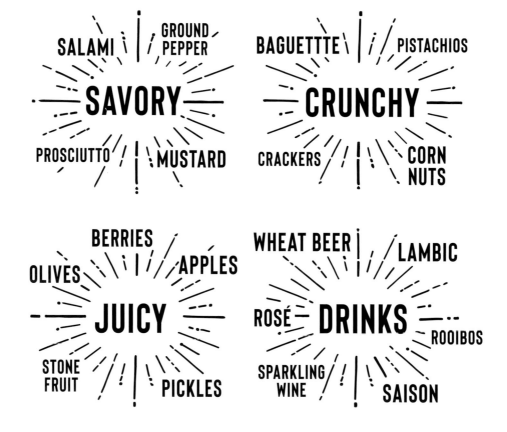

SALAMI | GROUND PEPPER

SAVORY

PROSCIUTTO | MUSTARD

BAGUETTTE | PISTACHIOS

CRUNCHY

CRACKERS | CORN NUTS

BERRIES
OLIVES | APPLES

JUICY

STONE FRUIT | PICKLES

WHEAT BEER | LAMBIC

ROSÉ ~ DRINKS
ROOIBOS

SPARKLING WINE | SAISON

SWEET SURRENDER

For a taste of the divine, pair the silky luxury of a mild bloomy with a little
something sweet. It's a simple and sophisticated combo that's guaranteed
to satiate any cheesecake craving.

PRESERVES • MARMALADES • CHUTNEY • HONEY • FIGS

Above: La Tur bites with Luxardo cherries and flaky salt

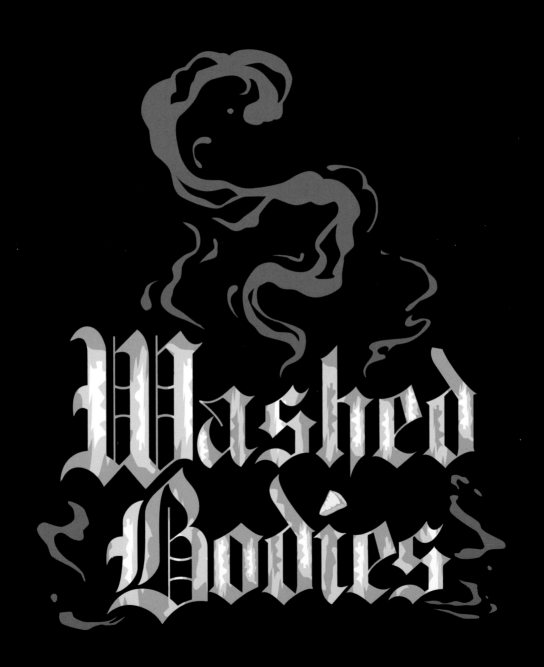

Washed Bodies

Welcome to the kinkiest, stinkiest realm of the cheese world: the washed rinds. These bold beef-cakes have reddish-orange, sticky rinds, golden pastes, and a pungency that varies from fresh onions and autumnal leaves to the uncanny, yet oddly enticing, stench of a corpse on the brink of decay. But underneath all that aggression lies a sensitive soul as savory and decadent as a freshly baked quiche.

Washed Wonders

WASHED-RIND CHEESES ARE NAMED FOR THEIR CEREMONIOUS BAPTISMS, EITHER IN BRINE OR A DILUTED ALCOHOL SOLUTION, WHICH WORK TO CONJURE COLONIES OF BACTERIA THAT RIPEN THE FLESH. AS THE BODY OF CHEESUS AGES, THE BACTERIA FLOURISH, CREATING A RUDDY RIND THAT STINKS TO HIGH HEAVEN AND TRANSFORMS THE INNER PASTE INTO SAVORY LUXURY.

THE MIRACULOUS TRANSFORMATION

The process of "washing" wheels to encourage bacterial growth is called putrefactive fermentation, and it essentially consists of a tightly controlled rot. A cheesemaker will wash or smear a body of Cheesus with a brine (usually a salt solution), a diluted alcoholic solution, or a thick, bacteria-laden paste, which blesses the rind with lively colonies of bacteria. Through a combination of science and, yes, divine intervention, this washing encourages bacterial growth. As they flourish in their salty environments, these angels digest the inner paste, spawning savory notes and an arresting pungency. Softer washed bodies of Cheesus turn oozy like a bloomy rind, while firmer bodies keep their solid forms but take on rich, savory flavors.

THE BODY ODOR OF CHEESUS

Some washed rinds smell like dirty gym socks, and there's a reason for that. *Brevibacterium linens* is one of the angels that works to transform washed-rind bodies of Cheesus by blessing them with a reddish color and an earthy stench. The resulting rosy-rinded wheels sometimes smell like steamy, sweaty sex because *B. linens* also lives on human skin. That bodily odor conjures feelings of lust partly because it reminds us of all our most sensuous earthly desires. The kinky stink just turns us on.

ANOINTED WITH ASHES

Some washed-rind bodies are blessed with a bisecting line of black ash, a ritual that began with Morbier, the classic stinker from France. This semi-firm washed rind hails from the Jura, where herdsmen pool together their yields of milk to produce gigantic wheels of Comté. Whenever the harsh mountain climate prevented them from pooling their milk, however, they'd each make a smaller wheel for personal enjoyment. Their herds were small, so the yield of milk from the evening wouldn't

Winnimere, a seasonal raw cow's milk body from Jasper Hill Farm

produce enough curds to fill the molds. To ward off insects overnight, the farmers would cover the exposed layer with vegetable ash. In the morning, they'd fill up the molds with curds from the morning milk, leaving the layer of ash in between. Although we have other ways of repelling pests nowadays, that chic shadowy streak has stuck around.

Ash is also used to help protect and develop the rinds of bloomy-rind bodies of Cheesus. It's an alkaline substance that absorbs moisture and reduces acidity, making a hospitable environment to the colonies of angels that develop these rinds.

WORSHIPPING WASHED CHEESUS

WHAT TO LOOK FOR: sticky, tacky rinds with a lively hue, even-colored paste, and an entrancing funk

WHAT TO AVOID: bloated, squashed, or splotchy cheeses with slimy, cracked, or bruised rinds that reek of corpse

SHELF LIFE: 7–10 days

STORAGE: cheese paper

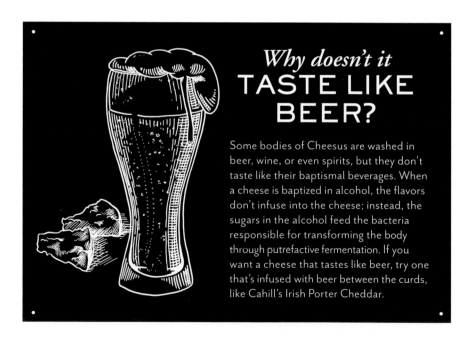

Why doesn't it TASTE LIKE BEER?

Some bodies of Cheesus are washed in beer, wine, or even spirits, but they don't taste like their baptismal beverages. When a cheese is baptized in alcohol, the flavors don't infuse into the cheese; instead, the sugars in the alcohol feed the bacteria responsible for transforming the body through putrefactive fermentation. If you want a cheese that tastes like beer, try one that's infused with beer between the curds, like Cahill's Irish Porter Cheddar.

Types of Washed Bodies

WASHED RINDS VARY WIDELY IN SIZE, TEXTURE,

AND PUNGENCY. SOME ARE PETITE AND JIGGLY, LIKE PERSONAL PUDDING CUPS, WHILE OTHERS ARE AGED GIANTS WITH A SEXY CRUNCH.

SUPER SOFT, LIKE ÉPOISSES These soft, oozing vixens are often the stinkiest of all washies. Underneath their flamboyant rind, their insides are as plush and luxurious as Brie, but their skins are sticky and stinky instead of pristine and downy. Buttery and mild when young, these stanky sirens can get murderous with age.

BARK-WRAPPED, LIKE VACHERIN MONT D'OR Some stinkies are so soft they need a bark corset to hold their supple bodies together, lest their oozing innards spill out of their rinds. They're best enjoyed at peak ripeness by the whole wheel, with the top peeled back and the silken insides scooped out or served as a transcendent dip for toast or potatoes.

PUDGY, LIKE TALEGGIO These squishy devils are more bouncy than spreadable. They won't ooze as much as relax into themselves, with their pudgy pastes ballooning outward like a breast spilling out of an undersized bra. These bodies of Cheesus have some of the most delicious rinds—savory and flavorful, with a toothsome, almost sugared texture.

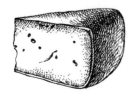

FIRM WASHIES, LIKE GRUYÈRE The least stinky of the family, these mature washies are aged for months or even years, which means they have less moisture and a softer, more incorporated funk. They're meltable with brothy notes of pot roast and caramelized onions. Glorious enough to take center stage on a platter, yet equally sacred when melted into oozing luxury, they include some of the most pleasurable lovers of the cheese world.

Oma, a raw cow's milk cheese made by von Trapp Farmstead and matured by Jasper Hill Farm, both in Vermont

FAMOUS VARIETIES

TALEGGIO PDO *Italy*

This gentle beefcake is the perfect introduction to the world of washies. Taleggio is delightfully tubby, with yeasty aromas of baking bread followed by earthy mushrooms and a delicate perfume of that signature funk that emits from any washed rind. The soft, squishy bodies are square-shaped with rusty orange rinds that develop stripes of grayish molds as they age. Mild and charming, Taleggio is both a cheese plate staple and an eager melter, aching to add custardy richness to everything from sauces to pizza. Keep an eye out for cave-aged or even raw milk varieties, which can sometimes be found at American cheese counters.

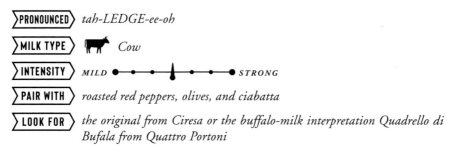

PRONOUNCED *tah-LEDGE-ee-oh*

MILK TYPE *Cow*

INTENSITY *MILD* ●—●—|—●—● *STRONG*

PAIR WITH *roasted red peppers, olives, and ciabatta*

LOOK FOR *the original from Ciresa or the buffalo-milk interpretation Quadrello di Bufala from Quattro Portoni*

VACHERIN MONT D'OR AOP *Switzerland*

This sensual seductress is an annual blessing, arriving at cheese counters at the start of every winter like a Cheesemas miracle. She's produced in the Alps during the autumn months, when the cows switch from fresh grasses to dried hay. This change in diet yields milk too fatty for Alpine cheeses like Gruyère. Instead, the lush milk is used for Vacherin Mont d'Or, a cheese so sinfully soft it needs a band of spruce to contain Her custardy insides. She's endlessly scoopable, boasting deep, bacony flavors and whispering with a sweet, piney essence. Find a wheel that's nearing the expiration date. She should feel like a water bed underneath Her rind.

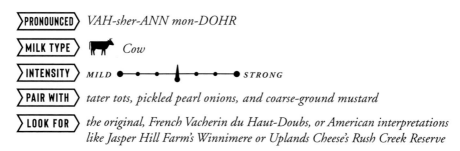

PRONOUNCED *VAH-sher-ANN mon-DOHR*

MILK TYPE *Cow*

INTENSITY *MILD* ●—●—|—●—● *STRONG*

PAIR WITH *tater tots, pickled pearl onions, and coarse-ground mustard*

LOOK FOR *the original, French Vacherin du Haut-Doubs, or American interpretations like Jasper Hill Farm's Winnimere or Uplands Cheese's Rush Creek Reserve*

LE GRUYÈRE AOP *Switzerland*

This muscular Alpine is a timeless stud that many of us first encounter bubbling over French onion soup or inside a pot of fondue. It's the most prolific and popular Swiss cheese, made by only 167 village dairies, pooling together local milk produced no more than twenty kilometers (12.4 miles) from the plant. Aging Gruyère is an art allocated to only ten affineurs in the region, who constantly tend to and taste the wheels to determine when they're ready to sell. The wheels are aged for a minimum of five months, with some selected to age for twenty-four months or more. The younger bodies are tender and miraculously meltable, while more aged beauties develop assertive meaty, herbal notes. In addition to christening this saintly Swiss varietal, the term "Gruyère" also classifies a whole family of related Alpine-style cheeses, including French Comté and Italian Asiago.

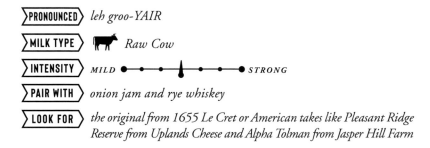

PRONOUNCED *leh groo-YAIR*

MILK TYPE *Raw Cow*

INTENSITY *MILD* ●—●—●—┃—●—●—● *STRONG*

PAIR WITH *onion jam and rye whiskey*

LOOK FOR *the original from 1655 Le Cret or American takes like Pleasant Ridge Reserve from Uplands Cheese and Alpha Tolman from Jasper Hill Farm*

MUNSTER-GÉROME PDO *France*

Dating back to the seventh century, Munster is one of the original gifts from monastic cheesemaking. Bearing no resemblance to the flabby, neon-rimmed slices from the deli, true Munster is much more elegant and complex. Handmade using copper cauldrons, the round wheels are rosy-red, semi-firm, and wafting with sweet, autumnal aromas followed by a pungent funk. Raw milk versions are always much more aggressive and runny, but the pasteurized wheels available in America are mild and buttery, with a gentle oniony savor.

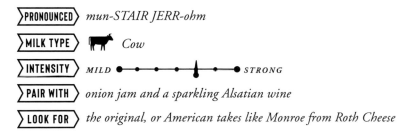

PRONOUNCED *mun-STAIR JERR-ohm*

MILK TYPE *Cow*

INTENSITY *MILD* ●—●—●—●—┃—●—● *STRONG*

PAIR WITH *onion jam and a sparkling Alsatian wine*

LOOK FOR *the original, or American takes like Monroe from Roth Cheese*

The LEGEND of the WASHIES

As the Roman Empire lapsed in the Middle Ages, an Italian monk named Benedict deserted the sinful temptation of the Eternal City, seeking solitude and enlightenment. Word spread of the pious rebel, and a devoted following of monks soon flocked to their new leader.

Supported by his entourage, Saint Benedict established his own monastery, and with it a scroll of rites entitled *The Rule of Saint Benedict*. This strict code of law damned the vices of Rome, calling for a self-sufficient lifestyle and rigorous routine anchored by work and prayer. It forbade the flesh of beasts, but sanctioned wine and victuals in moderation.

This lifestyle was perfect for the arduous art of cheesemaking, with which the monks experimented endlessly. However, they still yearned for the savory satisfaction only meat could appease. Struck with inspiration, one brave monk bathed a wheel with his ration of wine and left it to age in the cellars. The resulting body of Cheesus developed a putrid yet inexplicably alluring stench. The monk sliced into the wheel and discovered an inviting interior.

The taster tested fate, but he was soon absolved when rich, beefy flavors erupted on his palate. Enchanted, the monk shared the blessing with his brothers, who also fell under the spell cast from the strangely savory wheels. The monks worked tirelessly together to perfect the technique, and the world has been blessed by washed rinds ever since.

RACLETTE *Switzerland and France*

This boisterous, fleshy Swiss yearns to be melted into silken rivers of molten glory. Raclette is French for "scraper," which references the performative ritual of heating half wheels under a lamp or grill until browned and bubbling. The sizzling body is then scraped, cascading like a sensuous waterfall onto piles of potatoes, cured meats, and pickles. While this dramatic serving method is an essential experience for all dairy disciples, a good raclette is also a talented performer on a platter, boasting deep flavors of onions, salami, and butter. Raclette du Valais AOP is the only name-protected raclette, but there are many other delectable versions named after the villages in which they're made.

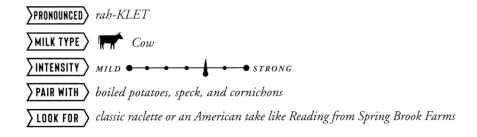

> **PRONOUNCED** *rah-KLET*

> **MILK TYPE** *Cow*

> **INTENSITY** *MILD* ●—●—●—|—●—●—● *STRONG*

> **PAIR WITH** *boiled potatoes, speck, and cornichons*

> **LOOK FOR** *classic raclette or an American take like Reading from Spring Brook Farms*

TÊTE DE MOINE AOP *Switzerland*

This rambunctious mountaineer might be petite, but what She lacks in girth She redeems with a roar of flavor. Her name is French for "head of the monk," referencing the wheel's resemblance to the bald spot on a monk's head when the top rind is shaved off with a *girolle*, a Swiss device designed exclusively for Tête. The machine is composed of a platform with a pointed rod that skewers the wheel and a sharp blade with a knobbed handle that lightly scrapes the top surface, shaving off ruffled blossoms. These razor-thin blooms have more surface area than a slice, allowing the rowdy flavors to unfold gently across the palate. The fiercely funky rind encases the savory golden paste that tastes of dried plums, toasted hazelnuts, beef stew, and animal funk.

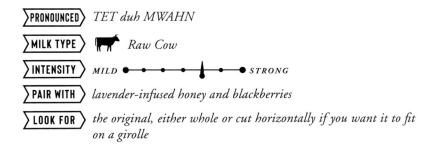

> **PRONOUNCED** *TET duh MWAHN*

> **MILK TYPE** *Raw Cow*

> **INTENSITY** *MILD* ●—●—●—●—|—●—● *STRONG*

> **PAIR WITH** *lavender-infused honey and blackberries*

> **LOOK FOR** *the original, either whole or cut horizontally if you want it to fit on a girolle*

A bouquet made out of Tête de Moine AOP

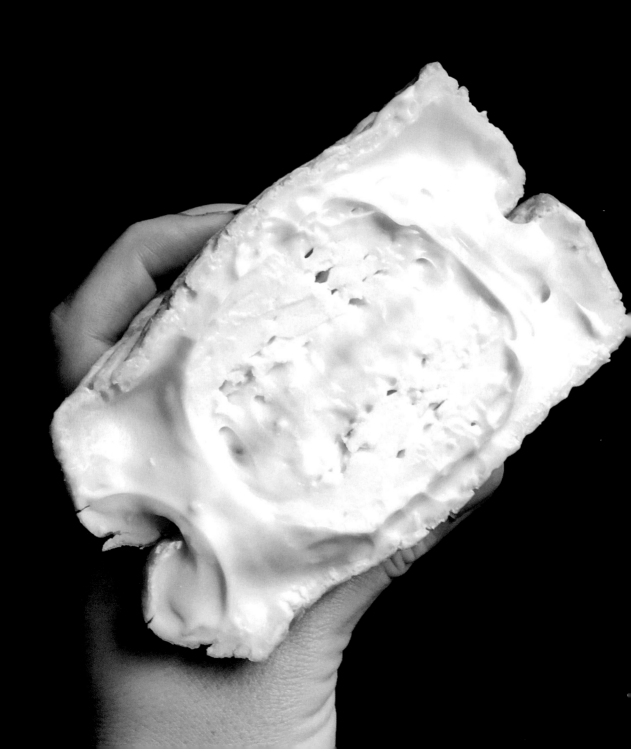

Foxglove, a triple cream washed rind from Tulip Tree Creamery in Indiana

GRAYSON *Virginia*

An American original, Grayson from Meadow Creek Dairy is a powerful, unapologetic dominatrix that'll obliterate your taste buds with the kind of bodily stank that'll make you fall to your knees in worship. She's a seasonal blessing, made only while the farm's herd of Jersey cows are out to pasture. The blush-colored rind is slightly tacky with a gentle crunch that feels almost candied against your teeth. She smells like your dirtiest, sweatiest body parts, while Her plump, golden interior tastes of bacon quiche, boiled peanuts, pork rillettes, and herbal bouquets. She's one of America's stankiest creations—a true wonder to behold.

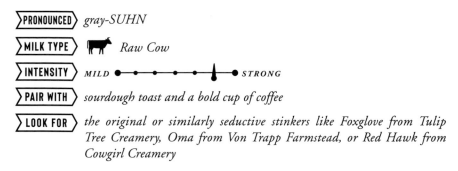

> PRONOUNCED ⟩ *gray-SUHN*

> MILK TYPE ⟩ 🐄 *Raw Cow*

> INTENSITY ⟩ *MILD* ●—●—●—●—|—● *STRONG*

> PAIR WITH ⟩ *sourdough toast and a bold cup of coffee*

> LOOK FOR ⟩ *the original or similarly seductive stinkers like Foxglove from Tulip Tree Creamery, Oma from Von Trapp Farmstead, or Red Hawk from Cowgirl Creamery*

ÉPOISSES DE BOURGOGNE AOC

Enjoying a ripe wheel of Époisses is akin to having mind-blowing marathon sex in the heat of summer when the air conditioner is broken. It's sweaty, stanky, yet addictively orgasmic. This classic French floozy is one of the most odiferous, sexiest bodies in the business. The petite wheels are washed with Marc de Bourgogne, a brandy made from the leftovers of winemaking. The resulting wheels range from auburn to brick red, fuming with a penetrating stench. Inside the rebellious shell lies a soft, custardy interior that becomes pudding-soft with age.

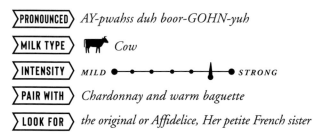

> PRONOUNCED ⟩ *AY-pwahss duh boor-GOHN-yuh*

> MILK TYPE ⟩ 🐄 *Cow*

> INTENSITY ⟩ *MILD* ●—●—●—●—|—● *STRONG*

> PAIR WITH ⟩ *Chardonnay and warm baguette*

> LOOK FOR ⟩ *the original or Affidelice, Her petite French sister*

Accompaniments and Pairings

THESE GUYS ARE BOLD AND STINKY, SO GO FOR RUSTIC, SAVORY FLAVORS TO COMPLEMENT THAT FUNK. EVEN THE STANKIEST BODIES OF CHEESUS FIND BALANCED NIRVANA WITH PICKLES.

HONEY | FIGS

SWEET

CARAMELIZED ONIONS | CHUTNEY

ROASTED VEGETABLES | SALAMI

SAVORY

PESTO | BACON
MUSTARD

PRETZELS
FRIED ONIONS | TOASTED PECANS

CRUNCHY

RYE TOASTS | POTATO CHIPS

APPLES | CUCUMBERS

GRAPES **JUICY**

BLACK CURRANTS | PICKLES

Pairing DRINK *with* STINK

To balance a bold washed body of Cheesus, a beverage needs a
backbone all its own. Opt for robust sippers like the selections below:

**DRY CIDER • MALTY BEER • FRUITY WHITE WINES
LIGHT-BODIED RED WINES • WHISKEY • COFFEE • BLACK TEA**

*Above: Sequatchie Coppinger and Nickeljack with
whole-grain mustard, pickle, and rye whiskey*

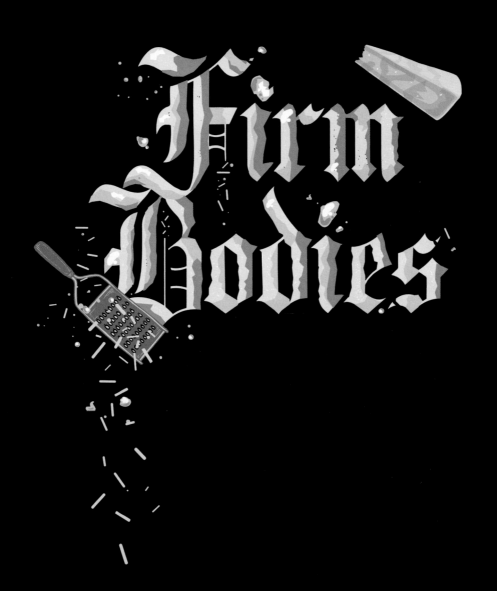

The broadest and most complex category, the firm family includes all the sturdy, hard bodies built to withstand months or even years of aging. As they ripen, they often form protective, rugged rinds over their more delicate inner pastes. While less frisky than youthful varieties, these more mature bodies of Cheesus reflect the glorious relationship

Foxy Firms

FIRM BODIES DON'T TRAP YOU IN ILLICIT LIAISONS

WITH SALACIOUS OOZE, BUT RATHER EMBRACE YOUR PALATE WITH DEEP, LAVISH STROKES THAT'LL PLEASURE YOU WITH AN EVERLASTING FINISH. DEVELOPING THEIR COMPLEX CHARACTER REQUIRES MONTHS OF AGING, WHICH MEANS FIRM BODIES OF CHEESUS ARE SOME OF THE MOST EXPENSIVE. ONE TASTE OF THAT PERSISTENT, MOUTH-FILLING FLAVOR WILL PROVE THEIR WORTHINESS.

ANGELS AND AFFINAGE IN THE AGING ROOM

These bodies spend a long time in their aging boudoirs, where the affineur pampers and cares for their every need. With the right combination of salt, airflow, and humidity, an aged body of Cheesus will develop Her rind all on Her own, sometimes using only the microflora miraculously present in the raw milk or aging environment.

It's the affineur's job to take care of the cheeses as they age. Techniques for affinage read like a menu of spa treatments. Some are brushed to remove excess mites; others are washed in brines to develop their aromatic skins. Some are massaged with oils, spices, and herbs, while others are rubbed with lard or butter and bound tightly with cloth.

Just like the bloomy and washed families, aged bodies of Cheesus have an active community of angels on the outer rind that work to ripen the cheese. The transformation looks much less dramatic compared to soft bodies. These angels don't soften or liquify the body; instead, they work to unlock flavors, build crunchy clusters of crystals, or blow gas bubbles, developing those famous round holes in bodies like Swiss Emmentaler.

ALPAGE, BLESSED BY THE SUN

Alpage is French for "mountain pasture." When you see it on a label, it means that the body of Cheesus has been blessed by the summer sun and the Alpine meadows. At the start of every spring, herds of cattle make their way up the Alps, following the receding snowline that unveils lush pastures. The climate and altitude make for a short, powerful growing season that produces an exquisite assortment of herbs, grasses, and flowers. This glorious, nutritious bouquet infuses the milk with rich

*A well-aged wedge of
Pleasant Ridge Reserve
from Uplands Cheese*

flavors, a golden hue, and native flora, all of which is reflected in the resulting body of Cheesus.

This ritual, known as transhumance, is so beloved that many farmers ceremoniously adorn their cattle with flowers and bells, parading them through the village as they embark on their journeys. After the season concludes, they're bedecked and paraded again in a festival called *Désalpes*, meaning "alpine descent." If you see *alpage* on the label, savor that wedge as if it were a perfect summer's day, preserved like a jar of peaches.

WORSHIPPING FIRM CHEESUS

WHAT TO LOOK FOR: a freshly cut wedge with an evenly colored paste and lively rind

WHAT TO AVOID: oily surface, splotchy coloring, or blue and white mold on the paste and an ashy, slimy rind

SHELF LIFE: 3–6 weeks

STORAGE: cheese paper

BUILT TO LAST

High moisture content leads to a shorter lifespan, thus firm bodies of Cheesus, which have a much lower water content than their softer relatives, live longer. All of the following techniques help to reduce their moisture level, prepping their bodies for long bouts of aging:

Milk is coagulated with rennet, causing the resulting baby curds to contract, expel whey, and fuse together.

Cheesemakers cut the baby curds very small, which helps them release more moisture.

The baby curds are molded and pressed to wring out the remaining moisture hiding in between.

Types of Firm Bodies

FIRM BODIES OF CHEESUS RANGE FROM YIELDING

AND MELTABLE TO HARD AND FLAKY, DEPENDING ON THEIR MOISTURE CONTENT. MANY OF THEM FIT INTO SEVERAL OF THE CATEGORIES BELOW, AND OTHERS DON'T FIT INTO ANY.

WASHED CURD, LIKE GOUDA Before the baby curds are molded and pressed into a body of Cheesus, they're baptized with water to rinse away extra whey. This lowers the acidity and produces a sweeter cheese with a more elastic texture that can age until crunchy.

TOMME, LIKE TOMME DE SAVOIE This category is pretty loose in general, encompassing stout wheels that are rounder than they are tall. There aren't any strict rules governing the term "Tomme," but these bodies are often creamy and pliable with grayish brown natural rinds.

ALPINE STYLE, LIKE COMTÉ AOC Developed as early as the first century, these hardy, rugged cheeses were built to weather long winters and rough transport. The curds are cut very small, cooked for a long time, pressed aggressively, and shaped into huge wheels. All of this results in a firm, durable body that melts smoothly and boasts complex, toasty flavors. Many Alpine bodies also have a washed rind, which contributes a meaty richness.

CHEDDAR, LIKE CLOTHBOUND CHEDDAR Originating in the English county of Somerset, these cheeses are made using an ancient ritual purportedly devised in medieval France. Known as cheddaring, this technique involves letting drained baby curds fuse together into a mass, cutting that into mats, and then continuously stacking and restacking the mats on top of each other to release moisture and develop acidity. It's a painstaking process, so some industrial producers use alternative methods to achieve similar results.

*Cheeses aging on wooden shelves at
Crown Finish Caves in Brooklyn,
New York*

GRANA STYLE, LIKE PARMIGIANO *Grana* means "grain" in Italian and refers to cutting the curds into tiny bits to release moisture and withstand lengthy aging periods. As they ripen, colonies of enzymes and angels within work to digest the proteins, fats, and sugars, releasing a plethora of orgasmically delicious flavors tucked inside crystal-studded hard bodies.

FAMOUS VARIETIES

HAVARTI *Denmark*

Plush and creamy with a charming sweetness and gentle tang, Havarti is playful and easy to love. Her mild buttery flavors are endlessly versatile, and Her yielding texture is equally pleasurable nestled between cold cuts on a sandwich or melted into cheese sauce. She might not be the most complex and nuanced in Her family, but She's never unwelcome and makes a gentle lover for timid worshippers.

> **PRONOUNCED** *huh-VAR-tee*

> **MILK TYPE** 🐄 *Cow*

> **INTENSITY** *MILD* ●——│——●——●——●——●——● *STRONG*

> **PAIR WITH** *a turkey club with a dill pickle*

> **LOOK FOR** *Danish Castello or an American take from Roth Cheese, especially the dill-infused version*

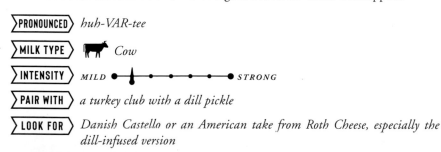

WOODEN SHELVES

Aging bodies of Cheesus on wooden shelves is an ancient ritual with mysteriously powerful effects on ripening. The wood not only brings a romantic and rustic aesthetic, it has a purpose. The angels build their colonies on the wood's surface and interact with the other angels that live on the cheese. Scientists don't fully understand the miraculous effects of these wooden shelves, but they are required for aging some famous PDO cheeses, including Comté and Roquefort.

Many people have questioned the safety of this ritual, but there is no record of foodborne illness being linked to wooden shelves. We don't know for sure, but some scientists believe it's due to antimicrobial compounds, which act like guardian angels and block pathogens.

EMMENTALER AOP *Switzerland*

When people hear "Swiss," they think of those plastic-like slices with big holes and bland flavor that vacillates between old milk and rubber. That desecration is a blasphemous adaption of Emmentaler, a burly body of Cheesus whose true form is a sight to behold. Done right, She's firm, supple, and studded with smooth holes the size of cherries, a result of bacteria releasing CO_2 bubbles inside Her elastic flesh. She's a mild cheese, with soft, buttery flavors of roasting nuts and cooked milk, all perfumed with mountain flora. If you find yourself with a piece that's weeping slightly from the round eyes, then rejoice. That's just a bit of butterfat rising to the surface, and it's a sign you've been blessed with a quality Emmentaler.

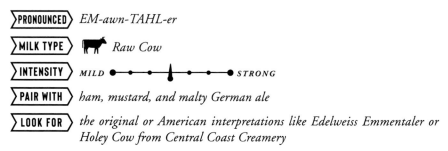

PRONOUNCED *EM-awn-TAHL-er*

MILK TYPE *Raw Cow*

INTENSITY *MILD* ●——●—•——|——•——●——● *STRONG*

PAIR WITH *ham, mustard, and malty German ale*

LOOK FOR *the original or American interpretations like Edelweiss Emmentaler or Holey Cow from Central Coast Creamery*

COMTÉ PDO *France*

The sweeter, fruitier version of Swiss Gruyère, Comté is the miraculous result of a cooperative effort between 3,000 farms, 170 fruitieres, and 20 affineurs sprinkled throughout the Massif du Jura region of France. The cheese is made exclusively with raw milk from handsome Montbéliarde and French Simmental cows, each blessed with two acres of their own lush Alpine pasture during the summer. This pristine milk travels from the farmers to the *fruitiere* (aka cheesemaker), where it's transformed into the Baby Cheesus, then sent to mature with the affineur. Like Gruyère, the flavor and texture depend heavily on the cheese's age, which varies anywhere from four months to three years. Noticeably quiet, mellow, and malleable when young, mature wheels develop an intricate mosaic of flavors that include toasted brioche, dried apricots, candied hazelnuts, and even chocolate.

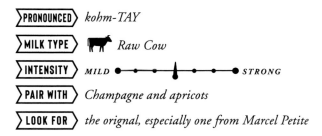

PRONOUNCED *kohm-TAY*

MILK TYPE *Raw Cow*

INTENSITY *MILD* ●——●—•——|——•——●——● *STRONG*

PAIR WITH *Champagne and apricots*

LOOK FOR *the orignal, especially one from Marcel Petite*

Slices of Comté PDO

BLOCK CHEDDAR *America*

As American as the apple pie it's melted on, block cheddars are more tender than their rugged clothbound cousins. The cheddared baby curds are formed into large blocks, then waxed or vacuum-sealed before aging to lock in moisture and prevent a rind from forming. This lockdown allows for almost endless aging potential. Hook's in Wisconsin, for instance, is one producer known to occasionally release a coveted twenty-year cheddar. There's a lot of bad block cheddar out there, with a gummy texture and the eggy, sulphurous aroma of brimstone. Quality block cheddars are a different animal—full of fruity flavors, tongue-tickling tang, and the occasional cluster of crunchy crystals.

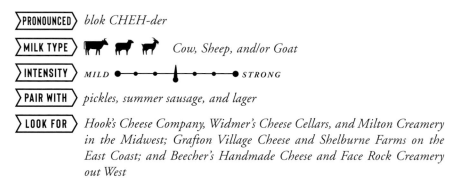

> **PRONOUNCED** *blok CHEH-der*

> **MILK TYPE** *Cow, Sheep, and/or Goat*

> **INTENSITY** *MILD* ●——●——●——|——●——●——● *STRONG*

> **PAIR WITH** *pickles, summer sausage, and lager*

> **LOOK FOR** *Hook's Cheese Company, Widmer's Cheese Cellars, and Milton Creamery in the Midwest; Grafton Village Cheese and Shelburne Farms on the East Coast; and Beecher's Handmade Cheese and Face Rock Creamery out West*

CLOTHBOUND CHEDDAR *England*

Clothbound cheddar bears very little resemblance to the commodity blocks Americans are used to. The young bodies are shaped into drum-like wheels, bound in cloth like a mummy, and coated with lard or butter. This breathable bandage protects the body of Cheesus while allowing Her to inhale and interact with the aging ambiance. These cheeses are expensive and labor intensive, but the result is often superior. Clothbound cheddars are dry and buttery, crumble like a scone, and showcase deeply complex flavors ranging from soil and grass to juicy tropical fruit.

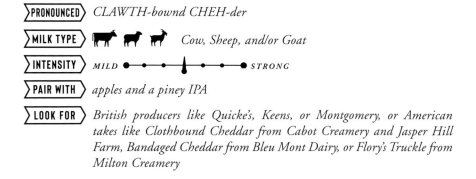

> **PRONOUNCED** *CLAWTH-bownd CHEH-der*

> **MILK TYPE** *Cow, Sheep, and/or Goat*

> **INTENSITY** *MILD* ●——●——●——|——●——●——● *STRONG*

> **PAIR WITH** *apples and a piney IPA*

> **LOOK FOR** *British producers like Quicke's, Keens, or Montgomery, or American takes like Clothbound Cheddar from Cabot Creamery and Jasper Hill Farm, Bandaged Cheddar from Bleu Mont Dairy, or Flory's Truckle from Milton Creamery*

Flory's Truckle, a clothbound cheddar from Milton Creamery in Iowa

GARROTXA *Spain*

This fashionable, unique gem stands tall amongst the sheep's and cow's milk cheeses for which Spain is known. Created in the 1980s, Garrotxa is made by ten family farms in the province of Girona, just north of Barcelona. The paste is bone-white, with a smooth, unctuous texture that toes the line of flakiness. The rind is a smoky gray and as smooth and velvety as a kitten's forehead. The mild, slightly sweet flavor is addictive—even to adamant haters of goat cheese—with flavors that roll from Meyer lemons to fresh mountain herbs and a toasty hazelnut finish that fills the mouth.

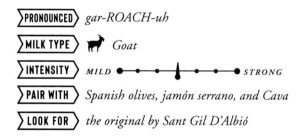

PRONOUNCED *gar-ROACH-uh*

MILK TYPE *Goat*

INTENSITY *MILD* ●——●——●——|——●——● *STRONG*

PAIR WITH *Spanish olives, jamón serrano, and Cava*

LOOK FOR *the original by Sant Gil D'Albió*

MIMOLETTE *France*

One of the most striking bodies of Cheesus, Mimolette is a glowing orange orb with a moonlike rind. Invented in the seventeenth century during the Franco-Dutch War, the French created Mimolette as a domestic replacement for Edam and Gouda. Mild and meltable when young, Her texture becomes crunchy and crystallized as She ages, boasting toasty notes of toffee and butterscotch followed by an impressive tang. Mimolette's most distinguishing feature is the dusty rind, cratered from the influence of tiny cheese mites that eat away at surface molds and help to age the cheese.

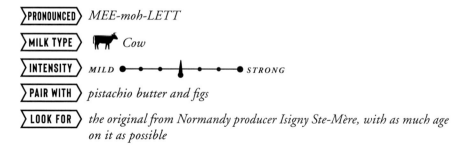

PRONOUNCED *MEE-moh-LETT*

MILK TYPE *Cow*

INTENSITY *MILD* ●——●——●——|——●——● *STRONG*

PAIR WITH *pistachio butter and figs*

LOOK FOR *the original from Normandy producer Isigny Ste-Mère, with as much age on it as possible*

A wedge of 24-month-old Mimolette from Isigny Ste-Mère

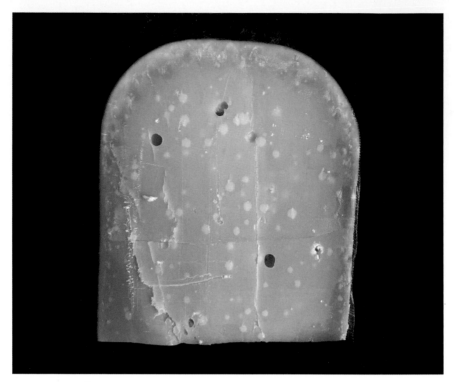

L'Amuse Gouda

GOUDA *Netherlands*

The iconic Dutch cheese is named after a large cheese market that dates back to medieval times, located in the town of Gouda. She's a smooth cheese with a sweet flavor profile, made by scalding the curds to form a dry, firm body that can age for long periods of time, producing an enormous range of flavors and textures. Young Goudas are flexible and spritely with a buttery flavor that oscillates between sweet and tangy. A well-aged gouda is an entirely different animal: crunchy and flaky, with notes of dried figs, butterscotch, and pecan toffee. The best goudas also sport herbaceous and savory flavors that balance the sweetness.

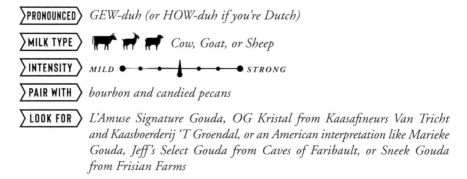

PRONOUNCED〉 *GEW-duh (or HOW-duh if you're Dutch)*

MILK TYPE 〉 *Cow, Goat, or Sheep*

INTENSITY 〉 *MILD* ●—●—•—|—•—●—● *STRONG*

PAIR WITH 〉 *bourbon and candied pecans*

LOOK FOR 〉 *L'Amuse Signature Gouda, OG Kristal from Kaasafineurs Van Tricht and Kaasboerderij 'T Groendal, or an American interpretation like Marieke Gouda, Jeff's Select Gouda from Caves of Faribault, or Sneek Gouda from Frisian Farms*

Queso Manchego PDO

QUESO MANCHEGO PDO *Spain*

Don Quixote himself pontificated about this Spanish legend, and today She takes up a third of the country's traditional cheese production. Made in the La Mancha region in central Spain, Manchego is aged for as few as two weeks and as many as a year, but most of the wheels you'll find in America are about three to six months old. She's pale, splattered with small holes, and imprinted with an iconic herringbone pattern, a nod to the woven grass molds originally used to form Her body. She's popular but shy, eager to play wallflower while accompaniments shine around her. There are a lot of industrial versions, which are pleasantly nutty albeit a bit plain. A truly great Manchego can stand on Her own, filling out Her figure with notes of dried figs, baking spices, wool sweaters, fresh grass, and a pleasantly piquant finish. She tends to perspire, so don't let Her lounge on a platter for too long.

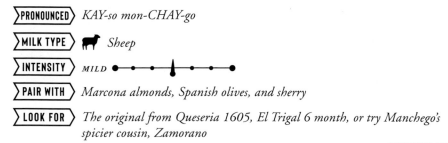

PRONOUNCED › *KAY-so mon-CHAY-go*

MILK TYPE › *Sheep*

INTENSITY › *MILD* ●━━●━━●━━┃━━●━━●━━●

PAIR WITH › *Marcona almonds, Spanish olives, and sherry*

LOOK FOR › *The original from Queseria 1605, El Trigal 6 month, or try Manchego's spicier cousin, Zamorano*

Pecorino Romano PDO, an ancient Italian hard body that dates as far back as the first century

PECORINO ROMANO PDO *Italy*

Pecorino, meaning "of sheep" in Italian, is a category of sheep's milk cheeses that include a wide variety of ages and textures, but this particular variety is a pillar of salt looking back at the rest. Named for Her hometown of Rome, Pecorino Romano is a dry, crumbly character that's so salty She'll paint your tongue with a fuzzy sensation. Take a bite and you'll be greeted with a punishing burn, but shave Her over pastas, salads, or pizza and Her canvas will awaken with strokes of salinity. If you want a Pecorino to gnaw on, get a wedge of Her sweet, buttery sister, Pecorino Toscano.

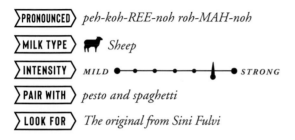

> PRONOUNCED 〉 *peh-koh-REE-noh roh-MAH-noh*

> MILK TYPE 〉 🐑 *Sheep*

> INTENSITY 〉 *MILD* ●—●—●—●—●—▾—● *STRONG*

> PAIR WITH 〉 *pesto and spaghetti*

> LOOK FOR 〉 *The original from Sini Fulvi*

PARMIGIANO-REGGIANO PDO *Italy*

Known as the "king of cheese," authentic Parmigiano is robust and pops with flavors that crackle across your palate like the finale at a fireworks show. References to this Italian royal date back to Roman times, and records suggest the recipe hasn't changed much in nine hundred years. There are about 350 sanctioned producers making Parm today, ranging from small family farms to large co-ops. Each of them delivers their yield to the cheesemaking plant within two hours of milking to preserve the fresh flavors. The partly skimmed raw milk is cultured, coagulated, and cooked in copper vats, then molded, brined, and imprinted with pin-dot letters that spell out "Parmigiano" and aged for a minimum of twelve months. All authentic Parmigiano is great, but some bodies are transcendent, bursting with euphoric notes of ripe pineapple in cottage cheese, vanilla bean, toasted walnuts, sea salt, and a mouth-filling, umami-laden finish. Buy a full wedge, chip off shards, and savor Her complex caresses.

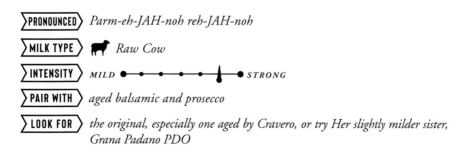

> PRONOUNCED 〉 *Parm-eh-JAH-noh reh-JAH-noh*

> MILK TYPE 〉 🐑 *Raw Cow*

> INTENSITY 〉 *MILD* ●—●—●—●—●—▾—● *STRONG*

> PAIR WITH 〉 *aged balsamic and prosecco*

> LOOK FOR 〉 *the original, especially one aged by Cravero, or try Her slightly milder sister, Grana Padano PDO*

Accompaniments and Pairings

AGED CHEESES ARE RECEPTIVE TO A WIDE ARRAY OF FLAVORS. MORE MATURE WEDGES ARE AUDACIOUS ENOUGH TO HANDLE SPIRITS, COCKTAILS, AND RED WINE.

SWEET
- BALSAMIC
- FIGS
- CARAMEL
- CARAMELIZED ONIONS
- QUINCE PASTE

SAVORY
- SALAMI
- ROASTED VEGETABLES
- CHUTNEY
- TINNED FISH
- MUSTARD

JUICY
- APPLES
- OLIVES
- PICKLES
- GRAPES
- STONE FRUIT

DRINKS
- SPIRITS
- FORTIFIED WINES
- RED WINE
- BEER
- GREEN TEA
- SPARKLING WINE
- COFFEE
- COCKTAILS

A HOLY UNION

The toothsome bite of a firm body meets its heavenly match with crunchy pairings.

POPCORN • POTATO CHIPS • TOFFEE • NUTS • FRIED CORN

*Above: Parmigiano-Reggiano PDO with candied walnuts,
black mission figs, aged balsamic, and prosciutto*

Blues are perhaps the most polarizing bodies of Cheesus: you either worship or despise that punchy funk. I'm a firm believer that haters simply haven't been with the right blue. Characterized by their piquancy and saltiness, the members of this family span the spectrums of texture, pungency, and appearance.

𝕭𝖑𝖊𝖘𝖘𝖊𝖉 𝕭𝖑𝖚𝖊𝖘

SOME BLUES ARE MILD AND GENTLE LOVERS, WHILE
OTHERS ARE REBELLIOUS, AGGRESSIVE BAD BOYS SET ON DOMINATING YOUR PALATE WITHOUT A SAFE WORD. THEN THERE ARE THE METALLIC-TASTING, OVER-SALTED, PRE-CRUMBLED SUPERMARKET BASICS THAT PALE NEXT TO THE TONGUE-TITILLATING BLESSINGS OF A TRUE BLUE. WITH SUCH A BROAD VARIETY, ONE CANNOT SIMPLY DISMISS THIS FAMILY ALTOGETHER.

THE MIRACULOUS TRANSFORMATION: HOW DOES A CHEESE BLUE?

Making a blue body of Cheesus is a carefully controlled process that starts in the vat. The cheesemaker sprinkles spores of mold, usually *Penicillium roqueforti*, straight into the liquid milk or curds. With a carefully curated combination of salt and oxygen, the angels will flourish, staining the pristine paste with blue pockets or streaks. Some bodies undergo a kinky ritual where cheesemakers pierce the wheels with needles, letting in oxygen and spurring the growth of thick blue veins. Others grow these molds only on their rinds, developing a glowing blue-colored dreamcoat.

As the wheel ages and blues, the angels within digest proteins and fats, creating soft, fudgy textures and unlocking a nuanced network of flavor. These blue molds work very quickly, and while cold temperatures will halt the transformation, they'll continue to develop new and exciting flavors even after they reach your fridge.

LOOK *for the* NAME

When shopping for blues, check for as many specifics as possible. If Her label omits details about the specific name, producer, or origin, there's no way of knowing what She's really like. If She's classified only as "Blue Cheese," you could end up with a false god—a metallic saltlick masquerading as divine dairy.

Bayley Hazen Blue, a raw cow's milk wonder from Jasper Hill Farm in Vermont

HOW TO LEARN TO LOVE BLUES

If you're curious about those kinky molds but averse to their aggressive advances, there's hope for you yet. You can groom your palate and acclimate your taste buds to that bold funk, opening up a whole new world of flavor erotica. Here's how:

- Try a mild blue, like Cambozola or Chiriboga (page 166). Avoid bodies with abundant streaks or pockets, which indicate boldness.

- Eat it cold to mellow the intense flavors.

- Pair with baguette, butter, and honey. The baguette brings carby comfort, the fatty butter softens the funk, and the honey balances the intensity.

CHEESE FIRST, BLUE SECOND

When tasting a variety of cheeses, always save the blues for last. They're usually the strongest and can blow out your palate with their aggressive funk. If you're enjoying a platter, eat your fill of the more delicate varieties before you play with a blue, lest you dull your palate and muffle the sacred nuances of the quieter bodies.

THESE MOLDS CAN'T KILL YA

Certain molds produce toxins that can make us sick, but not the ones used in making blues. A divine combination of highly controlled factors, including acidity, moisture, density, and temperature, create an environment that wards off toxins. Some say that it's not only safe to consume these molds but even beneficial, though the jury is still out on that.

WORSHIPPING BLUE CHEESUS

WHAT TO LOOK FOR: freshly cut wedges with a clean surface

WHAT TO AVOID: misshapen wedges with either pink or yellow molds, pale scum over the paste, or brown discoloration near the rind

SHELF LIFE: 7–14 days, depending on texture

STORAGE: cheese paper and a zip-top bag

Stilton and butter on baguette

The LEGEND *of* BLUE

Blue-blessed bodies are said to have been discovered many centuries ago by a humble French shepherd. The story begins on a beautiful summer's day, when our heroic herdsman sat down in a cave to enjoy a midday lunch of cheese and bread. As he began to rip into his crusty loaf, his eyes caught sight of a ravishing maiden in the distance. His heart aflutter, he abandoned his fare in the hopes of wooing her. His courtship lasted days, but eventually ended in rejection.

Devastated, he returned to the cave to discover that blue molds had overtaken his lunch, spreading from the bread to the cheese. Morose with rejection, yet strangely bewitched, he risked his life and took a bite out of the molding wedge. His mouth filled with smooth velvet—fruity, nuanced, and punctuated with piquancy. The euphoric sensation mended his broken heart and he fell head over heels in love with that funk.

News spread of the mold's miraculous effect on the body of Cheesus, and the world has worshipped blues ever since. Hallelujah!

Types of Blue Bodies

BLUES COME IN ALL SHAPES AND SIZES. SOME ARE CREAMY, SPREADABLE, AND FLECKED WITH VELVET POCKETS OF MOLD. OTHERS ARE DRY, CRUMBLY, AND STREAKED WITH THICK BLUE VEINS.

SOFT RIPENED, LIKE CAMBOZOLA These cheeses present as any old Brie-style cheese, but they're hiding a funky secret: their creamy inner pastes are kissed with flecks of blue molds. These eager-to-please bodies are mild and luscious, like butter with a little more attitude.

BLUE RINDED, LIKE SELLES-SUR-CHER The newest style of blue on the shelf, these bodies have that signature indigo hue only on the outside. Their moldy coats infuse the rinds with musty, piquant flavors, while their insides remain clean and pristine. Their textures range from a pound cake–like density to soft, custardy luxury.

FOILED, LIKE ROQUEFORT Wrapped in foil to prevent a rind, slow mold growth, and lock in moisture, these voluptuous vixens are smooth and velvety. They melt in your mouth with a wash of sweet cream, leaving your tongue stained with a peppery tingle. This category includes a lot of famous French blues from central and southern France.

NATURAL RINDED, LIKE STILTON These rugged, boisterous bad boys have sturdy, musky rinds that interact with their environment as they age. Their bodies are drier, firmer, and likely to emanate notes of barnyard and animals. Tread lightly: this category holds some of the most aggressive blues out there.

FAMOUS VARIETIES

GORGONZOLA DOLCE PDO *Italy*

Dolce is the creamiest, dreamiest blue in the family, bearing a closer resemblance to melting ice cream than cheese. Her name means "sweet" in Italian, and She's much softer and far less salty than Her spicier, firmer cousin Gorgonzola Piccante. Her body is voluptuous and jiggly, ornamented with modest, barely blue streaks. She's sweet as cereal milk and tangy as yogurt. When She reaches peak ripeness, Her figure becomes so supple you can spoon Her with an ice cream scooper.

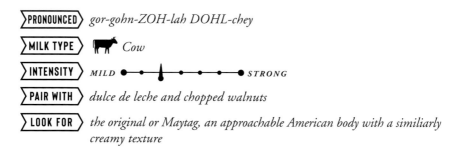

> PRONOUNCED 〉 *gor-gohn-ZOH-lah DOHL-chey*

> MILK TYPE 〉 🐄 *Cow*

> INTENSITY 〉 *MILD* ●———▮—●—●—●———● *STRONG*

> PAIR WITH 〉 *dulce de leche and chopped walnuts*

> LOOK FOR 〉 *the original or Maytag, an approachable American body with a similarly creamy texture*

CHIRIBOGA *Germany*

A gentle lover with the silky texture of cold butter, this heavenly gateway blue comes from Käserei Obere Mühle in Bavaria. Named after Her creator, Ecuadorian cheesemaker Arturo Chiriboga, this rindless blue is something of an anomaly. Unlike with other blues, Arturo doesn't add molds to the milk or curds. Instead, he pierces the wheels with mold-dipped needles, leaving most of the flesh untainted, save for a few sparse veins. Chiriboga tastes of crème fraîche with a hint of button mushrooms. Her delicate flavors and irresistibly creamy texture makes Her perfect for seducing blue skeptics and funk fans alike.

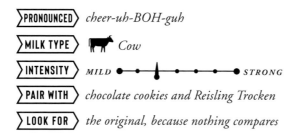

> PRONOUNCED 〉 *cheer-uh-BOH-guh*

> MILK TYPE 〉 🐄 *Cow*

> INTENSITY 〉 *MILD* ●———▮—●—●—●———● *STRONG*

> PAIR WITH 〉 *chocolate cookies and Reisling Trocken*

> LOOK FOR 〉 *the original, because nothing compares*

Chiriboga, a sinfully smooth blue from
Käserei Obere Mühle in Bavaria

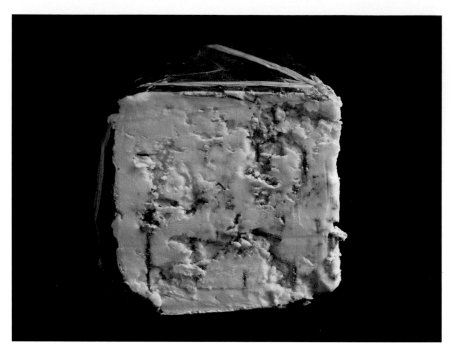

Rogue River Blue

ROGUE RIVER BLUE *Oregon*

This award-winning stunner comes from the blue masters at Rogue Creamery in Oregon. While their pedigree is decorated with several award-winning blues, none is worshipped like the ephemeral Rogue River Blue. This iconic body is a tribute to Her homeland. Made only in autumn, when the farm's certified organic milk is especially rich, each wheel is wrapped in local Syrah leaves, hand-picked and macerated in locally made pear brandy. Tied up with raffia ribbon, She resembles a gift-wrapped package, which is appropriate since She only comes out during the holiday season. Her interior is soft and yielding, speckled with tiny crystals and boasting notes of raisins, hazelnuts, and bacon. She's a pricey queen, but Her ability to pleasure a palate makes Her well worth the expense.

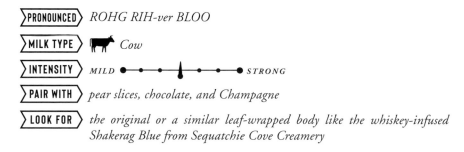

> **PRONOUNCED** *ROHG RIH-ver BLOO*

> **MILK TYPE** 🐄 *Cow*

> **INTENSITY** *MILD* ●–•–•–‖–•–•–● *STRONG*

> **PAIR WITH** *pear slices, chocolate, and Champagne*

> **LOOK FOR** *the original or a similar leaf-wrapped body like the whiskey-infused Shakerag Blue from Sequatchie Cove Creamery*

DUNBARTON BLUE *Wisconsin*

This American original from Roelli Cheese Haus combines the tanginess of cheddar with the pungency of blue to create a charming, gentlemanly hybrid. Fourth-generation cheesemaker Chris Roelli invented the recipe, which calls for pressing the cheese to form a sturdy, solid body before piercing with long needles to let in oxygen. Dunbarton is flush with savory, umami-laden notes of bacon that grow increasingly earthy as you near the rind. The cheddar characteristics dominate but never overwhelm the creeping blue funk that lingers with a faint piquancy.

Red Rock

PRONOUNCED	*dun-BAHR-ton bloo*
MILK TYPE	Cow
INTENSITY	MILD ●——●——|——●——●——● STRONG
PAIR WITH	*apples and malty brown ale*
LOOK FOR	*the original or Her sister, a glowing orange block called Red Rock, also from Roelli*

STILTON PDO *England*

Traditional Stilton is as noble as an English gentleman—brawny yet polite, with a firm texture that crumbles like a buttery biscuit. There is a cheese known as "White Stilton," which lacks the blue molding and is often sweetened and studded with fruit, but She doesn't belong in this family. The true blue variety is proper and sophisticated: earthy, rugged, and muscular with notes of buttery biscuits, barn, and chocolate. There are six producers licensed to create Stilton, but my favorite is from Colston Bassett Dairy. They create wheels using techniques that most resemble the original eighteenth-century recipe, conjuring a tender, buttery body with rolling flavors of fresh grass and flowers.

PRONOUNCED	*STILL-tin*
MILK TYPE	Cow
INTENSITY	MILD ●——●——●——|——●——● STRONG
PAIR WITH	*oat biscuits and port*
LOOK FOR	*The original, Her raw milk sister, Stichelton, or American interpretations like Bayley Hazen Blue from Jasper Hill Farm or Bay Blue from Point Reyes Farmstead Cheese Co.*

Roquefort PDO from Gabriel Coulet, a raw sheep's milk body from the South of France

ROQUEFORT PDO *France*

Christened the mother of blues, this matron saint serves as the namesake of the mold *Penicillium roqueforti* and is considered the original blue. She dates back to at least 1411, when King Charles VI granted exclusive aging rights to the village of Roquefort-sur-Soulzon, which are still honored today. Made in the South of France using milk from the elegant Lacaune sheep, this creamy, palate-obliterating icon goes down like a shot of artisanal gin: sweet at first, followed by a salty burn and waves of herbaceous flavors in the finish. Seven producers are allowed to make Roquefort, with differing levels of artisanship. The most transcendent bodies eat like praline ice cream, melting instantly on your tongue and leaving traces of crunchy crystals behind. Savor Her simply, with a sweet dessert wine and a few slices of ripe pear.

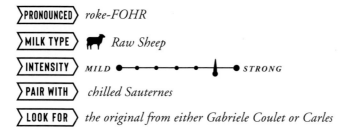

PRONOUNCED *roke-FOHR*

MILK TYPE *Raw Sheep*

INTENSITY *MILD* ●—•—•—•—•—|—● *STRONG*

PAIR WITH *chilled Sauternes*

LOOK FOR *the original from either Gabriele Coulet or Carles*

CABRALES PDO *Spain*

Biting and fierce, Cabrales is an aggressive dominatrix that's not for the faint of heart. A triple threat of raw cow, goat, and sheep's milks, this blue has a sharp pungency that singes the nose hairs with deep animal notes. Tread lightly and mellow Her boisterous sting with sweet accompaniments like honey or dried figs. If you're feeling bold, stuff Her into an olive and drop it into a dry gin martini.

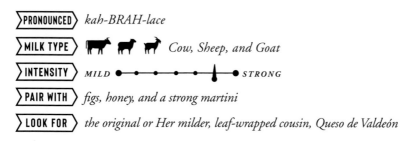

PRONOUNCED *kah-BRAH-lace*

MILK TYPE *Cow, Sheep, and Goat*

INTENSITY *MILD* ●—•—•—•—•—|—● *STRONG*

PAIR WITH *figs, honey, and a strong martini*

LOOK FOR *the original or Her milder, leaf-wrapped cousin, Queso de Valdeón*

Accompaniments and Pairings

YOU'RE WORKING WITH SALT, FUNK, AND OFTENTIMES A VERY RICH TEXTURE, SO FAVOR SWEET, CRISP PAIRINGS OVER SUPER-SALTY SNACKS. THE EXCEPTION TO THIS RULE IS COOKED MEAT, WHICH LOVES COZYING UP TO A BURLY BLUE.

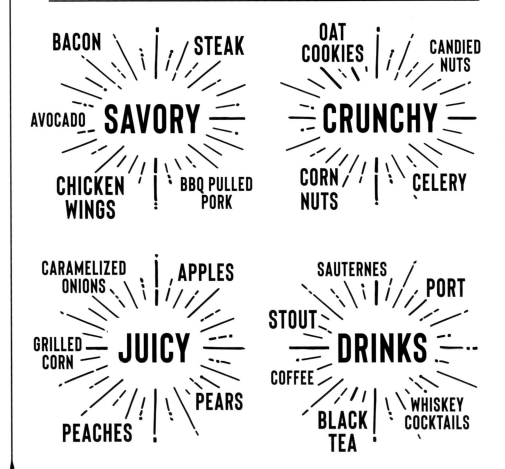

SAVORY
BACON · STEAK · AVOCADO · CHICKEN WINGS · BBQ PULLED PORK

CRUNCHY
OAT COOKIES · CANDIED NUTS · CORN NUTS · CELERY

JUICY
CARAMELIZED ONIONS · APPLES · GRILLED CORN · PEARS · PEACHES

DRINKS
SAUTERNES · PORT · STOUT · COFFEE · BLACK TEA · WHISKEY COCKTAILS

BLUES AND SWEETS:
A Love Everlasting

Pair the creamy, bold profile of a buxom blue with indulgent,
sweet flavors for a blissful balance on your palate.

FIG JAM • PEPPER JELLY • MARMALADE • HONEY • CHOCOLATE • SPICED CHERRIES

*Above: Bellamy Blue from Sequatchie Cove Creamery with caramel,
butter, roasted pecans, dark chocolate, and Effie's oatcakes.*

The
New
Testament
of Cheesus

The Books of:

Buying

Storing

Serving

Tasting

Pairing

Plating

Cooking

Give Us This Day Our Daily Cheesus

THE BODY OF CHEESUS IS AN EMBODIMENT OF MOTHER NATURE AND SACRED TRADITIONS, BUT SHE'S ALSO AN ENDLESS SOURCE OF MIND-BLOWING PLEASURE FOR YOUR PALATE. IT'S TIME TO TALK ABOUT YOUR ROLE IN THE MIRACLE OF CHEESUS: WORSHIP.

" Jésus, c'est du fromage. "

—*Salvador Dalí, interview, 1961*

Creating a body of Cheesus is a labor of love, but at the end of the day, it's food that's meant to be consumed. As a worshipper of Cheesus, your role is not only to support the hardworking cheesemakers but also to achieve the most pleasure out of your eating experience.

The New Testament will guide you in all ceremonious rituals: buying, storing, serving, tasting, pairing, plating, and cooking the body of Cheesus.

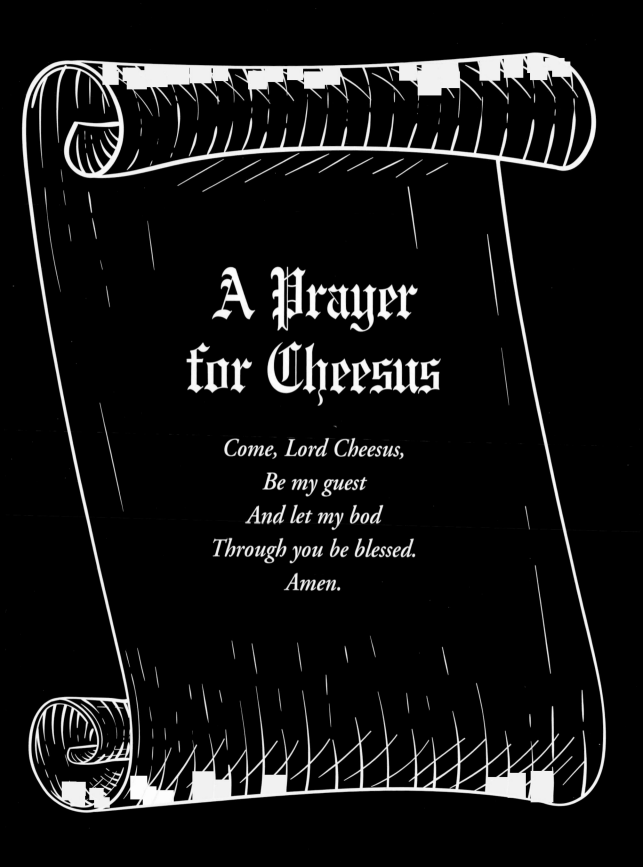

A Prayer for Cheesus

Come, Lord Cheesus,
Be my guest
And let my bod
Through you be blessed.
Amen.

The Book of
Buying

The cheese counter is a holy altar, but it can intimidate novice worshippers. At first, it's hard to navigate the diverse array of strange, smelly, and expensive bodies of Cheesus, each bedecked with labels and exotic, hard-to-pronounce names. Whether you're seeking to worship at a specialty shop or your everyday supermarket, let me teach you how to bring the body of Cheesus into your life.

The Holy Sacraments of Buying

FIND A CHEESE CHURCH: The cheese shop is your house of worship, so visit often and sing their praises.

GET INTIMATE WITH YOUR MONGERS: They're there to help you find the fromage of your fantasies, so let them guide you.

SUPPORT THE CHEESEMAKERS: Cheesus is expensive, but your dollars are supporting small businesses, time-honored traditions, and transcendently delicious bodies. Plus, a little goes a long way!

RECOGNIZE THE SIGNS OF DETERIORATION: Cheesus is sensitive to mishandling, but She'll always tell you when She's not happy.

LEARN THE LABEL: You can discover a lot about a body just by checking out the deets on Her label.

The best cheese shops function like nurseries, tending to Cheesus and sending Her off when She's ripe and ready. They also know how to take care of their customers, ensuring each devotee leaves with a selection that fits their budget, needs, and desires.

WHAT TO LOOK FOR IN A GOOD CHEESE SHOP

CUT TO ORDER: The shop will cut a wedge for you straight off the wheel, ensuring that Cheesus stays fresh and flirty. It also allows the monger to better customize your experience, since they are handling the bodies for you.

KNOWLEDGE: Your cheesemonger should be able to answer basic questions about creameries and varieties. If they don't know, they should offer to find out for you.

VARIETY: The selection should reflect the many forms of Cheesus, with several choices for fresh, soft, aged, and blue. They don't need a huge selection, but you want to have options.

HIGH TURNOVER: To ensure that Cheesus stays healthy and delicious, shops need to run through their inventory quickly, especially when they have lots of bodies to manage. Before you commit to a wedge, take a moment to check for signs of spoilage (see page 186).

WHAT'S A CHEESEMONGER?

Cheesemongers are the preachers behind the cheese counter. These disciples of Cheesus are equal parts nanny, shaman, and madame of fromage. They're the ones who care for Cheesus until someone takes Her home. They know all about each blessed body: who makes Her, where She's from, and how She's tasting today. They're also cupids, ready to play matchmaker between you and the fromage of your fantasies.

A good monger wants to make you happy. They don't want to judge your preferences or shame you for mispronouncing "Manchego." They want to share their tremendous wealth of knowledge with you, so that you may worship Cheesus to the best of your ability.

Find a cheesemonger near you, and build a relationship with them—an open one, but still a loving, trusting one. If you're lucky enough to have several great cheese shops in your town, make a pilgrimage to all of them. While you tend to get the best experience at a cut-to-order shop, many specialty supermarkets also have mongers ready to answer your questions and sample out the wedges in their case.

HOW TO TALK TO A CHEESEMONGER

Just like in any relationship, you must be open, honest, and trusting with your cheesemonger.

LET YOUR GUARD DOWN

Cheesemongers always know their selection best, because they're constantly tasting it. You have nothing to prove here. Sit back, relax, and let them guide you into new and exciting realms of pleasure.

ASK QUESTIONS

Cheesemongers know all the dirty details about any given body of Cheesus, Her maker, and how to best worship that wedge. They're usually eager to preach the curd word, too. Don't be shy to seek their guidance.

IDENTIFY YOUR NEEDS

Before you even enter the cheese shop, you should know three things: roughly how many bodies of Cheesus you want, how you intend to use them, and how many people you have to feed.

COMMUNICATE YOUR BUDGET

A cheesemonger wants you to leave happy, not feeling ripped off. Be up front, and they'll appreciate your honesty. They'll still let you sample the expensive bodies and might even seduce you into splurging on a sliver.

RECOGNIZE YOUR FROMAGE FETISHES

Know your likes and dislikes, or if you love all bodies of Cheesus, think about what you're in the mood for right now. Try to have a few descriptors ready, like "gooey, but not too pungent" or "fresh, tangy, and great on salads." For more descriptors, see Curdy Talk on page 228.

Never commit yourself to a cheese without having first examined it.

—*T. S. Eliot, quoted in* The Pound Era

Cheesemonger Nick Bayne at Fine Cheese Co. in London, England

KEEP AN OPEN MIND

Unlike most other lovers, Cheesus doesn't expect monogamy, so make sure to play the field. Don't stick to the same old cheddar—find some new bodies to worship. Keep an open mind; if you're shy, think of a wedge you already love, look for something similar, and expand from there.

SAMPLE, SAMPLE, SAMPLE

Tasting at the counter is an act of worship in itself. Don't hesitate to ask to try a body of Cheesus, and always be honest about your impressions. This will help the monger understand your palate. Cheesus is constantly changing, so try before you buy, even if you're familiar with a particular body. Just don't be greedy.

GIVE YOUR FEEDBACK

A good cheese shop openly communicates with the producers. As much as they love praise from mongers, cheesemakers need to know how the consumer feels about a body of Cheesus, too. Share your thoughts and feelings, like whether a body rocked your world or failed to pleasure your palate. Mongers know the difference between a defect and a polarizing trait, so be specific about what's not working for you.

QUESTIONS TO ASK A CHEESEMONGER

- What are you excited about today?
- What's in season right now?
- Is there anything particularly ripe at the moment?
- Can I try something local?
- Do you have something rare and exotic?
- What can you tell me about the cheesemaker?
- How long will it last?
- Can you cook with it?
- Do you have any recipe recommendations?
- What should I eat with it?
- What should I drink with it?

CHEESE SHOPPING WORKSHEET

Answer these questions before you leave for the cheese shop or grocery store, and you'll always be prepped and primed for a pleasurable shopping experience.

WHAT ARE YOUR INTENTIONS FOR CHEESUS? *(e.g., cooking, snacking, plating)*

HOW MANY DO YOU INTEND TO FEED?

HOW MUCH DO YOU NEED? *(plan approx. 2 ounces/55 g total per person for a snack, 4 ounces/115 g total per person for a meal)*

WHAT'S YOUR BUDGET? *(expect to pay between $15–$35 per pound for most bodies)*

Top: Cheesus for sale at Neal's Yard Dairy in London

Bottom: A variety of Cheesus in the case at Saxelby's Cheesemongers in New York City

HOW TO SPOT A GOOD CHEESE GONE BAD

Mishandling can turn a pristine body of Cheesus into an ammoniated corpse. Even under the best conditions, Cheesus can still become overripe. Here are the signs of deterioration, according to body type.

FRESH BODIES

These youngsters are meant to be eaten ASAP, so make sure they're fresh.

- Mold growth or discoloration
- Unappetizing, sour smell

SOFT-RIPENED BODIES

These damsels are the most delicate of all. Handle with the utmost TLC.

- Bloated and almost bursting out of its package
- Slimy, dry, or cracked rind
- Brownish or crusty paste
- Flattened, misshapen, or bruised
- Ammoniated smell

HOW TO KNOW
When a Bloomy or Washed Body Is Ripe

Check for ripeness by squeezing Her very gently, though not too hard or you'll bruise Her delicate body. It should feel slightly squishy, like a waterbed. If you want to worship a ripe body of Cheesus, wait until the week of the expiration date to cut into Her.

BLUE BODIES

Blues are less temperamental than softies but tend to weep moisture.

- Slimy or wet on the surface
- Patches of mold on the paste that differ from the bluish streaks and pockets
- Yellow or pink splotches
- Excessive brown discoloration near the rind
- Ammoniated smell

FIRM BODIES

These bodies are the most durable, but they can still be ruined by mishandling or poor storage conditions.

- Splotchy, uneven color
- Oily surface
- Blue and white mold on the paste
- Slimy or mushy rinds
- Ammoniated smell

THE PRICE OF GREATNESS: WHY CHEESE IS SO EXPENSIVE

Pampered cows at Uplands in Wisconsin

Cheesus is produced in two general forms: the sacred, artisanal bodies of Cheesus and Her inexpensive, industrial imitators. The good stuff costs more for a simple reason: artisan cheesemaking is labor intensive and requires a lot more resources than the industrial variety.

Artisan bodies of Cheesus might be expensive, but they're so worth it. Here's what's behind every dollar you're spending.

CARE FOR THE ANIMALS

Good milk comes from happy animals, and maintaining their room and board requires a lot of resources. This kind of pampering is more sustainable with a small herd, but that means less milk, which affects the price all the more.

You have to be a romantic to invest yourself, your money, and your time in cheese.
—*Anthony Bourdain, in* Medium Raw

Langres PDO, a washed rind body from the Champagne region of France

PREMIUM TRANSPORTATION

Cheesus is a delicate diva who requires first-class transportation services, complete with the right temperature and careful handling. This is especially important if She's a young, tender little thing.

AGING TIME

Cheesemakers have to account for the time that aged bodies spend ripening in the caves. You're also paying for all the labor they spend nurturing those aging bodies.

WINTER BREAK

Some artisan cheesemakers must adapt to the rhythms of nature. Even if they take the winters off from production, they still have to tend their animals and land year-round.

PRODUCTION *Categories*

INDUSTRIAL: emphasis on profitability. The result is consistent, relatively cheap, and often lacks personality.

ARTISAN: emphasis on complexity, milk quality, and well-being of land and animals. The result is inconsistent, relatively expensive, and holy.

SUPPORT FOR SMALL BUSINESSES

Making Cheesus is a labor of love that involves long hours, back-breaking work, and lots of inconsistencies. And both creameries and cheese shops cost a lot to operate, requiring massive overhead for labor, operations, inventory, and even rent. They're also businesses, so they need to make a profit on top of that.

When you think about all that goes into the creation of Cheesus, it doesn't seem that expensive. Plus, it is your civil and spiritual duty as a worshipper of Cheesus to protect and support small-production, artisan foods to counter the havoc that the industrial food system wreaks on the earth and our health. Pay your farmers, your makers, and your mongers. Every dollar counts.

That being said, there are a lot of bodies of Cheesus out there that are both delicious and affordable.

Cheesus for Cheap

ARTISAN CHEESE DOESN'T HAVE TO BE EXPENSIVE.
THESE COURTESANS WILL PLEASURE YOUR PALATE WITHOUT BREAKING THE BANK.

 **FRESH BODIES** Because they don't spend time in the aging room, freshies are generally cheaper than aged bodies. Look for an artisan goat cheese or an imported feta.

 DOUBLE- OR TRIPLE-CREAM BRIE STYLES These cream dreams are total crowd pleasers, and there are a lot of French brands making affordable wheels. Look for Fromager d'Affinois or Delice de Bourgogne.

 **TALEGGIO DOP** She looks fancy and indulgent, but this mild Italian stinker is quite the bargain. Get it cut to order from a cheese shop when possible. She's sensitive to mishandling.

STRAIGHT *from the* MAKER

Buying Cheesus directly from Her maker is a sacred experience. No one understands a body of Cheesus like the one who brought Her into existence, so they know how to best keep Her fresh and healthy until She's ripe and ready for worship. Because there are fewer distribution costs, you might pay less for the same amount, too.

The best part about buying directly is establishing a relationship with these saints of Cheesus. Sharing your appreciation and feedback helps makers perfect their rituals and understand what's resonating with consumers. They put their heart and soul into their sacred creations and want to know how you're enjoying them. By opening that line of communication, you get to play a part in the miracle of Cheesus. Visit a creamery's on-site or online store, or look for cheese stalls at your local farmers' markets.

 **YOUNG GOUDA** European imports are often cheaper than domestics, and some Goudas are ready for market in as little as six weeks. Young wheels take kindly to flavors like mustard seeds, fenugreek, and cumin. Look for wheels aged three months or less from Beemster and Marieke.

 **BLOCK CHEDDAR** This tangy tart is a staple at any corner store or supermarket. Buyer beware: there are some really bad cheddars out there, so don't go *too* cheap. Look for a mid-priced block from a cheddar capital, like Wisconsin, Vermont, or Ireland.

 **MANCHEGO DOP** This is the most affordable sheep's milk body out there. Even though She's made on a huge scale, She always delivers a buttery mouthfeel with notes of toasted nuts. Look for El Trigal or even Kirkland Signature Manchego.

 PARMESAN-CHEDDAR HYBRIDS These bodies pair the tanginess of a cheddar with the crumbly crunch of a parmesan. Look for MontAmoré from Sartori or Barely Buzzed, a coffee and lavender-rubbed wheel from Beehive Cheese.

HOW TO FIND CHEESUS AT THE SUPERMARKET

Nothing beats a trip to a real cheese shop, but you can score some hot bods from your average grocery store, too. Here's how to buy a body of Cheesus at any old supermarket.

CHECK THE LABEL FOR SPECIFICS

Look for details on region, maker, and age. The more a company reveals about itself, the better. If they're hiding something, that's a warning that it may be an industrial commodity product.

AVOID PRE-SHREDDED AND LOW-FAT CHEESE

Anything shredded or crumbled probably has artificial ingredients added to it, so you're better off purchasing whole wedges and shredding them yourself. Fat is also essential for creating those seductive flavors and textures, so reduced-fat products are never as delicious or luscious.

BEWARE FLAVORED BODIES

Herbs and spices are delicious, but they can also cover up signs of a low-quality cheese. Look for bodies with flavorings that enhance and complement the glory of Cheesus, not ones that overwhelm Her gentle complexities.

CHECK THE DATE

Supermarkets often can't care for Cheesus the way a cheesemonger can. Instead, you'll find Cheesus precut, confined to plastic, and set on display under harsh, fluorescent lights that damage Her precious flavor. Make sure the wrap date is within a week, and that the expiration date is at least two weeks out.

LOOK FOR SIGNS OF DAMAGE

A healthy, soft body of Cheesus should have an intact, fresh-looking rind. Aged bodies are much less vulnerable, but they can still suffer from light damage. See page 186 for signs of damage.

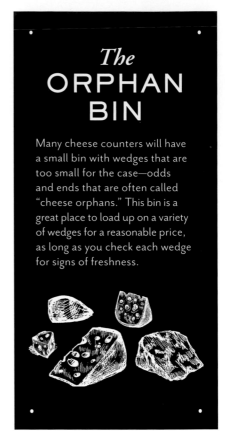

The
ORPHAN BIN

Many cheese counters will have a small bin with wedges that are too small for the case—odds and ends that are often called "cheese orphans." This bin is a great place to load up on a variety of wedges for a reasonable price, as long as you check each wedge for signs of freshness.

SHOW HER SOME LOVE

If Cheesus has spent a long time in plastic, slip off Her wrapper as soon as you get home. If She tastes like your fridge, lightly scrape the cut sides with a non-serrated knife until She tastes normal. Then, store Her in cheese paper or, if you don't have any, in parchment paper and a zip-top plastic bag.

DON'T BUY TOO MUCH AT ONCE

I'm not telling you to buy *less*, I'm just telling you to buy *more often*. Cheesus quickly deteriorates when She's cut from the wheel, and little pieces have the shortest shelf life. For the best flavor, only buy as much as you can eat within a few days, then buy some more.

WHEN IN DOUBT, GO PDO

Any body of Cheesus marked "PDO" on the label is usually a safe bet. This means that the cheesemaking rituals are recognized and protected by the European Union. PDO bodies can mostly survive mass production while remaining delicious and worthy of worship. (For more information on PDO, see page 195).

A cheese plate on the cheap, featuring block cheddar, salami, and pickles.

ANATOMY OF A CHEESE LABEL

SNOW MOUNTAIN FARMS

AWARD WINNING

· ESTD ·   · 2002 ·

Blessed Billie

GF GLUTEN FREE   **FARMSTEAD CHÈVRE**   VEG VEGETARIAN FRIENDLY

HANDCRAFTED IN TENNESSEE

INGREDIENTS: CERTIFIED ORGANIC PASTUERIZED GOAT'S MILK, SALT, CHEESE CULTURES, ORGANIC VEGETARIAN & GMO-FREE MICROBIAL ENZYME

NAME: American bodies often have whimsical names, while Old World bodies are typically named for the provinces where they're made.

REGION: This includes the country and maybe even the state or province.

MILK TYPE: This includes the animal type and whether the milk is raw or pasteurized.

RENNET TYPE: The choices are animal, vegetable, or microbial. The latter two are vegetarian, which is important for those with restrictive dietary preferences.

PRODUCER: Over time, you'll come to recognize specific creameries you favor. Look for their other creations, and give them a try as well.

AWARDS: If a body of Cheesus has won any notable awards, it'll be indicated on Her label, and often in glittering gold. Most notable are the World Cheese Awards and awards from the American Cheese Society.

CERTIFICATIONS: The most common are organic, GMO-free, animal welfare, and certified humane. The last two signal that the producers have met specific standards for humane treatment.

FARMSTEAD/FERMIER: This means that this body of Cheesus was made with milk from the cheesemaker's own herd. This gives them the most control.

THE EXPIRATION DATE

Always take an expiration date with a grain of salt. It's just an estimate and rarely dictates when a body has passed her palatable prime. However, it can help you estimate how ripe a cheese is. If you want an oozing Camembert, buy one that's near Her sell-by date. Keep in mind that there's also a wrap date, which tells you when a piece of cheese was cut. That one should be fairly recent, because fresh cuts are sacred. Remember to always use your best judgement and check for the signs of a cheese that's past Her prime (page 186).

PROTECTED ORIGIN DESIGNATIONS

Whenever you see PDO, AOC, DOP, or another such acronym on Cheesus's label, that means this body is protected by the national government to preserve its history and production method. This practice was started by the French, who wanted to protect their wine and later extended it to other foods and countries. In 1925, Roquefort became the first body of Cheesus to receive this protected status.

These rites regulate everything about production, including region, breed, recipe, and affinage practices. If a cheesemaker doesn't follow this sacred code, they cannot label the body of Cheesus with that protected name.

For example, "parmesan" is made all over the world using a variety of techniques. On the other hand, "Parmigiano-Reggiano DOP" must be made specifically with raw cow's milk using copper vats, among countless other rules.

You'll find the designation in different languages across Europe, but they all mean the same thing.

PDO (English): Protected Denomination of Origin

AOC (French): *Appellation d'Origine Contrôlée*

DOP (Italian): *Denominazione di Origine Protetta*

DOP (Spanish): *Denominación de Origen Protegida*

AOP (Swiss): *Appellation d'Origine Protégée*

PGI (English): Protected Geographical Indication

In Cheesus's NAME

Cheesus's names can be hard to pronounce, even for a monger. It helps to understand a bit about how makers name the fruits of their labors. Don't worry too much about butchering a cheese's name. Just do your best, then laugh it off and put some in your mouth.

To capitalize, or not? The name of Cheesus is only capitalized when She is:

- Named after a place, such as Gouda
- Named after a person, such as Brillat-Savarin
- Designated with a PDO, like Parmigiano-Reggiano
- Christened with Her own personal moniker, like Humboldt Fog

Cheese Pantry Essentials

STOCK THESE FEW ESSENTIALS, AND YOU'LL ALWAYS

HAVE WHAT YOU NEED TO CREATE A MASTERFUL PLATTER—
NO MATTER WHAT BODY OF CHEESUS YOU'RE WORSHIPPING.
FOR A FULL LIST OF ACCOMPANIMENTS, SEE PAGE 255.

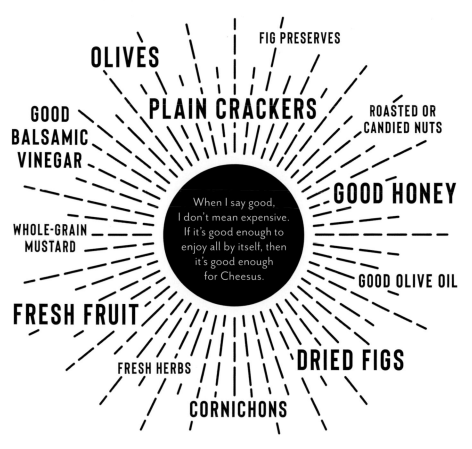

FIG PRESERVES

OLIVES

PLAIN CRACKERS

ROASTED OR CANDIED NUTS

GOOD BALSAMIC VINEGAR

GOOD HONEY

When I say good, I don't mean expensive. If it's good enough to enjoy all by itself, then it's good enough for Cheesus.

WHOLE-GRAIN MUSTARD

GOOD OLIVE OIL

FRESH FRUIT

DRIED FIGS

FRESH HERBS

CORNICHONS

Opposite page: A luxurious platter featuring French cheeses and classic accompaniments

Brabander Reserve, an extra-aged goat's milk Gouda from L'Amuse

The Book of
Storing

Storage is next to godliness. Do it wrong and you'll turn a beautiful, luscious wedge into a hideous, slimy demon patched with unwanted molds. Cheesus is a sacred, delicate creation that requires TLC both at the cheese shop and in your fridge. Fortunately, proper storage is easy and only takes a few minutes of actual effort. This book will teach you how to properly wrap and store the body of Cheesus, and detail Her shelf life according to body type. Do right by Cheesus, and She shall do right by you.

The Holy Sacraments of Storing

SHUN PLASTIC WRAP: Nonporous plastic wrap cuts off airflow and traps moisture, leading to utter ruin.

WRAP HER TIGHTLY IN CHEESE PAPER: Make sure She's fully covered to prevent dry patches and cracking.

BUY LESS, MORE OFTEN: Cheesus always tastes best when eaten fresh from the shop, so only buy as much as you can worship within a couple days.

PLASTIC *at the* CHEESE SHOP

Cheese shops often rely on plastic wrap to meet the health department's demands while allowing customers to ogle the bodies before they buy. Although Cheesus needs oxygen, She's also really good at holding Her breath for a few days. As long as the shop can quickly turn over their inventory, Cheesus will survive unscathed.

THE SIN OF PLASTIC WRAP

To wrap Cheesus in plastic is to damn Her to hell. Store Her correctly, however, and She'll take you to heaven.

IT SUFFOCATES HER

The body of Cheesus is brimming with active microbial angels that need oxygen to survive. Plastic wrap cuts off the air supply, which eventually suffocates Her. The exceptions are fresh bodies of Cheesus, such as mozzarella, which spoil more quickly with ample oxygen.

IT TRAPS IN MOISTURE

Cheesus needs humidity, but not too much. Excess moisture makes Her slimy, moldy, and the wrong kind of smelly.

IT LETS IN LIGHT

Harsh fluorescent lights are able to pierce through translucent wrap, bleaching Cheesus's gorgeous color and oxidizing Her fat. This light damage transforms Her delicious complexities into waxy, crayon-like flavors.

HOW TO STORE CHEESUS CORRECTLY

Cheese prefers the cool, dank environment of a cave, even when She's out in the world. It is our duty to follow these rites at home and emulate the aerated, humid environment She desires and deserves.

USE SPECIALTY CHEESE PAPER, OR SEMIPERMEABLE PAPER AND A ZIP-TOP BAG

Specialty cheese paper blocks light, provides perfect airflow, and maintains optimal humidity. Plus it's easy to find at homeware stores and cheese counters. You can also use another kind of semipermeable paper (like wax, parchment, or butcher paper) together with a zip-top plastic bag to capture humidity. Seal the bag completely, keeping a bit of air in there so Cheesus can breathe comfortably.

MAKE SURE SHE'S SNUG AND FULLY COVERED

Wrap the body of Cheesus tightly and neatly, just like a little present. While you're tucking Her in, don't leave any parts exposed. The fridge will dry out Her tender flesh, leaving Her dull and crusty.

STORE IN THE CRISPER OR DELI DRAWER

Designed to keep vegetables fresh, the crisper drawer has ample humidity for Cheesus as well. It also blocks out aromas from other foods, leaving Cheesus to relish in Her own sacred stink.

TAKE OUT ONLY AS MUCH AS YOU PLAN TO EAT

Cheesus loves consistent temperatures, so take out only as much as you intend to eat in one sitting and keep the rest stored. This also discourages you from eating the whole wedge in one sitting. Of course, if that's your intention, get at it.

DON'T SHARE PAPER ACROSS TYPES

Molds love to jump onto other bodies of Cheesus, even when they're detrimental to their host. To prevent unwanted mold growth, don't share the same sheet of cheese paper across different body types.

IF YOU FIND MOLD, JUST SCRAPE IT OFF

The body of Cheesus hosts all kinds of molds and bacteria. Don't blame Her if a few stray white or blue molds bloom over Her inner paste. Just scrape them off with a non-serrated blade, and if you want to be extra careful, change the wrapper as well. These molds are harmless, but they are a sign that you should worship this body of Cheesus sooner rather than later.

The only exceptions to this rule are fresh bodies. If those get moldy, it's best to throw them away completely. Fresh bodies aren't built to age and spoil instead of ripen.

REUSABLE WAX FOOD WRAPS

These sheets are a wonderful, eco-friendly alternative to single-use plastic wrap, but they're not my favorite option for storing Cheesus. The waxed surface is stiff and difficult to seal, which lets out too much moisture. They're adequate for a twenty-four-hour stint, but over time they cause Cheesus to dry out and lose Her oomph.

Chiriboga, a creamy-as-sin blue from Bavaria

Two Methods for Wrapping Cheesus in Paper

THE GIFT

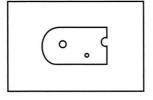

- Place the wedge in the center of the paper, with the long sides of the cheese running parallel to the long sides of the paper.

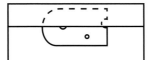

- Pull one of the long sides of the paper over the wedge until taut, and make a crease.

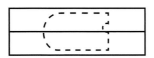

- Repeat with the other long side.

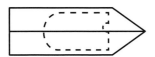

- On one of the short sides, pull each corner of the paper toward the center, creating two 45-degree flaps. Crease along the flaps.

- Repeat on the other short side, then tuck both flaps under the cheese to create a loose seal.

THE FRENCH PLEAT

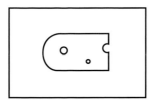

- Place the wedge in the center of the paper, with the long sides of the cheese running parallel to the long sides of the paper.

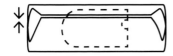

- Bring the edges of the long sides of the paper together, over the top of the wedge, so that they meet.

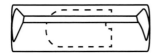

- Pinch the long sides of the paper together and carefully fold them over to create about a half-inch (12-mm) wide hem. Make a crease.

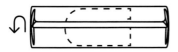

- Roll the hem downward, toward the center, until it's tight against the top surface of the cheese.

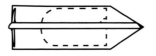

- On one of the short sides, pull each corner of the paper toward the wedge, creating two 45-degree flaps. Crease along the flaps.

- Repeat on the other short side, then tuck both flaps under the cheese to create a loose seal.

The Shelf Life of of Cheesus

DIFFERENT TYPES OF CHEESUS HAVE DIFFERENT STORAGE PREFERENCES AND SHELF LIVES. SOFT BODIES HAVE MORE MOISTURE AND SPOIL FASTER, WHILE AGED FIRM BODIES ARE BUILT TO LAST.

FRESH

Fresh Cheesus has the shortest shelf life and should be worshipped as soon as possible after the package is opened. High-acid bodies like chèvre have a slightly longer shelf life than other fresh bodies, while sweet, milky ricotta will perish in just a few days.

Storage: Store in airtight bags or in tub containers with lids. If She comes stored in brine, keep Her in there until She's consumed.

Average Shelf Life: 1–5 days

SIZE MATTERS

The smaller the wedge of Cheesus, the shorter its average shelf life. If you find yourself with a plethora of slivers, worship them as soon as possible. Then go buy more.

SOFT-RIPENED

These delicate damsels are always in flux, with active rinds constantly ripening and transforming the inner paste. If the wheel is intact, then the shelf life depends on the level of ripeness, which can typically be estimated by the expiration date on the package. If you're dealing with an oozing wedge, store Her in a sealed container with a small piece of damp paper towel folded behind Her back rind to keep Her supple.

Storage: Store in cheese paper or other semipermeable paper and a zip-top bag.

Average Shelf Life: 7–10 days

Can you FREEZE CHEESUS?

Freezing is a practice I strongly discourage. Cheesus loves consistent temperatures, and freezing Her forever disfigures Her delicate flavors and textures. If you must, it's best to turn Her into a finished dish, like lasagna, before freezing.

Never freeze a delicate bloomy, like this Sappy Ewe from Nettle Meadow Farm.

BLUE

Too much exposure to oxygen, and She'll continue to blue, so it's best to use a tight-fitting zip-top bag. This will limit airflow and barricade Her bold funk from spreading throughout your fridge. The shelf life of a blue depends on Her texture, with softer blues perishing more quickly than firmer varieties. If She's weeping moisture, lay a dry paper towel around Her body, wrap Her in parchment paper, and place Her in a zip-top bag or tub container with a lid.

Storage: Store in cheese paper or other semipermeable paper and a zip-top bag.

Average Shelf Life: 7–14 days

FIRM

The harder the body, the sturdier the Cheesus. That said, firm, aged bodies are by no means indestructible. With enough time, they'll lose their vivacious flavor and texture. If you notice She tastes like the inside of the refrigerator, use a non-serrated chef's knife to gently scrape off that little glossy layer on the paste, and proceed with your worship.

Storage: Store in cheese paper or other semipermeable paper and a zip-top bag.

Average Shelf Life: 2–6 weeks

The Book of
Serving

Now that you understand how to buy and store Cheesus, it's time to learn how to prepare Her for the altar and share Her with your congregation. Serving Cheesus properly is an act of respect to all those who have sacrificed to bring that body to you, from herdsmen, milkers, cheesemakers, affineurs, mongers, and everyone in between. It's also an opportunity to learn, discuss, and worship in holy communion.

The Holy Sacraments of Serving

PERSONAL WORSHIP IS BEAUTIFUL, BUT THERE'S NOTHING LIKE THE BONDING EXPERIENCE OF SHARING CHEESUS WITH THOSE YOU LOVE MOST. WHETHER IT'S A PLATTER AT THE CENTER OF A PARTY OR AT AN INTIMATE TASTING SESSION WITH A FEW FRIENDS OR LOVERS, THE ACT OF WORSHIPPING CHEESUS HAS AN UNRIVALED ABILITY TO BRING US TOGETHER IN HOLY COMMUNION.

SERVE THE RIGHT AMOUNT: If Cheesus is your appetizer, serve 2 to 3 ounces (55 to 85 g) total per person. If She's the main course, aim for 4 to 6 ounces (115 to 170 g).

CUT WITH RESPECT: Let Her body shape tell you how She wants to be cut (for more info, see page 212), and always wait to slice Her until just before serving.

USE ONE KNIFE PER BODY: If you use the same blade for everything, the flavors will mix and sully their seductive nuances.

BRING CHEESUS TO ROOM TEMPERATURE: Refrigeration dulls Her flavor and makes Her texture brittle, so temper soft bodies for at least twenty minutes and firm bodies for forty minutes.

SERVING SIZE

Understanding serving size is the key to worshipping Cheesus every day. Portioning prevents overindulgence, keeping your habit affordable and sustainable. Cheesus is a powerful seductress: when She offers Her body to you, the temptation to devour Her whole may overpower you. Your only mode of defense is preparation, so always portion before tempering.

INDIVIDUAL SERVING SIZE:

For an appetizer: 2 to 3 ounces (55 to 85 g) total cheese per person

For the main course: 4 to 6 ounces (115 to 170 g) total cheese per person

SERVING SIZE FORMULA:

Use the following formula to calculate about how much to serve of each cheese.

(A × B) / C = total ounces per body of Cheesus

A = individual serving size

B = number of people

C = number of cheeses

If you're melting the body of Cheesus, increase the serving size by an ounce or two. You can easily take down a lot more when She's hot and gooey.

HOW MUCH CAN YOU WORSHIP IN A DAY?

The proper daily portion is different for everyone. I usually enjoy around 3 to 4 ounces (85 to 115 g) of cheese daily, either all at once or spread out over several meals. Sometimes it's less, but sometimes it's a lot more. See what works for you, and make sure you get a lot of plants in there, too. You'll be grateful for all that blessed fiber.

TAKE OUT WHAT YOU NEED, KEEP THE REST IN THE FRIDGE

While Her flavors shine at room temperature, Cheesus prefers consistency during storage. When She warms up, Her body softens, oozes, and even sweats. She'll lose a bit of Her plump spring every time She tempers, so only take out as much as you intend to eat in one sitting. Keep the rest safely stored in the fridge.

Cutting the Cheese

PREPARING A BODY OF CHEESUS ISN'T JUST ABOUT

AESTHETICS. HOW AND WHEN YOU CUT A WEDGE OR WHEEL AFFECTS THE TASTE, TEXTURE, AND THE ENTIRE WORSHIP EXPERIENCE. EVERY CHEESE HAS A PREFERENCE FOR HOW IT WANTS TO BE CUT, AND YOU CAN ALWAYS TELL BASED ON ITS SHAPE.

Once you understand the basic rites behind the ritual, cutting Cheesus becomes joyful and therapeutic. For maximum freshness, slice Her up just before serving.

THE CUT ACCORDING TO BODY SHAPE

SOFT BODIES **These bodies usually have delicious rinds, so aim for a consistent rind-to-paste ratio between slices. Think of it like a pie: that flaky crust is just as important as the sweet filling.**

ROUND WHEELS, LIKE CAMEMBERT Start by slicing in half, then turn 90 degrees and cut in half again so you have quarters. Continue bisecting into smaller pieces, depending on the wheel's overall size. I also use this technique on large-diameter logs that are purchased in round disc shapes, like French Bûcheron.

CHEESE LOGS, LIKE FRESH CHÈVRE Slice into coins about ¼ inch (6 mm) thick. For a super clean cut on fresh goat cheese, freeze it for about ten minutes before slicing.

SQUARE WHEELS, LIKE ROBIOLA BOSINA Bisect diagonally, from corner to corner. Turn and repeat on the opposite corners so that the wedge is in quarters. Then, slice perpendicularly, from top to bottom and side to side, to make triangular wedges. I use this technique on square blocks of cheddar, too.

ANATOMY *of the* PERFECT SLICE

CONSISTENT RIND-TO-PASTE RATIO

EDIBLE IN 1 TO 2 BITES

CONVENIENT HANDHELD SIZE

Garroxta sliced into triangles

A perfectly portioned slice of Red Rock from Roelli Cheese Haus

PYRAMID CHEESES, LIKE VALENÇAY While this is the most intimidating shape to cut, you can use the same pie-slice technique as you would on round wheels. Keeping the bottom flat, cut into diagonal quarters from corner to corner. Then, slice perpendicularly, from top to bottom and side to side.

SPRUCE-WRAPPED ROUND WHEELS, LIKE VACHERIN MONT D'OR These bodies are so soft and gooey, they need a belt of bark to keep their voluptuous insides from oozing all over the place. Use a paring knife to carefully slice all the way around the top rind, just inside the bark. Slowly peel back and remove the top rind, reserving it for snacking after you've finished the rest. Then stick a spoon in Her creamy center. You can also leave half of the top rind intact, which makes for a sexy, scantily clad presentation.

SLICING TIP

You always want to eat Cheesus at room temperature, but slicing Her is a different story. Cut soft bodies and crumbly wedges while cold, and slice any pliable, semifirm bods at room temperature.

The cold makes Cheesus stiffer and more brittle, which keeps soft gooey bodies intact and helps crumbly wedges break apart more easily. If you're slicing a semifirm body like Comté, however, bring Her to room temperature first. She'll be more flexible and less likely to stick to your blade that way.

FIRM BODIES These bodies spend months in the cave developing deeply complex, lingering flavors. To unlock all that potential pleasure, you need lots of surface area in the form of thin slices.

RECTANGULAR WEDGES, LIKE GRUYÈRE These gals are made in huge wheels, which a monger will break down into a large wedge, then into smaller rectangles of varying sizes. Use a very sharp knife to slice them lengthwise into ⅛ inch (3 mm) slices.

TRIANGULAR WEDGES, LIKE MANCHEGO The triangular wedge is a common shape that's easy to break down. Cut off and discard the top and bottom rind. Then, slice into thin triangles. Leave the back rind on to use as a handle, like a pizza crust.

CRUMBLY CHEESES, LIKE PARMIGIANO No matter how hard you try, you'll never get a clean cut from a super fudgy blue or a crunchy aged cheese. These bodies just want to crumble apart, so embrace their inclinations. Insert the tip of a knife straight into a wedge and gently wiggle it to release snackable chunks.

A GUIDE TO CHEESE KNIVES AND OTHER TOYS

The texture of the cheese you're eating determines which knife to use when cutting Her. This choice is vital; a thick blade will smush a soft body, while a dull spreader is useless against a hard, crunchy wedge. And while there are a lot of cheese knives out there, you really only need two basic kitchen knives. For best results, be sure to sharpen them regularly.

ESSENTIAL PREP KNIVES

A THIN-BLADED KNIFE for soft cheeses

A CHEF'S KNIFE for firmer cheese (6 to 10 inches/15 to 25 cm long, whatever's most comfortable for you)

SERVING KNIVES

Specialty cheese knives are adorable and convenient for adorning platters, but they're mostly ornamental. If you don't have them, just use butter knives for soft bodies and steak knives for firm bodies. However, if you want to equip yourself with some sacred tools designated only for the body of Cheesus, then get yourself a couple serving knives that fit the different body types.

1 *THE FORK-TIPPED KNIFE* lets you cut semi-firm bods like Havarti, then stab a slice and bring it straight to your mouth.

2 *THE OFFSET CHEESE KNIFE* has a skinny blade, which is great for delicately slicing through softies. It also rests lower than the handle, so your knuckles don't hit the cutting board.

3 *THE SPEAR KNIFE* is great for chipping snackable chunks off of crumbly bodies like Gorgonzola or Parmigiano.

4 *THE CHEESE PLANE* is used to shave off razor-thin slices from flavorful firm bods like Comté. It's a sexy tool, but it's not my favorite because it scars the body of Cheesus with unsightly divots and valleys.

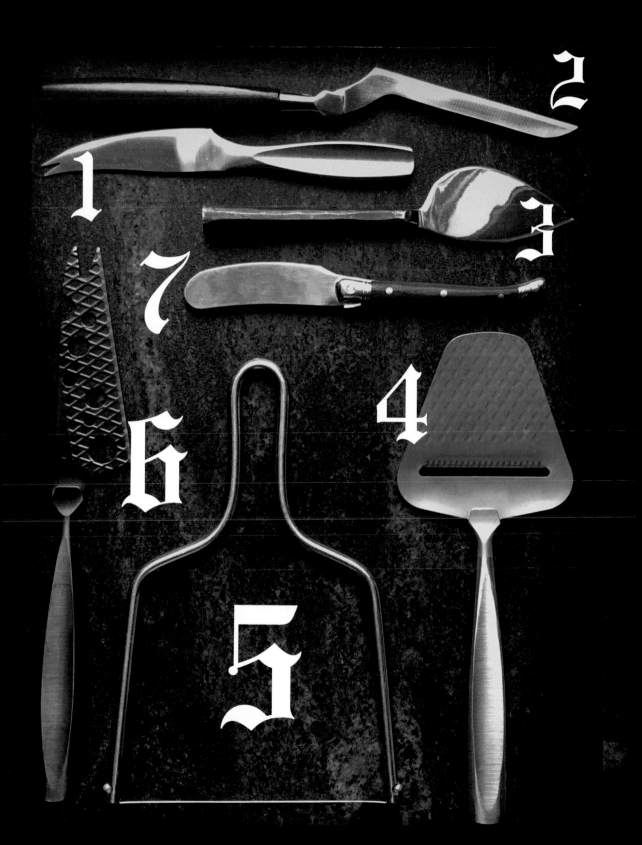

⑤ **THE CHEESE WIRE** creates the cleanest cut, perfect for creating pristine slices of delicate bodies like fresh chèvre logs or super ripe Bries. You can also use unflavored dental floss, but it's not as handy.

⑥ **THE SKELETON KNIFE** has holes in the blade to reduce drag and prevent the cheese from sticking.

⑦ **THE CHEESE SPREADER** has a blunt edge that is great for spreadable cheeses like ricotta, fresh chèvre, and burrata.

FUN SWISS TOYS

The Swiss are so devoted to Cheesus that they've invented a smattering of fun toys, each crafted for a specific body in mind. They say it's sacrilegious to employ these instruments on bodies other than those which they were designed for, but sometimes it's fun to break the rules.

The **girolle cheese curler** creates perfect blossoms out of Tête de Moine. It consists of two pieces: a platform with a pole in the middle and a rotating blade with a handle that slides on top of the pole. It can be used on any firm body that's of similar stature to Tête.

The **raclette grill** heats raclette until it's melty enough to scrape onto a plate of accompaniments. Full-size grills can hold an entire wheel of raclette, but there are also mini versions available that produce personal servings. Firm, melty bodies like Morbier and Emmentaler love getting the raclette treatment as well.

The **fondue pot** is a small pot used to keep fondue warm and dippable. It's a sexy toy, but any enameled pot does the job. Fill it with a classic fondue (see page 330 for my fondue recipe) or beer cheese for a sacrilegious spin.

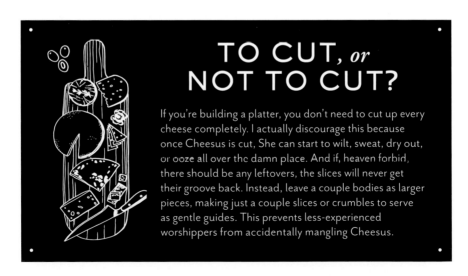

TO CUT, *or* NOT TO CUT?

If you're building a platter, you don't need to cut up every cheese completely. I actually discourage this because once Cheesus is cut, She can start to wilt, sweat, dry out, or ooze all over the damn place. And if, heaven forbid, there should be any leftovers, the slices will never get their groove back. Instead, leave a couple bodies as larger pieces, making just a couple slices or crumbles to serve as gentle guides. This prevents less-experienced worshippers from accidentally mangling Cheesus.

What to SERVE CHEESUS ON

You can make a cheese plate on top of any flat surface, such as:

**PLATES • SERVING PLATTERS • ROASTING DISHES • BAKING SHEETS
CUTTING BOARDS • SLATES • MARBLE SLABS • CAKE STANDS**

Below: Cheese plate with Pleasant Ridge Reserve, Montagnard des Vosges, and Blu di Bufala paired with a Manhattan

The Book of Tasting

Approached as an indulgent ritual, tasting Cheesus not only pleasures our palates but also stimulates our intellects, stirs our emotions, and awakens our spirits. When done with intention, savoring our Lord and savior is a ceremonious act that fully engages all of our senses. Whether you're worshipping solo or with a congregation, take the time to give yourself, body, mind, and soul, to Cheesus.

Opposite page: The author worshipping Grand Cru from Roth Cheese

The Holy Sacraments of Tasting

BRING CHEESUS TO ROOM TEMPERATURE: The cold dulls Her flavors and makes Her textures brittle. Remember: twenty minutes for soft bods, forty for hard ones.

EMPLOY ALL YOUR SENSES: Behold Her beauty, stroke Her body, meditate on Her aromas, and then let Her enter your mouth.

TASTE FROM MILD TO STRONG: This progression helps your palate fully appreciate the gentle nuances of shy bodies before the bold personalities dominate your palate.

TRY CHEESUS NAKED FIRST: Cheesus is divine on Her own, so honor Her au naturel before kinking things up with accompaniments.

RESPECT HER RIND: Unless they're coated with wax or plastic, all rinds are edible, and some are even delicious.

CLEANSE BETWEEN BITES: Rich butterfat quickly builds up on your palate, so keep your taste buds sharp with bubbly beverages or juicy, acidic accompaniments.

HOW TO TASTE CHEESUS

To fully appreciate the blessed and highly flavored body of Cheesus, you must taste Her mindfully. Take your time, be present, and transcend.

PREPARE YOUR TEMPLE

Set the mood for worship. Put on some music, dim the lights, and pour yourself a beverage. Set out a bouquet of flowers, or pull up a picture of the farm from whence this body of Cheesus came.

Do whatever you need to do to make yourself comfortable, but be wary of heavily scented candles, lotions, soaps, or sanitizers, which can interfere with your ability to enjoy the natural aromas of Cheesus.

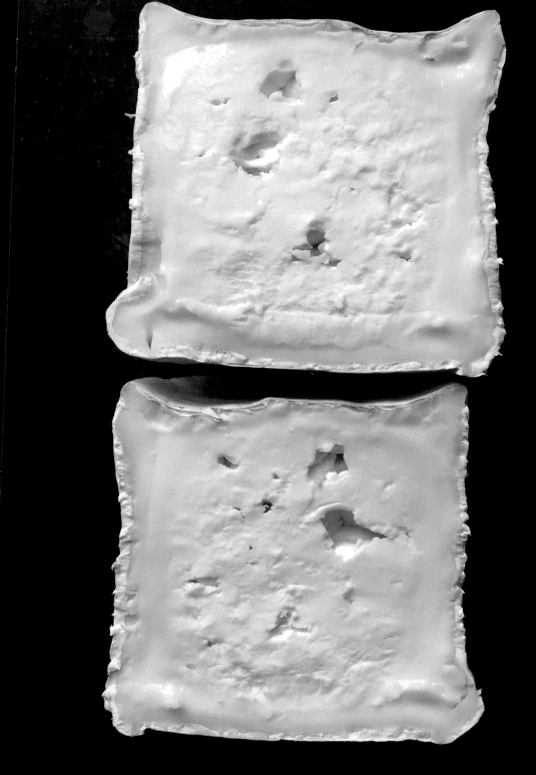

Little Lucy Brie from Redhead Creamery in Minnesota

Fingers dipped in the blessed body of Harbison

MEDITATE BRIEFLY

Take a moment to ease your mind, open your senses, and prepare yourself to receive the body of Cheesus. If you're not present, you will miss out on a world of pleasure.

Breathe deeply and close your eyes. Recite the prayer on page 177, if you wish. Give thanks to our Mother Earth, the animals, the microbial angels, and all the saints and disciples that labored and sacrificed to bring this holy curd to thy table.

BEHOLD HER BEAUTY

Your eyes eat first, so let them feast. Examine Her body, taking note of Her rind, paste, color, size, and shape. Imagine how She'll smell, feel in your hands, and taste in your mouth. Let that tingle of excitement ripple through your own body.

TOUCH HER BODY

Cut yourself a piece, feeling the way your knife slices into Her. Pick up a portion with your fingers and give Her a gentle squeeze, letting Her soften in your hand.

Take note of how Her body reacts to your fingers. Is She giving or resistant, flexible or brittle? Enjoy the sensation of your hands on Her body, and fantasize about how She'll feel inside your mouth.

Personally, I enjoy the sensuality of worshipping Cheesus with my bare hands. The warmth of your touch helps release Her perfumes. If you're not into that, feel free to use a spoon, fork, or knife.

WORSHIP HER SCENT

Next, flood your olfactory system with Her perfume. Contemplate Her unique fragrance. Smell Her paste, then sniff Her rind and see if you detect any differences. For some bodies, the bark is much stronger than the bite. If She's coming off a little aggressive, She'll probably taste much milder. Breathe in and out a few times, paying attention to how Her aromas shift as you become a little more intimate with Her.

TASTE HER BODY, AND TRANSCEND

Finally, put the body of Cheesus inside your mouth, all on Her own without any accompaniment or pairing. Inhale before chewing, letting your breath aerate your palate. Chew slowly, observing how Her body breaks apart. Feel Her fill your mouth and embrace your entire palate. Close your eyes and meditate on the pleasure that washes over you. Cherish this first wave of flavor, breathing in and out through your nose to flood your palate with Her aromas.

Allow the sensation to transport you to the terroir that birthed this body of Cheesus, picturing the farmland, terrain, animals, and season. Let the flavors climax, then appreciate Her finish, taking note of how long Her flavors linger. Allow yourself to moan with pleasure, letting the rush of air aerate your palate. Then, go at it again: taste Her rind and paste separately, then both parts together. Note how Her flavors shift and transform.

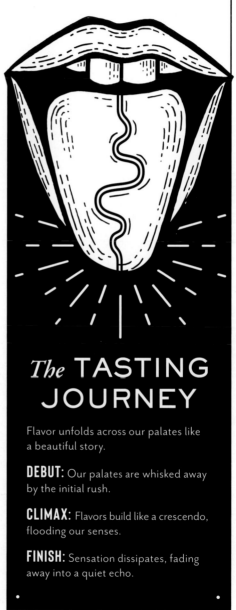

The TASTING JOURNEY

Flavor unfolds across our palates like a beautiful story.

DEBUT: Our palates are whisked away by the initial rush.

CLIMAX: Flavors build like a crescendo, flooding our senses.

FINISH: Sensation dissipates, fading away into a quiet echo.

Burrata with prosciutto, olive oil,
pink salt, and freshly cracked pepper

REJOICE AND DISCUSS

Once your feet return to Earth, share your first impressions: Did your palate explode with pleasure, or did She fail to get you off? Try to identify Her dominant flavors: is She sweet, sour, salty, bitter, or umami? Then expand from there and pinpoint a few specific flavors. Maybe She tastes sweet and fruity like apples, or sour and tangy like yogurt.

Preach your impressions of flavor and texture, and share any feelings or memories that emerge. The more you discuss, the more you aerate your palate, further arousing your taste buds. You can also record your tasting notes in a log or journal.

CLEANSE YOUR PALATE

When you taste a body of Cheesus, Her butterfat coats your mouth, causing the flavors to cling to your palate. They build up quickly and eventually dull your taste buds, so you should regularly cleanse your palate. Champagne, beer, and other effervescent beverages cut through the richness like scrubbing bubbles, keeping your palate sharp. Plain bread and crackers, or even just sips of water, also help to reset your taste buds. Whatever your method, do it every couple of bites, and you'll have much more tasting libido.

ANOINT HER WITH ACCOMPANIMENTS

Once you've fully enjoyed the naked body of Cheesus, spice things up with a playful pairing. Swirl Her in your mouth with a libation, dollop Her body with a seductive spread, or chase Her with a candied nut or tart pickle. Observe how the pairings mingle with and enhance Her flavors. Explore, indulge, and don't be afraid to get a little kinky with Her. (See the Book of Pairing, page 234.)

QUESTIONS *for* WORSHIP

What's Her name?

How old is She?

What's Her homeland like?

What milk is She made with?

What's the story of Her maker?

What type of body is She? Fresh, bloomy, washed, firm, or blue?

How does She feel in my hands?

What color is She?

Does She have a rind?

What does Her rind look like? Soft, sticky, flaky, or something else entirely?

How wet is She? How much moisture does She have?

Does She smell more sweet or more savory?

Does Her rind smell different from the rest of Her body?

What does She taste like?

Do I like how She tastes?

What pairings would complement her?

Curdy Talk

BUILDING A VOCABULARY FOR CHEESUS HELPS YOU

IDENTIFY WHAT YOU LIKE, WHAT YOU DON'T, AND WHAT TO ASK FOR AT THE CHEESE COUNTER. IT ALSO HELPS YOU DETERMINE WHAT'S A NORMAL FUNKY SMELL VERSUS A BAD SIGN OF DECAY.

Professionals love to toss out eccentric descriptors like "basementy" and "fresh forest floor," which can sound really fancy and intimidating. But you don't have to do all that (unless you want to). This is about creating your own sacred language with Cheesus, and it should be personal and enjoyable. Consider what feelings and sensations She inspires within you, and do your best to describe them.

DESCRIPTORS

Use these as a jumping-off point, then form your own sacred language with Cheesus.

MILKY: fresh cream, cultured butter, clotted cream, boiled milk, white chocolate

FRUITY: apples, plums, cherries, apricots, grapes, strawberries

FLORAL: orange flower, lilac, lavender, roses, honey, vanilla

TANGY: yogurt, buttermilk, sourdough, lemon, pineapple

VEGETAL: potato, cabbage, broccoli, bell peppers, leeks, garlic

HERBACEOUS: rosemary, thyme, sage, chives, mint

SPICY: peppercorn, nutmeg, allspice, cloves, cumin, coriander, fennel

TOASTY: roasted nuts, baking bread, caramelized onions, coffee, chocolate, smoke

EARTHY: fresh soil, wet grass, dried hay, leather, cave, tobacco

FUNKY: animal, barnyard, miso, mushrooms, armpits, feet

TEXTURES

SPREADABLE	*CHALKY*	*FLEXIBLE*
CREAMY	*CAKEY*	*FIRM*
SILKY	*SPRINGY*	*CRUMBLY*
SPONGY	*STICKY*	*CRUNCHY*
OOZY	*PUDGY*	*FLAKY*
SQUISHY	*CURDY*	*FUDGY*

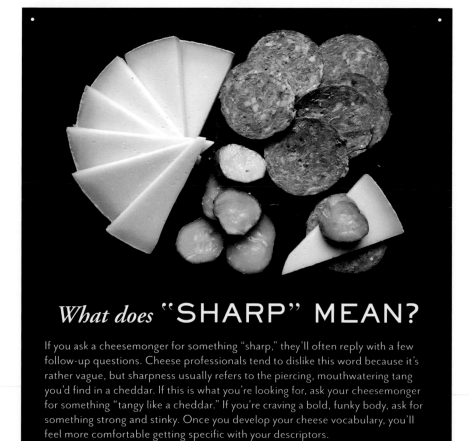

What does "SHARP" MEAN?

If you ask a cheesemonger for something "sharp," they'll often reply with a few follow-up questions. Cheese professionals tend to dislike this word because it's rather vague, but sharpness usually refers to the piercing, mouthwatering tang you'd find in a cheddar. If this is what you're looking for, ask your cheesemonger for something "tangy like a cheddar." If you're craving a bold, funky body, ask for something strong and stinky. Once you develop your cheese vocabulary, you'll feel more comfortable getting specific with your descriptors.

DID YOU HATE IT?

Here are three things to consider before you condemn a body of Cheesus.

FLAVOR IS IN THE PALATE OF THE TASTER

Everyone's palate is as different and unique as their fingerprint. If you don't vibe with a particular body of Cheesus, that doesn't mean She's no good—it just means She's not right for you (at least at the moment). Our palates also change and develop over time, so the two of you might find everlasting love down the line.

NOT YOUR BATCH

Cheesus is constantly changing. Each body, especially ones made with raw milk, are snapshots of the circumstances under which they were made. The same recipe can taste different depending on the season, weather, time of day, and other factors that affect milk composition. Flavor also changes dramatically as She ripens, and sometimes a wedge in your fridge can even fluctuate from one day to the next. It's important to try the same cheese at different ages to see if there's a stage of ripeness that you favor in particular.

SHE'S A GOOD CHEESE GONE BAD

If that body of Cheesus smells revolting, She may have passed Her prime. Even the stinkiest bodies have a freshness to them when they're healthy. Trust your instincts and familiarize yourself with the difference between a bold flavor and a sign that Cheesus has passed.

DOES SHE TASTE LIKE YOUR FRIDGE?

Fat readily absorbs odors, so Cheesus often takes on the scent of her surrounding environment. This can be pleasant like when a cave-aged body gets those dank, cavey notes, but it also means that she's susceptible to soaking in that cold, stale flavor of your refrigerator. If this happens, just give her a gentle exfoliating facial by lightly scraping her surface with a non-serrated blade. Once you remove that slightly shiny layer of film, try Cheesus again to see if she's back to tasting like Her fabulous self.

NOT FOR ME *vs.* NOT GOOD

If Cheesus is tasting downright offensive, those flavors are likely not intentional.
Here's a list of some potential tasting defects.

VIRTUE *vs.* DEFECT

VIRTUE	DEFECT
Tangy	Sour
Herbaceous	Unpleasantly Bitter
Fruity	Rotten
Smoky	Sulphuric
Nutty	Rancid Crayon
Fresh Soil	Dirty Barn
Mushroomy Funk	Ammoniated
Complex and Balanced	Flat and One-Noted

Bonne Bouche, an ash-ripened goat cheese from Vermont Creamery

How Tasty Is Thy Rind?

IT'D BE A SHAME TO GO YOUR WHOLE LIFE WITHOUT

DABBLING IN THE PLEASURES OF EATING RIND. ALL RINDS ARE EDIBLE—UNLESS THEY'RE COATED WITH PLASTIC, CLOTH, OR WAX—AND THEY EVEN CAN BRING EXCITING DIMENSIONS TO YOUR WORSHIP. YOU SHOULD ALWAYS TASTE A RIND. IF IT'S NOT YOUR THING, THAT'S TOTALLY FINE. YOU DON'T HAVE TO EAT IT AGAIN, AS LONG AS YOU'VE GIVEN CHEESUS A CHANCE. HERE'S A CHEAT SHEET FOR THOSE EAGER TO EAT RIND.

DELICIOUS

Bloomy rinds, like on Brie: mushroomy and peppery

Wrinkly rinds, like on Chabichou: yeasty like a baguette

Washed rinds, like on Taleggio: savory like steak

Young natural rinds, like on Stilton: earthy like caves and soil

EDIBLE BUT NOT THAT GREAT

Tough natural rinds, like well-aged Alpines: chewy, slightly bitter, and rather unpleasant (unless you're into it!)

Extremely hard rinds, like Parmigiano: waxy and unpalatably dry (but they can add sacred flavor to broths and stew.)

DON'T EAT IT

Anything that's clearly inedible, like wax, cloth, plastic, leaves, bark, or straw: you should avoid ingesting (however, the rind beneath might tickle your fancy, so feel free to peel off the outer material and carry on.)

Cumberland from Sequatchie Cove Creamery

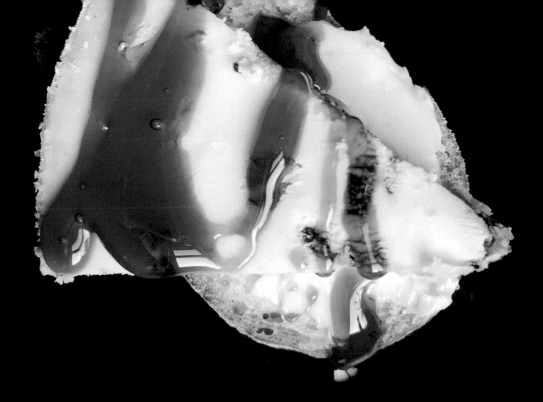

SENSORY ANALYSIS

If you want to tune up your taste buds before worship, try this short palate reset that will help you better identify sweet, salty, sour, and bitter flavors.

YOU WILL NEED:

Sugar water: ½ teaspoon sugar dissolved in 2 tablespoons water

Salted water: scant ⅛ teaspoon salt dissolved in 3 tablespoons water

Wedge of lemon

Soy sauce water: ¼ teaspoon soy sauce in 2 tablespoons water

Glass of plain water at room temperature

Cup for spitting (optional)

Above: Bridgman Blue from Jasper Hill Farm with butter, bread, and buckwheat honey

INSTRUCTIONS:

After each step, spit or swallow, then rinse with plain water.

- Start sweet: Sip the sugar water and swish it around your entire mouth. Take note of how the sweetness feels cool and sticky on your tongue.

- Sip the saltwater and swirl it in your mouth. Notice how your taste buds come alive.

- Bite into the lemon flesh and swirl it around. Feel the subtle burn of acidity as your mouth waters.

- Bite into the lemon rind this time, and feel the aching bitterness fill your mouth.

- Sip the soy sauce water and swish it around. Notice how the buzzing savory sensation arouses your taste buds.

The Book of Pairing

Once you've worshipped Cheesus au naturel, it's time to bless Her with a pairing. Your goal is to elevate the body of Cheesus so that the sum is even greater than its parts. If you get lucky, you'll even achieve the "third taste," a new flavor profile born of the climatic union between individual elements. This miraculous sensation rolls across your palate like an orgasm, signaling that you've reached pairing nirvana.

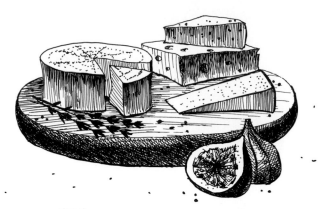

It Is Right to Give Our Thanks and Pairings

A PERFECT BODY OF CHEESUS EASILY STANDS ON HER OWN, BUT EVEN THE BEST LOVE AFFAIRS BENEFIT FROM A LITTLE KINK. THIS BOOK PREACHES THE FUNDAMENTALS OF PAIRING AND OFFERS RECOMMENDATIONS FOR BOTH BEVERAGES AND ACCOMPANIMENTS.

THE CATECHISMS OF PAIRING CHEESUS

Understanding a few general principles will provide you with the skills you need to break out on your own and freely explore this world of infinite possibility. Once you build a foundational understanding of the pairing arts, you'll have the confidence and experience you need to venture beyond these basic tenets.

PAIR WITH INTENTION: Amplify Cheesus's sexiest qualities with contrasting and complementary flavors and textures.

FIND A BALANCE: Don't obscure Cheesus's sacred flavors with overly loud or complex pairings.

BRING EVERYTHING TO ROOM TEMPERATURE: All flavors are more pronounced at room temperature, *including* those of beverages and accompaniments.

KEEP AN OPEN MIND: Play around often, get a little kinky, and break the rules.

THERE IS NO SUCH THING AS A PERFECT PAIRING: All of us have unique palates and personal preferences, so the way we experience flavors is subjective. The same pairing can't possibly pleasure all of us, and you might find that some of the following recommendations won't work for you. Trust your impressions and don't be afraid to dislike something.

THERE IS, HOWEVER, SUCH A THING AS A BAD PAIRING: As you explore all of the pairing possibilities, you will inevitably discover one that really doesn't work. There are varying degrees of an unsuccessful pairing. Sometimes the flavors stay independent, like oil and vinegar, so you taste them separately. It's not unpleasant, but it lacks that revelatory moment.

When you have a truly bad pairing, the components will bring out each other's worst qualities. Occasionally, you might even get a burst of a nasty lingering metallic flavor. Because everyone's palate is different, it's hard to predict whether or not a pairing will taste offensive to you. Don't let that keep you from exploring all the possible flavor combinations; it's a risk any worshipper must be willing to take.

HOW TO PAIR CHEESUS

The following guidelines will help you set up a foundation for balancing the body of Cheesus with an array of pairings, from a communion with wine to ingredients in a composed meal.

LOOK FOR CONTRASTS

Bringing together opposite flavors tends to subdue Cheesus's more dominant flavors, creating a balanced pairing.

EXAMPLES OF CONTRASTS:

Salty with Sweet: Blue Cheese with Honey

Tangy with Bitter: Fresh Chèvre with Orange Marmalade

Fatty with Salty: Burrata with Prosciutto

Funky with Tangy: Raclette with Pickles

LOOK FOR COMPLEMENTS

Bringing together similar flavors tends to accentuate one or more of Cheesus's flavors, leading to a heightened experience.

EXAMPLES OF COMPLEMENTS:

Fatty with Fatty: Burrata with Olive Oil

Meaty with Meaty: Gruyère with Salami

Nutty with Nutty: Manchego with Marcona Almonds

Caramelly with Caramelly: Gouda with Bourbon

BALANCE INTENSITY

Never let a strong accompaniment overwhelm a delicate body of Cheesus, and avoid matching bold bodies with subtle pairings. Match the intensity, but beware of pairing complex wedges with an equally complex wine. Their personalities can clash.

EXAMPLES OF BALANCE:

Mellow with Mellow: Fresh Chèvre with Wheat Beer

Bitter with Bitter: Bandaged Cheddar with IPA

Bold with Bold: Stilton with Stout

Rich with Rich: Époisses with Dubbel

What GROWS TOGETHER, *Goes* TOGETHER

This age-old saying advocates for the sacred relationship between terroir and culinary tradition. While there's a ton of variation and it doesn't always work, it's a fun theme to play with. Here are some of my favorites:

TUSCANY, ITALY: Chianti & Pecorino Toscano

LOIRE VALLEY, FRANCE: Sancerre (Sauvignon Blanc) & Valençay

SOMERSET, ENGLAND: English Pale Ale & Clothbound Cheddar

MILWAUKEE, WISCONSIN: Miller High Life & Cheese Curds

PLAY WITH TEXTURE, TOO

Textures bring all sorts of pleasurable sensations: soft condiments fill your mouth, while crunchy ones tickle your palate. Employ them in both contrasting and complementary ways.

*Sourdough toast with
Chabichou, fresh figs, honey,
rosemary, and pepper*

Rogue Creamery Original Blue
with dark chocolate

EMPLOY YOUR PERSONAL EXPERIENCE

Pairing is personal, so investigate your individual preferences. Explore pairings with your favorite childhood snacks, or replicate the flavors of your favorite meals. If you love Flamin' Hot Cheetos, try them with some cheddar. If you love cheeseburgers, pair a beefy washed-rind cheese with tangy cornichons. Don't be afraid to get a little freaky.

QUALITY > PRICE

Even if you splurged on your cheese, you don't need to shell out on the beverage pairing. What matters is that you love what you're drinking. For example, I'm a slut for a Miller High Life. It's a cheap lager, but it's delicious with cheddar and always makes me happy. Your personal pleasure is what matters most when you worship Cheesus.

When it comes to accompaniments, go with what's looking good, which doesn't necessarily mean the most expensive option. I'm a big proponent of supporting small-scale farmers and artisan producers. They not only craft sacred, delicious foods worthy of blessing the body of Cheesus, they also have smaller carbon footprints, especially when they're local to you. But don't feel like you have to buy the topshelf option: just get something that looks good and is within your budget. Sometimes, that's just your favorite brand of potato chips. Remember: always prioritize pleasure!

Winnimere with Fritos and cornichons

*Mont St. Francis from Capriole
perched on a pale ale*

The Holy Sacraments of Beverage Pairing

PAIRING THE BODY OF CHEESUS WITH A SACRED

LIBATION IS AN ANCIENT RITUAL. THE TWO ELEMENTS HAVE THE POWER TO BRING OUT THE BEST IN EACH OTHER, CREATING A NEW, MIRACULOUS TASTING SENSATION. THIS HOLY COMMUNION BLESSES US WITH LIMITLESS PAIRING OPTIONS. THIS SECTION WILL HELP YOU FIND THE PERFECT BODY OF CHEESUS, WHATEVER YOUR POISON.

The following suggestions are broad and based on personal favorites, so they might not pleasure your body the way they do mine. The only way to find out is to try, so experiment often and don't get too stuck on specifics. The thing that matters most is that you like what you're drinking and enjoy yourself.

EMPLOY ALL YOUR SENSES: Taste your libation just as you would Cheesus, acknowledging its color, texture, smell, and flavor on its own.

MARRY THE FLAVORS: Take a sip and a nibble and swirl them together to make a saucy potion in your mouth.

EMBRACE ACID AND EFFERVESCENCE: Acidity and bubbles promote balance and longevity, while bitter elements, like the tannins in wine, can overpower.

The ART of COMMUNION

Begin by tasting both components separately, using all of your senses to fully familiarize yourself with the individual flavors and mouthfeels. Whether you begin with Cheesus or the beverage is a matter of personal preference, but I usually worship Cheesus first. After you've tasted both, try them together. Keep a bit of cheese in your mouth as you sip your beverage, and swirl them around your palate to marry the flavors. Meditate on the combined sensations, then cleanse your palate and go at it again. You have to try a pairing at least three times before you really know whether or not it works.

BEER

Cheesus and beer have a spiritual connection. Beer is made with fermented wheat and barley, and these seeds sprout grasses, which feed the animals that make Cheesus. That's a foundational quality that few other beverages share, which helps give these two a particularly palatable chemistry.

Beer takes two main forms: *ale* and *lager*. Ale is made with top-fermenting yeasts, generally at a warm temperature, while lager is made with bottom-fermenting yeasts, usually at a cool temperature. From there, they branch out into a crazy range of styles with flavors that can taste like anything from pine trees to coffee. They also feature bitter hops and effervescence, both of which cut through a luscious body of Cheesus like a knife.

PILSNERS AND LIGHT LAGERS crisp, refreshing, and drinkable

> VARIETIES > *pilsners, Mexican lagers, and American macros like Budweiser*

> PAIR WITH > *mozzarella, queso fresco, and cheese curds*

LIGHT-BODIED ALES light, fruity, and effervescent with citrusy notes

> VARIETIES > *blonde ales, wheat ales, and saisons*

> PAIR WITH > *tangy young chèvres and creamy Brie styles*

PALE ALES medium bodied with light malty flavors and a hoppy finish

> VARIETIES > *American pale ales, English bitter ales, and Belgian pale ales*

> PAIR WITH > *buttery Tommes, tangy clothbound cheddars, and nutty Alpine styles*

INDIA PALE ALES bold, hoppy, and widely varied, often featuring tropical, grassy, or malty flavors

> VARIETIES > *West Coast IPAs, New England IPAs, and English IPAs*

> PAIR WITH > *grassy bandaged cheddars, Parmigiano-Reggiano, and creamy blues*

SOUR BEERS tart and funky, due to activity from bacteria and wild yeasts

> VARIETIES > *lambics, goses, Berliner weisses, and American wild ales*

> PAIR WITH > *funky washed rinds and fruity cheddars*

FULL-BODIED ALES rich and malty with fruity yeasts and a lingering caramelized sweetness

> VARIETIES ⟩ *amber ales, brown ales, and dark Belgians like dubbels and tripels*

> PAIR WITH ⟩ *soft and stinky washed rinds, well-aged sheep's milk bodies, and buttery blues*

FULL-BODIED LAGERS amber or brown in color with heavy malts and rich notes of brown sugar

> VARIETIES ⟩ *Maibocks, Märzens, and Dunkels*

> PAIR WITH ⟩ *goat's milk Goudas or any wedge with deep nutty notes, like Alpine styles*

DARK ALES rich, toasty, and powerful with intense toffee flavors

> VARIETIES ⟩ *stouts, porters, and barley wines*

> PAIR WITH ⟩ *toffee-sweet aged Goudas and rich, salty blues*

BLESSINGS
of BEER *and* CHEESUS

Many insist that wine is the best beverage for Cheesus, but I believe beer makes a better pairing. It lacks mouth-coating tannins and has a bubbly effervescence that cleanses the palate.

Left: Red Rock from Roelli Cheese Haus with a juicy IPA

WINE

Wine is the most iconic companion to Cheesus, but it's also the hardest pairing to master. The staggering variety makes generalizing difficult, complex flavors can create clashes, and the tannins can overwhelm Cheesus. The most cheese-friendly wines are often high-acid with fruity flavors, and white wines are almost always more forgiving then reds. When in doubt, Cheesus always loves sparkling wine, and nearly every wine loves a good Parmigiano.

SPARKLING WINES bubbly and playful, ranging from bright and fruity to rich and toasty

> VARIETIES ⟩ *Champagne, Prosecco, and Cava*

> PAIR WITH ⟩ *everything, but especially luscious Brie styles, aged Alpines, and crunchy hard bods like Parmigiano-Reggiano.*

LIGHT-BODIED WHITES refreshing and easy to drink, ranging from floral and herbaceous to tart and citrusy

> VARIETIES ⟩ *Pinot Grigio, Albariño, Grüner Veltliner, and Sauvignon Blanc*

> PAIR WITH ⟩ *creamy burrata and tangy fresh goat's milk bodies*

FULL-BODIED WHITES rich, smooth, and often oaked

> VARIETIES ⟩ *Chardonnay and Viognier*

> PAIR WITH ⟩ *creamy Camembert and meaty bodies like Gruyère*

AROMATIC WHITES fruity, floral, and fragrant with a range of sweetness

> VARIETIES ⟩ *Riesling, Moscato, and Gewurztraminer*

> PAIR WITH ⟩ *fruity cheddars, Comté, and herbaceous sheep's milk bodies*

BLUSHING WINES bright and acidic like a white, but fuller bodied like a red

> VARIETIES ⟩ *rosé and orange wines*

> PAIR WITH ⟩ *creamy burrata, semi-firm sheep's milk bodies, and chèvres of all ages*

*Bonne Bouche from
Vermont Creamery with rosé*

LIGHT-BODIED REDS bright, fruity, and herbaceous

> VARIETIES > *Pinot Noir, Gamay, Grenache, and Lambrusco*

> PAIR WITH > *creamy Brie styles, stinky washed rinds, aged Alpines, and fruity cheddars*

MEDIUM-BODIED REDS berry forward, floral, and sometimes spicy

> VARIETIES > *Cabernet Franc, Sangiovese, Barbera, and Tempranillo*

> PAIR WITH > *grassy, aged sheep's bodies like Pecorino, fruity Parmigiano, or mild blues*

FULL-BODIED REDS jammy with dark, earthy notes like tobacco and figs

> VARIETIES > *Zinfandel, Syrah, Malbec, and Cabernet Sauvignon*

> PAIR WITH > *well-aged Alpine styles, aged Goudas, and blue cheese (especially on a steak)*

DESSERT WINES aromatic, full-flavored, complex, and often quite sweet

> VARIETIES > *Eiswein, Port, sherry, and Sauternes*

> PAIR WITH > *creamy Brie styles, aged sheep's milk bodies, and salty blues like Roquefort*

CIDER

Cheesus loves a little cider, which is blessed with a natural acidity and range of sweetness and effervescence. Thanks to a recent surge in artisan cideries, the market boasts a staggering variety that includes some deliciously nuanced options. As long as you avoid super-sweet, flat-tasting ciders, you'll be hard pressed to find an unfavorable pairing.

FRENCH-STYLE CIDER slightly sweet and funky

> PAIR WITH > *rich Brie styles and nutty Alpines*

PERRY sweet, floral, and made with pear juice

> PAIR WITH > *tangy goat's milk bodies and creamy blues*

Flory's Truckle from Milton Creamery with an English-style cider

ENGLISH-STYLE CIDER dry and sometimes slightly smoky

⟩ **PAIR WITH** ⟩ *a crumbly clothbound cheddar and an earthy Stilton*

SIDRA a briny Basque cider with low effervescence

⟩ **PAIR WITH** ⟩ *Spanish classics like Manchego and Garrotxa*

*Fresh chèvre, Ossau-Iraty,
and Chiriboga on a platter
with Nigori sake*

SAKE

Sake rice experiences a similar transformation as the Virgin Milk: it's fermented with yeasts and mold, and it sometimes even contains lactic acid bacteria. To the naked eye, filtered sake looks similar to white wine, but the alcoholic content is higher, the acidity is lower, and it often booms with savory umami flavors. The different types of sake are categorized by their brewing method and the level of polishing that the rice undergoes. The more polishing, the more delicate the flavor, with Daiginjo sake being the highest level.

JUNMAI classic sake with high acid and full flavor

> PAIR WITH > *tangy fresh and soft-ripened chèvre*

NIGORI a roughly filtered, cloudy, and slightly sweet sake

> PAIR WITH > *buttery blue bodies*

KIMOTO a funky sake made in a time-consuming traditional method

> PAIR WITH > *funky Brie styles like Camembert*

DAIGINJO an artful premium sake with delicate aromas and a light, fruity flavor

> PAIR WITH > *nutty aged sheep's milk bodies*

SPIRITS

Spirits might not be everyone's first thought when it comes to pairing Cheesus, but they're surprisingly amicable and a joy to play with. Favor aged spirits, and be wary of anything that has a harsh burn. Those are best when mellowed with a few drops of water or mixed into a cocktail that has enough sweetness to balance the bite.

VODKA grain based, neutral flavored, and sometimes spicy or citrusy

> VARIETIES > *wheat, corn, rye, potato, and barley based*

> PAIR WITH > *mix into a Bloody Mary to pair with cheddar or dill Havarti, or take a shot alongside rye bread with pickled onions and a stinky Limburger*

GIN botanical based, herbaceous, and clean

> VARIETIES ⟩ *London Dry, Genever, Old Tom, and Plymouth*

> PAIR WITH ⟩ *try a gin and tonic with a leaf-wrapped goat's milk cheese, like O'Banon, or pair a gin martini with olives stuffed with Roquefort or a nutty sheep's milk body like Pecorino*

TEQUILA agave based, grassy, and earthy

> VARIETIES ⟩ *blanco, reposado, añejo, and variations like smoky mezcal*

> PAIR WITH ⟩ *pair a margarita with a chile-infused cheddar, or sip an aged reposado with a grassy aged sheep's milk cheese like Manchego*

RUM sugar cane based and ranging from light syrup to deep molasses, depending on the age

> VARIETIES ⟩ *white, gold, dark, blackstrap, and rhum agricole*

> PAIR WITH ⟩ *mix into a daiquiri and pair with a crunchy bod that tastes of pineapple, like Grana Padano, or drink a well-aged variety straight up with an aged Gouda or a rich, creamy blue*

WHISKEY grain based, wood-aged, and spicy with sweet caramel notes

> VARIETIES ⟩ *bourbon, Tennessee, rye, Scotch, Irish, and Japanese*

> PAIR WITH ⟩ *toffee-sweet aged Goudas, spicy Alpines, grassy clothbound cheddars, and earthy blues like Stilton*

COFFEE

Bold, rich, and often complex, a good cup of coffee loves cozying up with Cheesus. The pairing makes an efficient, transcendent breakfast or afternoon pick-me-up. In Columbia and some Scandinavian countries, people even drop cubes of soft, spongy cheeses straight into their hot cups, letting it soften and soak in the rich, earthy coffee flavor. No matter how you go about it, get yourself a bag of something freshly roasted or splurge on a pour-over or espresso.

> PAIR WITH ⟩ *triple-cream Brie styles, pudgy washed rinds, crunchy aged Goudas, and bold blue bodies*

A rye Manhattan with Pleasant Ridge Reserve from Uplands

TEA

The variety of flavors in tea and herbal infusions run a similar gamut as wine. Some are high in acid, some are fruity, and some are even rich with delicate tannins. Unlike wine, tea is much more forgiving when it comes to pairing with Cheesus.

HERBAL INFUSIONS, like chamomile and rooibos

> PAIR WITH ⟩ *tangy fresh bodies and soft-ripened goat's bodies*

WHITE TEA, like white peony and silver needle

> PAIR WITH ⟩ *fresh bodies like sheep's milk ricotta and triple-cream Brie styles*

GREEN TEA, like sencha, genmaicha, and matcha

> PAIR WITH ⟩ *tangy fresh chèvres, grassy clothbound cheddars, and nutty sheep's milk bodies*

BLACK TEA, like Earl Grey, oolong, and pu'erh

> PAIR WITH ⟩ *earthy bodies like Camembert, creamy blues, and well-aged Alpine styles*

Earl Grey tea with Roquefort PDO and fresh figs

The Holy Sacraments
of Playing with
Accompaniments

ACCOMPANIMENTS ARE LIKE SEX TOYS, SPICING UP YOUR WORSHIP WITH TITILLATING TEXTURES AND NEW LEVELS OF FLAVOR. THE LIST OF POSSIBLE COMBINATIONS ARE TRULY ENDLESS, SO I'VE BROKEN DOWN THE OPTIONS INTO CATEGORIES AND OFFERED SUGGESTIONS TO HELP GUIDE YOUR EXPLORATION. DON'T LIMIT YOURSELF TO MY RECOMMENDATIONS—USE THEM AS A JUMPING-OFF POINT AND EXPERIMENT OFTEN. REMEMBER: THE ONLY THING THAT MATTERS IS THAT YOU ENJOY YOURSELF.

TRY CHEESUS NAKED FIRST: Allow Her natural glory to shine before getting kinky with an accompaniment.

DON'T OVERWHELM HER: Anything extremely spicy, sweet, sour, or bitter risks outshining Her complexities and nuances.

PAIR WITH INTENT: Identify Her specific flavors and textures, then complement or contrast them with a pairing.

BREAD

Glorious, glutinous bread is an ancient food, just like Cheesus. It brings a transcendent texture and neutral flavor profile that lets Cheesus shine, especially with a dollop of jam or honey. The pairing possibilities are infinite, but I usually prefer bread with soft bodies. Enjoy it fresh, toasted, or grilled, but avoid dark toast, which can be too bitter.

*An extra ripe wheel of Saint-Félicien
with toasted sourdough*

HERBED BREAD with mild milky bodies like ricotta

CIABATTA with creamy freshies like burrata

BAGELS with tangy spreadables like fresh chèvre

FOCACCIA with flaky hard bodies like Parmigiano

CORNBREAD with tangy cheddars

SEEDED BREAD with young Goudas

RYE BREAD with nutty Alpines like Gruyère

PUMPERNICKEL with burly Swisses like Emmentaler

FRENCH COUNTRY BREAD with washed rinds like Vacherin Mont d'Or

FRUIT AND NUT BREADS with salty blues like Gorgonzola Dolce

BAGUETTE with ripe, oozing Brie-style bodies like Camembert

SOURDOUGH with soft goat's milk bodies

CARBS *Are Not* REQUIRED

Cheesus doesn't always benefit from bread and crackers, especially hard bodies like aged Gouda, Alpines, and cheddars. I'm not telling you to shun the blessings of gluten, I just want you to taste Cheesus in all Her naked glory first. There are some bodies so soft they seem to require a crunchy carb bed, but sometimes it's fun to get your fingers dirty instead.

CRACKERS

Few pairings can compare to the delightful contrast between a crisp cracker and a supple body of Cheesus. Because of their signature crunch, crackers shine best when bedding soft, spreadable, and semi-firm bodies. Plain crackers are the most versatile, but there's a time and a place for flavored varieties. Be careful of strong additives like chives or onion, which can overpower complex bodies and clash with other accompaniments.

WATER CRACKERS with creamy Brie styles

WAFERS with soft goat's milk bodies

BUTTER CRACKERS with tangy cheddars

CRISPBREAD with mild spreadables like fromage blanc

RYE CRACKERS with pudgy washed rinds like Taleggio

MATZO with buttery firm bodies like dill Havarti

OAT BISCUITS with earthy blues like Stilton

PRETZEL CRISPS with nutty Alpine styles

HONEY

Good honey is a miraculous accompaniment. It blesses Cheesus with a nuanced sweetness that contrasts Her salty richness and acts as a bridge to other pairings like beverages or bread. There are more than three hundred different types of honey in the US alone, but it's hard to find a bad pairing between these two. Look for raw, unfiltered honey, which has the most complex flavor.

DELICATE FLORAL HONEY, like Dutch clover

> PAIR WITH ⟩ *goat's milk bodies of all ages and creamy bloomies like Brie styles*

RICH DARK HONEY, like buckwheat

> PAIR WITH ⟩ *complex bodies like aged cheddars and nutty aged bodies like Mimolette*

WAXY HONEYCOMB

> PAIR WITH ⟩ *earthy blues and firm sheep's milk bodies*

SPICY, CHILE-INFUSED HONEY

> PAIR WITH ⟩ *grilled Halloumi and anything with a bloomy rind*

LUXURIOUS TRUFFLE HONEY

> PAIR WITH ⟩ *well-aged sheep's milk bodies and creamy blues*

JAMS AND PRESERVES

Preserves offer a playground of pleasure. Compared to fresh fruits and vegetables, they have a richer, sweeter flavor and a jammy, mouth-filling texture that complements softies and contrasts with crunchy aged bodies. That smooth texture shines best when balanced with something toothsome, like a cracker or a crystal-studded hard body. Here's a breakdown of the different types of preserved fruits and my favorite pairings within each category.

JELLIES: smooth, firm, and sweet

> PAIR > *strawberry jelly with creamy blues like Maytag*

JAMS: pulpy and spreadable

> PAIR > *onion jam with nutty Alpines like Gruyère*

PRESERVES: syrupy with whole or large chunks of fruit

> PAIR > *fig preserves with soft-ripened chèvre like Humboldt Fog*

FRUIT BUTTERS: thick and smooth with deep, cooked flavors

> PAIR > *apple butter with tangy young Gouda*

MARMALADES: a bittersweet relish made with citrus fruits

> PAIR > *orange marmalade with spreadable freshies like ricotta*

CHUTNEYS: a savory condiment made with vinegar, spices, and fruits or vegetables

> PAIR > *mango chutney with clothbound cheddar*

MOSTARDAS: a spicy spread made with candied fruit and mustard seeds

> PAIR > *pear mostarda with salty bodies like Pecorino*

MEMBRILLO: a thick, sliceable paste made with quince fruit

> PAIR WITH > *aged Spaniards like Manchego*

FRESH FRUIT

While preserves amp up the flavor, fresh fruits bless Cheesus with bursts of refreshing juice, bright colors, and hearty fiber. Their ample acidity cleanses the palate between bites and helps balance the richness. Fresh fruit is pretty easygoing, which makes room for abundant pairing potential, but some combinations are more transcendent than others.

STRAWBERRIES with young tangy chèvres like Bûcheron

RASPBERRIES with milky sweet spreadables like ricotta

BLUEBERRIES with rich triple-cream Brie styles

BLACKBERRIES with stinky washed rinds

CURRANTS with buttery Tommes

APRICOTS with funky bloomies like Camembert

PLUMS with salty aged sheep's milk bodies like Pecorino

PEACHES with creamy blues like Gorgonzola Dolce

MELONS with briny feta

PINEAPPLES with milky cottage cheese

GRAPEFRUITS with salty queso fresco

ORANGES with tangy fresh chèvre

LEMONS with grilled Halloumi

PEARS with aged Parmigiano

MOST VERSATILE

APPLES with anything, but especially cheddar and Camembert

CHERRIES with anything, but especially Alpine styles and blues

GRAPES with anything, but especially Taleggio and young Gouda

FIGS with anything, but especially chèvre and Parmigiano

St. Albans from Vermont Creamery with cherry preserves and baguette

DRIED FRUIT

Dried fruits sacrifice their refreshing juices for deep, complex sweetness. Their chewy textures and concentrated flavors shine most with firm aged bodies.

RAISINS with stinky softies like Taleggio

DRIED CRANBERRIES with crumbly bandaged cheddar

DRIED CHERRIES with buttery Tommes

DRIED APRICOTS with fruity Alpines like Comté

DRIED CURRANTS with fresh spreadables like chèvre

CANDIED GINGER with creamy mild blues

DATES with firm sheep's milk bodies like Manchego

DRIED FIGS with anything

NUTS

Nuts have a rich, mellow flavor and crunchy texture that work with nearly any body of Cheesus. Their ability to tease out the roasted nutty flavors in aged bodies is truly unmatched, but they also add a titillating textural contrast to creamy softies. Enjoy them toasted, roasted, fried, or candied.

ALMONDS with semi-firm sheep's milk bodies like Manchego

PECANS with crunchy aged Gouda

CASHEWS with buttery Tomme

PISTACHIOS with chèvre of all ages

HAZELNUTS with nutty Alpines like Gruyère

PEANUTS with stinky washed rinds like Grayson

WALNUTS with crumbly blues like Roquefort

PINE NUTS with hard Italian bods like Parmigiano

PICKLED VEGETABLES

Tangy, juicy pickles are best employed next to bodies that love swinging on the savory side. They're excellent palate cleansers and have the power to mellow out even the funkiest washed rinds. Add them to a charcuterie board with mustard and crunchy, salty snacks.

PICKLED SHALLOTS with meaty Alpines like Gruyère

PICKLED CARROTS with salty sheep's milk bodies like Pecorino

CORNICHONS with funky bloomies like Camembert

CAPERS with rich, creamy mascarpone

PICKLED OKRA with smoked Gouda

PICKLED SWEET PEPPERS with tangy chèvre

KIMCHI with fruity block cheddars

KRAUT with stinky washies like raclette

CAPER BERRIES with unctuous firm bodies like Manchego

Rush Creek Reserve from Uplands with French fries and cornichons

*Meredith Dairy Sheep &
Goat Cheese with olives
and baguette*

FRESH VEGETABLES

While fresh veggies are less common accompaniments than their pickled brethren, they bring refreshing crunch and a bit of contrasting bitterness. They make a lovely addition to a platter, but this complement is best showcased on a good salad. (See Sacred Salads on page 320.)

RADISHES with dill Havarti

CUCUMBERS with briny feta

BELL PEPPERS with tangy fresh chèvre

CELERY with creamy blues like Buttermilk Blue

TOMATOES with fresh bodies like mozzarella

COOKED VEGETABLES

Not all vegetables can complement Cheesus when served raw, so heat them up to release their deep, flavorful potential before blessing your platter.

CARAMELIZED ONIONS with nutty Alpine styles like Gruyère

ROASTED PEPPERS with salty feta

ASPARAGUS with crunchy hard bodies like Parmigiano

ROASTED POTATOES with melty washies like raclette

SAUTÉED MUSHROOMS with creamy Brie styles

ROASTED BROCCOLI with crumbly blues like Maytag

MARINATED ARTICHOKES with hard sheep's milk bodies like Manchego

OLIVES

Juicy, briny, and salty olives are a beloved companion to Cheesus. Avoid super salty bodies like blue—unless, of course, you're stuffing that olive with a blue body. Here are some common varieties of olives.

KALAMATA OLIVES: purple-black with a deep fruity flavor

> PAIR WITH ⟩ *briny feta*

CASTELVETRANO: bright green with a mellow buttery flavor

> PAIR WITH ⟩ *tangy fresh chèvre*

PICHOLINE: light green and firm with notes of lemon

> PAIR WITH ⟩ *firm, buttery Tomme styles*

OIL-CURED OLIVES: black and wrinkly with deep, salty flavors

> PAIR WITH ⟩ *complex hard bods like Parmigiano*

GORDAL: fat and meaty with rich, briny flavors

> PAIR WITH ⟩ *nutty Spanish bodies like Manchego*

SWEET TREATS

Soothe Cheesus's salty side with a little something sweet and decadent. There's a lot of room to get kinky with dessert-themed pairings, but avoid cloying candies, like Skittles or rock candy. Their sugar content can overwhelm the nuances in Cheesus.

TOFFEE with crunchy aged Gouda

PRALINES with aged hard bods like Parmigiano-Reggiano

CARAMEL with goat's milk Gouda

DARK CHOCOLATE with earthy blues like Stilton

FIG AND ALMOND CAKE with salty hard bodies like Pecorino

MERINGUES with hard goat's milk bodies

NOUGAT with nutty Alpines like Comté

LEMON CURD with soft-ripened goat's milk bodies like Bûcheron

POMEGRANATE MOLASSES with grilled Halloumi

MAPLE SYRUP with crumbly bandaged cheddar

COOKIES

Cookies bless Cheesus with a playful crunch and buttery sweetness. Like crackers, their texture shines best with soft bodies. It's an indulgent pairing that's delightful with coffee, tea, and sippable spirits like whiskey.

SHORTBREAD COOKIES with soft-ripened chèvre like Humboldt Fog

MOLASSES COOKIES with creamy blues like Gorgonzola Dolce

CORN COOKIES with fruity cheddar like Prairie Breeze

BISCOTTI with rich spreadables like mascarpone

MACAROONS with nutty Alpines like Pleasant Ridge Reserve

PEANUT BUTTER COOKIES with crunchy aged Gouda

CHOCOLATE CHIP COOKIES with triple-cream Brie styles

SNICKERDOODLES with semi-firm sheep's milk bodies

CHOCOLATE WAFER COOKIES with tangy chèvre

Midnight Moon from Cypress Grove with caramel

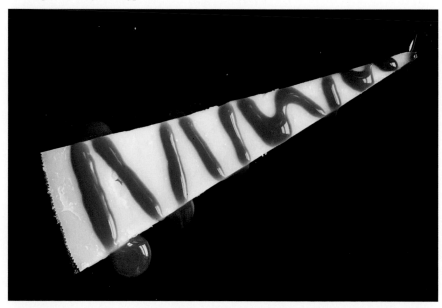

Prairie Breeze from Milton Creamery with Flamin' Hot Cheetos

SNACKS

Don't be afraid of getting lowbrow—you're here to have fun! Be wary of pairing complex bodies with super-strong flavorings like sour cream and onion. You never want to overpower the nuances in Cheesus.

SPICY CHEESE PUFFS with fruity block cheddars

POTATO CHIPS with firm washed rinds like raclette

BBQ CHIPS with creamy blues like Maytag

CORN CHIPS with soft washed rinds like Taleggio

POPCORN with hard, salty sheep's milk bodies like Pecorino

CORN NUTS with buttery Tomme styles

FRENCH FRIES with spruce-wrapped bodies like Harbison

SAVORY SAUCES

Like sweet preserves, savory sauces add a luscious texture to the body of Cheesus, but these guys have a salty side that complements the funky notes. Play around with their mouthwatering complexity, but watch out for aggressive garlic or heat, which can burn out your taste buds.

OLIVE TAPENADE with aged sheep's milk bodies like Manchego

PESTO with fresh, milky bodies like mozzarella

HUMMUS with briny feta

OLIVE OIL with fresh, creamy burrata

BALSAMIC with hard, crunchy Parmigiano

MUSTARD with stinky washed rinds like raclette

MARMITE with crumbly clothbound cheddar

HOT SAUCE with tangy blues like Buttermilk Blue

MISO with triple-cream Brie styles

FISH

A lot of cheese lovers scoff over this surf-and-turf pairing, but it's a time-honored tradition. In ancient Rome, for instance, people grated hard bodies into fish-based stews and sauces all the time. If you're nervous, start with mild freshies and salty hard bodies, then expand from there.

SALMON LOX with tangy fresh chèvre

TINNED FISH with salty hard bodies like Pecorino

ANCHOVIES with umami-rich Parmigiano

CAVIAR with creamy spreadables like fromage blanc

LOBSTER with melty young Gouda

MUSSELS with crumbly blues like Roquefort

MEAT

Cured and cooked meats are the quintessential savory accompaniment, blessing Cheesus with satisfying sustenance and palate-pleasing umami. Dress up this holy coupling with pickles, roasted veggies, mustard, onion jam, radishes, olives, apples, figs, and breads.

WHOLE MUSCLE CURED MEATS, like Prosciutto di Parma and Jamon Serrano

> PAIR WITH 〉 *milky sweet mozzarella, firm washed bodies like Gruyère, and nutty sheep's milk bodies like Manchego*

SALAMI, like saucisson sec, finocchiona, and Spanish chorizo

> PAIR WITH 〉 *firm Alpines like Comté, stinky washies like Taleggio, and nutty hard bodies like Pecorino Toscano*

SOFT SPREADABLES, like pâté, 'Nduja, and rillettes

> PAIR WITH 〉 *stinky Alpines like Gruyère, hard sheep's milk Italians, and firm goat's milk bodies*

CLASSIC COOKED MEATS, like steak, pastrami, and bacon

> PAIR WITH 〉 *creamy blues like Roquefort, firm Swiss bodies like Emmentaler, and tangy cheddar*

CANNABIS

Everything tastes better when you're high, and Cheesus is no exception. There's a scientific approach to pairing up this dynamic duo: both Cheesus and Saint Mary Jane have terpenes, which are aromatic oils with distinct flavors like citrus, pine, and berries. Terpenes are found in plants like hops, flowers, and herbs, and they are even produced by microbial bacteria. They're non-psychoactive, but they can promote calming and uplifting effects. While there isn't a regulated system to classify the different strains, many databases do list the prominent terpenes in common varietals of cannabis. Once you identify which terpenes are present, you can use the basic pairing techniques to go forth and worship. For the best flavor, I recommend using a clean glass pipe, rolled joints and blunts, vaporizers, and infused edibles.

*Couple from Vermont
Creamery with prosciutto
and fig preserves*

L'Amuse Gouda with a Girl Scout Cookies joint

CALMING

MYRCENE: HERBAL AND MUSKY

COMMON STRAINS: Blue Dream and Purple Haze

> PAIR WITH > *crumbly bodies with dank notes like bandaged cheddar*

PINENE: FRESH AND WOODSY

COMMON STRAINS: OG Kush and Harlequin

> PAIR WITH > *spruce-wrapped bodies like Harbison*

CARYOPHYLLENE: PEPPERY AND SPICY

COMMON STRAINS: Girl Scout Cookies and LA Confidential

> PAIR WITH > *crunchy hard bodies like aged Gouda*

LIMONENE: CITRUSY AND HERBACEOUS

COMMON STRAINS: Sour Diesel and Wedding Cake

> PAIR WITH > *tangy bodies like fresh chèvre*

TERPINOLENE: FRUITY AND FLORAL

COMMON STRAINS: Jack Herer and Dutch Treat

> PAIR WITH > *creamy Brie styles*

ENERGIZING

Five Pairings That Will Never Fail You

WHEN YOU FEEL OVERWHELMED BY ENDLESS PAIRING

POSSIBILITIES, IT HELPS TO HAVE A FEW DEPENDABLE COMBINATIONS IN YOUR BACK POCKET. WHETHER YOU'RE LOOKING FOR A SAVORY CHARCUTERIE BOARD OR AN INDULGENT DESSERT-THEMED PLATTER, THESE FIVE CHEESE PAIRINGS WILL NEVER LET YOU DOWN.

ANY CHEESE + GOOD HONEY

Salt is a crucial step in cheesemaking, so all cheeses are naturally salty. Counter the savory with a quality honey, preferably something local.

BRIE + BERRY JAM

I've never met a Brie that didn't love a dollop of sweet, fruity preserves. Enjoy this coupling atop baguette or crackers.

STINKY BODIES + PICKLES

This combination is basically a cheeseburger in paradise, especially when paired with a good salami.

AGED BODIES + NUTS

Cheeses that age for long periods of time often have complex, toasty flavors, and nuts are the perfect way to tease those out.

BLUE BODIES + DARK CHOCOLATE

Both blues and chocolate have an earthy flavor and fudgy texture that naturally complement each other.

CHEAT SHEET

for when you feel lost and overwhelmed

FRESH BODIES +
Honey + Wheat Beer

BLOOMY BODIES +
Jam + Champagne

WASHED BODIES +
Pickles + Malty Beer

FIRM BODIES +
Nuts + Dark Spirits

BLUE BODIES +
Chocolate + Stout

The Book of
Plating

*Like a beautiful church, a cheese plate is
about more than aesthetics; it's the altar
at which we gather to worship our Lord
Cheesus. It sparks conversation, smooths
awkward moments between strangers at
parties, and it even buys you time if
dinner runs late. (Thank you, Cheesus!)*

The Holy Sacraments of Plating

PEOPLE ARE OFTEN TOO INTIMIDATED TO CREATE A CHEESE PLATE ON THEIR OWN, BUT ONCE YOU GET THE HANG OF THE BASIC STEPS, IT'S AN INSTANTLY GRATIFYING FORM OF CREATIVE EXPRESSION. DON'T WORRY ABOUT MAKING IT LOOK PERFECT; JUST ENJOY THE PROCESS OF PREPARING AN OFFERING FOR YOURSELF OR YOUR LOVED ONES. WORSHIPPING CHEESUS IS A CELEBRATION.

CURATE AN ARRAY OF DELICIOUS THINGS: Look for a variety of textures, colors, and flavor profiles.

BRING IT ALL TO ROOM TEMP: As always, temper both Cheesus and Her accompaniments before serving.

PLATE WITH PURPOSE: Arrange each body from mild to strong, place their favorite accompaniments nearby, and give everything its own utensil.

ENJOY YOURSELF: Plating is an act of worship, so set aside enough time so you can enjoy the process and express yourself.

TYPES OF CHEESE PLATES

A cheese plate can be anything you want. It can be as casual as a single wedge on a plate or as sophisticated as a grazing board. It can serve as an appetizer, main course, brunch, dessert, or happy-hour snack. All this possibility can get overwhelming, so let's break it down into three different presentations.

PERSONAL PLATE: an individual offering, served as a snack or full course

COMMUNAL PLATTER: an altar meant for intimate worship among a small group

GRAZING BOARD: a cathedral meant for worshipping with a crowd

Once you know what kind of cheese plate you're assembling, you just need to choose a variety of delicious things to put on it.

WHAT TO PUT ON YOUR CHEESE PLATE

LET'S START WITH CHEESUS

Select three to six bodies featuring a variety of milk types, regions, styles, ages, colors, and flavor profiles. This ensures a nice assortment without overwhelming worshippers. Alternatively, you can showcase a single body to worship.

NOW FOR ACCOMPANIMENTS

Aim for one accompaniment per body and go from there. You can also feature a single condiment that goes with everything, or let one body share a selection of pairings.

FOCUS ON VARIETY

A broad selection of textures, colors, and flavors brings excitement to your cheese platter. Make sure you provide something light and refreshing—like fresh fruit—to break up the richness and increase snacking stamina.

TASTY *doesn't have to mean* PRICEY

If you have great ingredients, it's impossible to make a bad cheese plate. That doesn't mean you need to spend a lot of money— just make sure that each element is delicious enough to stand on its own. Here's a tip: buy a small wedge of a pricey showstopper, then fill out the board with a couple more affordable bodies, like crumbly block cheddars or fresh chèvre, and simple snacks like crackers and fresh fruit.

THE PERFECT CHEESE PLATE FORMULA

This cheese plate formula is designed to provide you with the right variety of cheeses, accompaniments, and pairings. Fill it in like a Mad Lib and refer to the serving sizes on page 211 to tailor it to fit any size party.

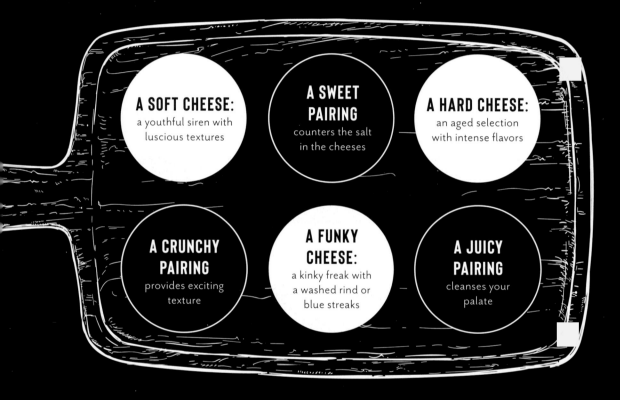

A SOFT CHEESE: a youthful siren with luscious textures

A SWEET PAIRING counters the salt in the cheeses

A HARD CHEESE: an aged selection with intense flavors

A CRUNCHY PAIRING provides exciting texture

A FUNKY CHEESE: a kinky freak with a washed rind or blue streaks

A JUICY PAIRING cleanses your palate

Regional Examples of the Perfect Cheese Plate

FRANCE

soft: Brie

hard: Comté

funky: Roquefort

sweet: honey

crunchy: baguette

juicy: cornichons

ITALY

soft: Burrata

hard: Parmigiano

funky: Taleggio

sweet: balsamic reduction

crunchy: toasted focaccia

juicy: cherry tomatoes

SPAIN

soft: Cana de Cabra

hard: Manchego

funky: Queso de Valdeón

sweet: membrillo paste

crunchy: Marcona almonds

juicy: olives

ESSENTIAL CHEESE PLATE EQUIPMENT CHECKLIST

CUTTING BOARD

Always prep Cheesus on a separate cutting board, so you keep the serving platter clean and ready for worship.

SERVING PLATE

Consider the size of the group you're feeding. You can include a selection of plates or one massive board, but remember: the bigger the better. Cheesus hates being crowded. (See the Book of Serving on page 208.)

SERVING KNIVES

Use a separate knife for every cheese. Even if She's already sliced, equip your guests with options in case they want to cut one more blessing for themselves. (See the knife guide on page 216.)

VESSELS

Any dollopy spread or briny pairing needs to be contained, lest it taint the pristine body of Cheesus. Use mini jars, casuelas, ramekins, or tiny bowls.

UTENSILS

To prevent your plate's flavors from cross-contaminating, provide little spoons and forks for every accompaniment that needs one.

GARNISH

Fresh herbs and edible flowers bless your platter with vivid colors, rich aromas, and a touch of ambiance. It's like setting the mood with a scented candle. Just make sure your garnishes are food-grade and nontoxic.

Taking that
CHEESE PLATE TO-GO?

Put it together on a rimmed cookie sheet or baking dish and wrap it tightly for safe transport. Bring utensils and garnish it separately upon arrival.

Julianna from Capriole Goat Cheeses, Mimolette from Isigny Ste-Mère, and Keep Dreaming from Dorothy's Cheese on a platter with citrus, pistachios, grapes, and honey

How to Build a Cheese Plate

PLATING IS AN ACT OF WORSHIP—ENJOY IT. PUT ON SOME MUSIC, TAKE A DEEP MEDITATIVE BREATH, AND SET ASIDE ENOUGH TIME SO YOU WON'T FEEL RUSHED.

MISE EN PLACE

French for "set in place," mise en place refers to preparing all your equipment and ingredients for ease of assembly. Temper your ingredients, gather your boards and knives, set out your accompaniments, fill your ramekins, and cut your cheese.

PUT IT TOGETHER

Now for the fun part: you have all the tools and supplies before you, so let yourself get creative and have fun. Don't worry about making mistakes. Cheese plates are art, and art is subjective.

THE ART OF THE CHEESE LANDSCAPE

Cheesus is a holy creation of the earth, and the most beautiful platters pay homage to the beauty of a natural landscape: a winding trail of crackers, crumbles cascading from a mountain of Parmigiano, or a rippling stream of prosciutto.

TRAILS AND RIVERS divide the plate and can be made with vegetables, meats, crackers, bread, or even Cheesus Herself.

PONDS AND LAKES fill in the gaps between other elements and are easy to refill. Small, loose items like nuts, berries, and chips work well here.

MOATS act as barriers preventing strong flavors like blue cheeses from funking up the rest of the plate and can be made with anything, including crackers, nuts, chocolate squares, and sliced vegetables.

MOUNTAINS AND HILLS add height and act as centerpieces. Use a large wedge of aged cheese or pile up cuts of salami.

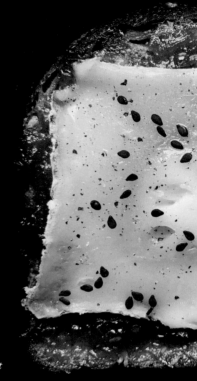

What to do with LEFTOVERS

When a body of Cheesus sits out at room temperature, Her body changes. Some bodies start to ooze, and others will sweat, their precious fats pooling on the surface in little beads. While She's still safe to eat, Her texture is forever compromised and She will never shine as brightly on the plate. However, She'll still pleasure your palate in the kitchen. In the unlikely event that you ever have cheese plate leftovers, incorporate them into a recipe, like the Monger's Mac 'N' Cheesus (page 326) or Seven Blessed Toasts (page 318). Beware of leaving out fresh bodies: their high-moisture content makes them more perishable, so they should be discarded if left out for more than a few hours.

Right: A slice of Dirt Lover from Green Dirt Farm with plum preserves on toast

ASSEMBLY:

- **Start by laying out any jars and bowls**, so you can build around their shapes.
- **Add Cheesus**, evenly spacing the bodies and arranging them from mild to strong.
- **Position accompaniments near their recommended cheese pairing** to help guide worshippers.
- **Finish with garnishes and utensils.** Stick the garnish in any sparse spots and lay utensils around the perimeter for easy access.
- **Keep extra crackers, bread, and nuts on hand** so you can easily refill and reload as you worship.

PLATING LORD CHEESUS

A few suggestions for how to lay the body of Cheesus on the plate.

The Fan

The Zigzag

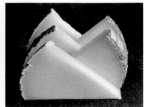

The Interlace

The Staircase

The Cascade

The Cheese Shell

The Swirl

The Presentation Piece

PLATING CHARCUTERIE

Prosciutto: gently lay each slice down, twisting your hand slightly to create a rippling effect.

Large-format salami: fold into quarters for easy pickup.

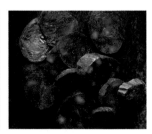

Small-format salami: either shingle into a river or pile into a small hill.

Eight Holy Cheese Plate Offerings

THE SEASONS SHAPE THE WAY WE EAT AND THE FOODS

AVAILABLE TO US. LIKEWISE, THE RHYTHMS OF MOTHER NATURE INFLUENCE THE BODY OF CHEESUS. I CURATED THESE CHEESE PLATES AS A NOD TO THE THE ANNUAL CYCLE OF FESTIVALS THAT CELEBRATES THE PASSING SEASONS. USE THEM AS BLUEPRINTS TO INSPIRE YOUR OWN ALTAR AS YOU WORSHIP THROUGHOUT THE YEAR.

TRAVELING *with* CHEESUS

Here's how to be equipped to make a cheese plate at the beach, on a roadtrip, or even on a plane.

GO WITH A FIRM BODY: Aged bodies are more durable and often less stinky.

SLICE BEFORE YOU LEAVE: Get Her ready for worship before you head out.

WRAP HER RIGHT: Make sure She's well protected on Her journey with specialty cheese or parchment paper, which doubles as a plating surface.

BRING NON-MESSY PAIRINGS: Jams and honeys are a sticky nuisance on the road, so favor dried fruits, crackers, nuts, or whatever you can find at the gas station or airport.

DRIED FIGS complement the caramelized notes in firm bodies, while contrasting against salty blues.

LUXARDO CHERRIES tease out the fruity notes in both whiskey and Alpine-style bodies.

THE CHEESES

➊ ALPINE STYLE

Alpine-style cheeses taste brothy and herbaceous, with deep flavors that glorify the pleasing spiciness of rye whiskeys.

RECOMMENDED: Uplands Pleasant Ridge Reserve (pictured), Gruyère 1655, or Roth Grand Cru Surchoix

➋ CREAMY BLUE

Creamy blues blanket your mouth with an abundance of butterfat and punchy funk, prepping your taste buds for bold whiskeys like Scotch.

RECOMMENDED: Rogue Creamery Oregon Blue (pictured), Bleu d'Auvergne, or Sequatchie Cove Creamery Shakerag Blue

➌ AGED GOUDA

Aged Gouda's sweet, toasty notes of butterscotch tease out the best qualities in bourbon.

RECOMMENDED: Cypress Grove Midnight Moon goat's milk Gouda (pictured), Ewephoria sheep's milk Gouda, or L'Amuse Signature Gouda

CORN NUTS are satisfyingly crunchy and evoke the corn used to make bourbon.

JUICY ORANGE SLICES
cleanse the palate between bites.

TOASTED PECANS
flirt with the nutty notes in Goudas and Alpines.

WHISKEY PLATE

As luxurious and sophisticated as a velvet smoking jacket, this cheese plate is built to flatter an array of whiskeys. The chosen bodies of Cheesus are distinctly rich and complex with long-lasting flavors that enrobe your palate while complementing the depth of this dark spirit. The accompaniments are more than sublime pairings: they each represent vital whiskey ingredients and classic cocktail garnishes. Best enjoyed fireside while clad in your coziest robe.

BEVERAGE PAIRING:
Manhattan, old fashioned, or a flight of bourbon, rye, and scotch

EFFIE'S OATCAKES
act as a crunchy chariot for creamy blues.

SPRING CHEASTER PLATE

This celebratory platter is alive with the bright, vibrant flavors of nature's annual resurrection. The chosen bodies of Cheesus embody a pasture at bloom, blessed with herbaceous flavors that evoke warm sunshine and dewy grass. The accompaniments are classic and simple, inspired by springtime in France. Enjoy on a patio or make a picnic in the park.

FRESH BAGUETTE sops up the oil-soaked chèvre and lovingly beds the creamy blue.

1

LOCAL HONEY evokes the sweet promise of summer while contrasting with the salty bodies of Cheesus.

SALTED PISTACHIOS provide a splash of vivid green and complimentary floral flavor.

DRIED APRICOTS complement the fruity qualities in Comté.

RADISHES balance the rich butter and cleanse your palate.

BEVERAGE PAIRING: Chilled rosé or Riesling

THE CHEESES

❶ FRENCH BLUE

French blues have a tender, creamy body and a mellow, salty funk that longs for a drizzle of sweet honey.

RECOMMENDED:
Saint Agur (pictured), Roquefort, or Fourme d'Ambert

❷ MARINATED FRESH CHÈVRE

Marinated fresh chèvre is lush and herbaceous—the quintessential cheese of springtime, especially when lubed up with herb-spiked olive oil.

RECOMMENDED:
Use the recipe on page 312 to marinate some lavender-infused Purple Haze from Cypress Grove (pictured), or try a premade version like CHEVOO or Meredith Dairy Sheep & Goat Cheese

❸ SUMMER MILK COMTÉ

Summer Milk Comté is the embodiment of an Alpine meadow, flush with mountain flora and blossoming with flavors of herbs, grasses, and flowers.

RECOMMENDED:
Summer Milk Comté (pictured), Alp Blossom, or Uplands Pleasant Ridge Reserve

CULTURED BUTTER is intoxicating when slathered onto crunchy spring radishes or layered beneath a slice of funky blue.

SEEDED CRACKERS offer a satisfying crunch and a poetic homage to the sprouting seeds of springtime.

FRESH CUCUMBERS
break up the
intense flavors.

POPCORN
offers something
satisfying to munch
and crunch between
bites of cheese.

THE CHEESES

① SPREADABLE FRESH BODY

Spreadable fresh bodies flavored
with chives add luscious texture and
a savory tease that complements
crunchy chips and crackers.

RECOMMENDED:
Boursin (pictured) or flavored
chèvre logs from Vermont Creamery
or Cypress Grove

② FRESH CHEESE CURDS

Fresh cheese curds are as snackable
as popcorn and delightful when
dipped straight into spicy honey.

RECOMMENDED:
Cheddar Curds from Ellsworth
Creamery (pictured) or something
from a cheddar capital like
Wisconsin or Vermont

③ FRUITY BLOCK CHEDDAR

Fruity block cheddar breaks apart
into crumbles and brings a sweet,
tangy flavor with enough zing to
stand up to mouth-buzzing MSG.

RECOMMENDED:
Prairie Breeze from Milton
Creamery (pictured),
MontAmoré from Sartori,
Promontory from Beehive
Cheese, or Beecher's Flagship

BUTTER CRACKERS
are a light and flaky
chariot for the
spreadable cheese.

CORN NUTS
add an irresistible crunch
and complementary
flavors of sweet corn.

2

**BEVERAGE &
CANNABIS PAIRING:**
Miller High Life and
a couple joints

MUNCHIE PLATE

SPICY HONEY
brings a sweet heat
that complements
nearly any cheese.

**FLAMIN' HOT
CHEETOS**
bring salty tang
and an addictive,
building heat.

Worshipping our Lord Cheesus doesn't mean you have to limit yourself to fancy artisan accompaniments. Some people think pairing so-called junk food with Cheesus is sacrilegious, but I disagree. If pairing Cheetos with cheddar makes you happy, then that can't be blasphemous. Let loose, get a little lowbrow, and light up a fatty to pair with this munchie-filled platter. Just please pair responsibly: while I fully condone junk food pairings, artificial flavors can overwhelm gentle, nuanced complexities. Save extra sacred bodies for another plate.

3

SUMMER PICNIC PLATE

1

Ideal for enjoying at a picnic or poolside, this solstice offering is filled with juicy, refreshing accompaniments and bodies of Cheesus that can handle the heat. Hard bodies, especially sheep's milk ones like Manchego, sweat in the sun, and their fat pools on the surface, creating an unflattering, greasy texture. The chosen bodies here can keep their cool and relax in the heat. The accompaniments are both seasonal and refreshing, perfect for cleansing your palate and cooling your bod between bites of indulgence.

PEANUTS
offer a salty crunch and a familiar earthy flavor that balances bold stinkers.

BASIL
offers a vibrant burst of green, a zesty piquancy, and a delicious complement to the creamy burrata.

BLACKBERRY JAM
mellows and complements funky rinds while blessing milder bods with a mouthfilling dollop of brambly sweetness.

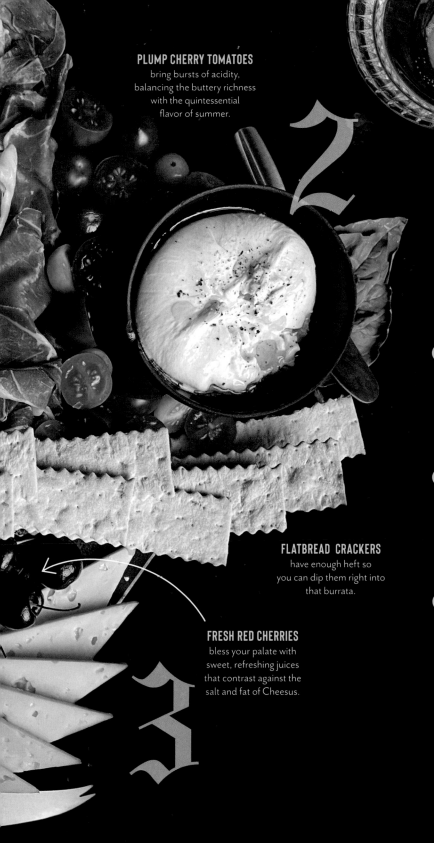

PLUMP CHERRY TOMATOES
bring bursts of acidity,
balancing the buttery richness
with the quintessential
flavor of summer.

BEVERAGE PAIRING:
Wine spritzer, shandy,
or spiked seltzer

FLATBREAD CRACKERS
have enough heft so
you can dip them right into
that burrata.

FRESH RED CHERRIES
bless your palate with
sweet, refreshing juices
that contrast against the
salt and fat of Cheesus.

THE CHEESES

1 SOFT STANKY

Stinky cheeses relax in the sun,
becoming ever-more yielding,
custardy, and inviting.

RECOMMENDED:
Taleggio (pictured), Willoughby
from Jasper Hill Farm, or Grayson
from Meadow Creek Dairy

2 FRESHY

Fresh bodies reflect the glory
of summertime, especially when
finished with olive oil and salt.

RECOMMENDED:
Burrata (pictured) or another
fresh cheese like mozzarella or
marinated feta

3 RAW MILK TOMME

Raw milk Tommes are lush with
the flavors of earth and pasture,
buttery and satisfying with a kiss
of mushroomy funk that blossoms
near the rind.

RECOMMENDED:
Tomme de Savoie (pictured),
Thomasville Tomme from Sweet
Grass Dairy, or Cumberland from
Sequatchie Cove Creamery

PRETZELS
are ideal for dipping
directly into the
cheese spread.

THE CHEESES

1 BEER-WASHED BODY

Beer-washed bodies have a savory,
funky quality that shines against
toasty malts.

RECOMMENDED:
Chimay (pictured), Mont St.
Francis from Capriole Goat
Cheese, or Good Thunder
from Alemar Cheese

2 CLOTHBOUND CHEDDAR

Clothbound Cheddars have a fruity,
earthy flavor and persistent tang that
yearns to cuddle up with bitter hops.

RECOMMENDED:
Montgomery's Cheddar by
Neal's Yard Dairy (pictured),
Cabot Clothbound from
Jasper Hill Farm, or Bleu
Mont Bandaged Cheddar

3 COLD PACK CHEESE

Cheese spread was originally
created as a tavern snack
and is always eager to
accompany a pint.

RECOMMENDED:
A cold-pack cheese spread,
like Widmer's Aged Brick
Spread (pictured), or Merkt's

CORNICHONS
bring juicy bursts that
cleanse the palate and
mellow funky flavors.

THYME
adds cozy fragrance.

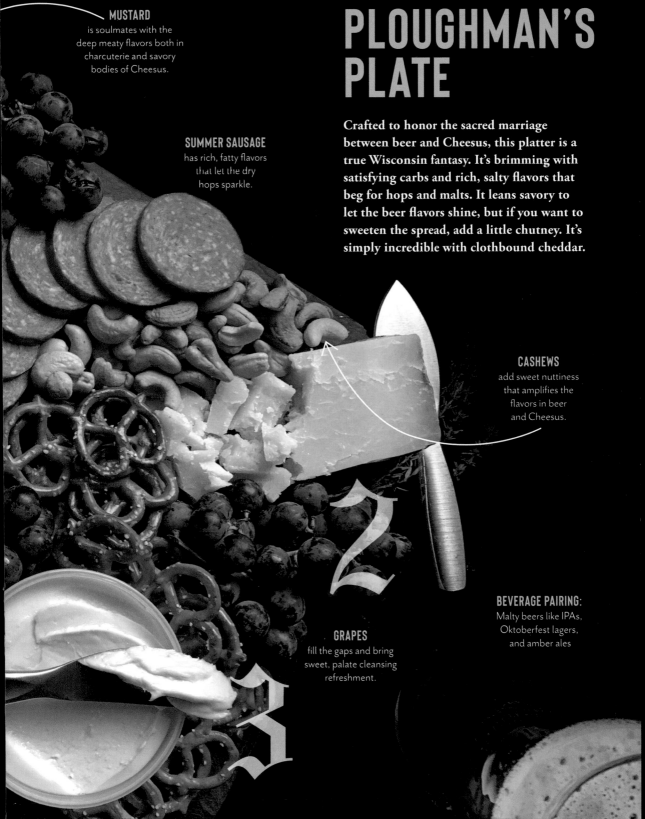

MUSTARD
is soulmates with the deep meaty flavors both in charcuterie and savory bodies of Cheesus.

SUMMER SAUSAGE
has rich, fatty flavors that let the dry hops sparkle.

PLOUGHMAN'S PLATE

Crafted to honor the sacred marriage between beer and Cheesus, this platter is a true Wisconsin fantasy. It's brimming with satisfying carbs and rich, salty flavors that beg for hops and malts. It leans savory to let the beer flavors shine, but if you want to sweeten the spread, add a little chutney. It's simply incredible with clothbound cheddar.

CASHEWS
add sweet nuttiness that amplifies the flavors in beer and Cheesus.

BEVERAGE PAIRING:
Malty beers like IPAs, Oktoberfest lagers, and amber ales

GRAPES
fill the gaps and bring sweet, palate cleansing refreshment.

FALL HARVEST PLATE

The sweet, crisp flavors of fall naturally complement luscious, salty bodies of Cheesus. This platter is a celebration of cozy and indulgent autumnal flavors— a feast made with the fruits of the harvest. The featured bodies are eye-catching and bursting with bold, complex flavors that hold their own next to the luxurious fall accompaniments.

PIZZELLE
are a whimsical and enticing vehicle for the soft bodies.

SAGE
imbues the plate with a soft green hue and festive aroma.

FIG JAM
brings a deep sweetness that mellows and marries all of the strong flavors on the plate.

BEVERAGE PAIRING:
A farmhouse cider, rich porter, or a strong, stirred cocktail

APPLE SLICES refresh the palate with a crisp, juicy crunch.

DRIED CRANBERRIES add a sweet-tart contrast to the luscious flavors.

CANDIED WALNUTS bring a delightfully sugary crunch and complementary nuttiness.

BABY SQUASH are a cute, ornamental touch.

DARK CHOCOLATE is an indulgent, orgasmic pairing with

THE CHEESES

① MIMOLETTE

Mimolette brings a nutty butter-scotch flavor and a blazing orange color reminiscent of pumpkins.

RECOMMENDED: Mimolette (pictured) or aged Gouda as an alternative

② SMOKED BLUE

Smoked blues are rich, creamy, and infused with the smell of bonfires and burning leaves.

RECOMMENDED: Smokey Blue from Rogue Creamery (pictured), Moody Blue from Roth Cheese, or Smoked Kentucky Bleu from Kenny's Farmhouse Cheese

③ ASH-RIPENED CHEVRE

Ash-ripened chèvre is an eye-catching enchantress and a talented dance partner with the sweet, spicy accompaniments.

RECOMMENDED: Humboldt Fog from Cypress Grove (pictured), Sofia from Capriole Goat Cheeses, or French Valençay

ROSEMARY
adds a rich,
woody fragrance.

PICKLED CARROTS
bring a rush of crisp,
palate-cleansing acidity.

**WHOLE GRAIN
MUSTARD**
blesses the plate
with a decadent kiss
of savory tang.

TATER TOTS
are comforting and truly
divine when dipped directly
into Her soft, gooey interior.

DRIED FIGS
bring sweet respite that
complements the
foresty savior.

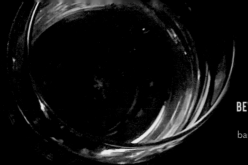

BEVERAGE PAIRING:
French cider,
barrel-aged sour ale,
or whiskey

VACHERIN VATICAN

Some bodies demand the spotlight all to themselves, especially spruce-wrapped sirens like Vacherin Mont d'Or or any of Her American interpretations. Worshipping these self-contained cheese Jacuzzis is an indulgent, ceremonious ritual that will pleasure all of your senses. When you're building an altar for a single body of Cheesus, surround Her with a plethora of pairings to keep things exciting. Serve the wheel whole with the bark intact, lest She ooze all over the place.

THE CHEESE

1 SPRUCE-WRAPPED BODY

Spruce-wrapped bodies are like a hot tub of instant fondue—pure silken luxury that bursts with notes of custard and forest.

RECOMMENDED:
Vacherin Mont d'Or, Rush Creek Reserve from Uplands Cheese (pictured), or Harbison from Jasper Hill Farm

PREPARING A SPRUCE-WRAPPED BODY OF CHEESUS

CHECK FOR RIPENESS: Give Her a gentle squeeze. If She feels soft and yielding, She's good to go.

HEAT HER UP: If She feels a bit firm, give Her a little oven lovin'. Preheat your oven to the lowest temperature and place the wheel on a parchment-lined baking sheet. Gently heat for 8 to 10 minutes, until She feels like a waterbed.

TAKE HER TOP OFF: Use a paring knife to carefully slice off the top rind. Insert your knife just above the bark and slice all the way around the wheel. Slowly peel back and remove the rind, reserving it as a snack for later. Then, stick a spoon in Her creamy center. You can also leave half of the top rind intact, which makes for a sexy, scantily clad presentation.

CHEESEMAS PLATE

A climactic celebration of holiday indulgence, this festive board is packed with the merry flavors of Yuletide. Dressed to impress with accompaniments, the pairings are as satisfying and sultry as a mug of spiked hot chocolate. It's the kind of extravagance you need as you usher in the end of the calendar year and the cold, bitter winter sets in. Serve alongside a platter of cookies and party on with caloric abandon.

THE CHEESES

❶ LEAF WRAPPED BLUE

Leaf-wrapped blues look like little presents, blessing your platter with gifts of salty, earthy funk.

RECOMMENDED:
Rogue River Blue from Rogue Creamery, Shakerag Blue from Sequatchie Cove Creamery (pictured), or classic Spanish Queso de Valdeón

❷ SHEEP'S MILK HARD BODY

Sheep's milk hard bodies are unctuous and rich with complex, roasty notes.

RECOMMENDED:
Pecorino Toscano, Manchego, or Moliterno al Tartufo (pictured), an Italian stallion with veins of black truffle

❸ TRIPLE-CREAM BRIE

Triple-cream Brie is the ultimate decadence, like butter inside a rind.

RECOMMENDED:
Delice de Bourgogne (pictured), Mt. Tam from Cowgirl Creamery, or Trillium from Tulip Tree Creamery

BEVERAGE PAIRING:
Champagne, dark stout, or Cognac

BAGUETTE
provides a crunchy bed for the spreadable Brie and fudgy blue.

CHOCOLATE-COVERED PRETZELS
bring sweet, earthy crunch to complement the blue.

MARCONA ALMONDS
add salty crunch and complement the nutty sheep's milk bodies.

ROSEMARY AND SAGE
bless your board with festive flair.

A SALAMI MOAT
contains the briny olives.

SECKLE PEARS
are bursting with floral, palate-cleansing juices.

SPICED CHERRY PRESERVES
bring warm, spicy flavors that complement all three bodies.

OLIVES
cut through the richness of the triple cream and complement the briny qualities of the aged sheep's milk.

The Book of Cooking

Cheesus is transcendent when savored alone, but something miraculous happens when you incorporate Her into a composed dish. A hot, melty body of Cheesus has the power to hypnotize and captivate: our inhibitions fall away, rendering us powerless and quivering with lustful desire.

The Holy Sacraments of Cooking with Cheesus

CHEESUS WILL BLESS ANY COMPOSED DISH WITH HER SALTY SAVOR, NO MATTER THE TIME OF DAY OR YEAR. YOU DON'T EVEN NEED TO BE A GREAT COOK—JUST START WITH GOOD INGREDIENTS, AND EVERYTHING YOU MAKE WILL BE DELICIOUS. COOKING WITH CHEESUS IS A FORM OF WORSHIP, SO DON'T RUSH OR WORRY ABOUT MISTAKES. JUST ENJOY YOURSELF.

AVOID PRE-SHREDDED CHEESE: Pre-sliced or pre-shredded cheese is filled with preservatives and declumping agents that affect flavor and meltability.

BRING HER TO ROOM TEMP: Adding a cold body of Cheesus to a hot sauce will cause Her to seize and form a blasphemous rubbery mass.

DO NOT OVERCOOK: If the heat is too high or you cook Her too long, the oils will separate and Cheesus will become tough and stringy.

> " *Many's the long night I've dreamed of cheese—toasted, mostly.* "
> —*Robert Louis Stevenson, in* Treasure Island

THE SCIENCE OF MELTING CHEESUS: THE HOLY TRINITY OF WATER, FAT, AND THE CASEIN WEB

Not all bodies of Cheesus are meant for melting. The Immaculate Coagulation of the Virgin Milk creates a web of casein protein that traps water and fat, held together by a calcium "glue." The flexibility of this web and the amount of water and fat held inside it determine whether or not a body of Cheesus can melt.

Here's a rundown of which bodies melt into hot, gooey nirvana, and which ones don't.

MAJESTIC MELTERS

The best melting bodies have lots of moisture and fat. When tempted with heat, their webs unknot, unravel, and flow into a thick, molten liquid. Examples include:

YOUNG, SEMI-FIRM BODIES, WHICH ARE SUPPLE AND MOIST:

Gruyère, raclette, Fontina, Emmentaler, Havarti, Chihuahua, Monterey Jack, Colby, and young Gouda

PASTA FILATAS, WHICH GET SEDUCTIVELY STRETCHY:

mozzarella, Oaxaca, Provolone, and string cheese

SOFT-RIPENED BODIES, WHICH LIQUIFY INTO AN INSTANT SAUCE:

Vacherin Mont d'Or, Brie, Camembert, Taleggio, and Reblochon

MELTING TIP: CHERISHED CHEDDAR

Cheddar is a popular melting cheese, but Her high acid levels can actually cause Her to separate and become oily. If you're craving that signature tang, get a young block cheddar with a texture that's more smooth than crumbly and combine her with a Majestic Melter like Gruyère.

NON-MELTING BODIES

HIGH-ACID FRESH BODIES, LIKE FRESH CHÈVRE

The acid content in these supple fresh bodies makes the proteins clump together, preventing their bodies from fully melting. Instead, they soften and relax, making them ideal for stirring into sauces or turning into cheesecake (see page 332).

*A grilled cheese with bacon,
pepper jelly, and cheese curds*

LOW-ACID FRESH BODIES, LIKE HALLOUMI

These taut little bodies have lots of calcium glue that keeps their webs tight and rigid. They soften but never liquify, which makes them ideal for grilling.

HARD BODIES, LIKE PARMIGIANO AND AGED GOUDA

As Cheesus ages, Her web solidifies and She loses the holy water that lets Her curds melt and flow. When heated, She leaks a greasy puddle of oil. Instead, these bodies are ideal for turning into Parmigiano Crisps (page 314) or encrusting an egg in a toast basket (page 319).

SACRED SHREDDING

Shredding the body of Cheesus is a sacred ritual. It creates evenly sized pieces with a large surface area, allowing everything to melt at the same rate. Shredding Cheesus fresh off the block is essential for an optimal flavor and texture experience. Pre-shredded cheese won't hurt you, but it's tainted with preservatives and declumping agents that affect its flavor and ability to melt. Plus, with all that grating you'll get a nice arm workout and burn a few calories, which you can immediately make up for with a handful of fresh shreds straight to the mouth.

SHREDDING QUANTITY QUICK CHART

THE FOLLOWING YIELD 1 CUP, PACKED

4 ounces (115 g) coarsely grated cheese

3 ounces (85 g) medium grated cheese

2 ounces (55 g) finely grated cheese

Note that the rinds on hard bodies are too dry to melt, so you'll want to remove them before cooking to avoid a gritty texture. Start by cutting off the top and bottom rinds, leaving on the back to use as a handle. Reserve any Parmigiano rinds, which can be used to add deep, seductive flavors to broths and soups.

ARE ALL BODIES GOOD FOR COOKING?

Look for bodies of Cheesus that are delicious enough to eat on their own, but aren't so divine that it would be blasphemous to compromise their form. Complex bodies of Cheesus often demand the spotlight, and incorporating them into a recipe overshadows their nuances. Cooking with them also gets rather expensive. However, if you find yourself with the desire to cook with an extra bougie bod, then go for it. Conversely, if you want to make a grilled cheese using classic American slices, get at that, too. Personal pleasure *always* takes priority.

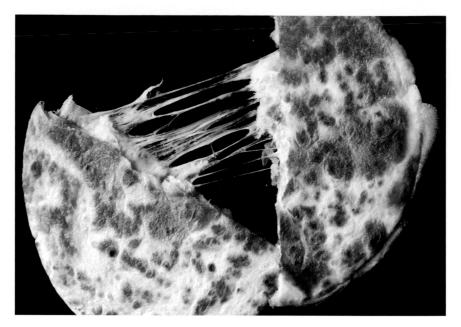

Classic quesadilla with Oaxaca and cheddar

ESSENTIAL COOKING BODIES TO ALWAYS HAVE ON HAND

Fresh chèvre for spreading

Young Gruyère for melting

Parmigiano-Reggiano DOP for grating (get the real stuff!)

Crumbly blue for sprinkling

TOOLS FOR COOKING WITH CHEESUS

Remember to clean your graters right after use, and keep your knives sharp.

CITRUS ZESTER for making silky, feathery shreds

BOX GRATER with small holes to grate crunchy hard bodies and the larger ones for shredding semi-firm wedges

FOOD PROCESSOR for grating and shredding large amounts

CHEF'S KNIFE for slicing cheese

BEFORE YOU BEGIN...

All of the recipes I've included in this book are simple to make. However, cooking with Cheesus is a form of worship—make sure you're prepared so you stay relaxed and don't get frazzled. Here's how to set yourself up for success.

READ THE RECIPE TWICE: Make sure you have all the right ingredients, equipment, and enough time. You don't want to run into any unwanted surprises.

SET UP YOUR MISE EN PLACE: Proper preparation keeps you focused on the ritual. Set out all of your tools and ingredients before you start cooking.

USE GREAT INGREDIENTS: All of the following recipes are simple and require very little cooking, so it's important to choose high-quality ingredients.

TASTE FOR SALT: Cheesus is a salty gal, so be careful of adding too much salt before She takes center stage. Taste as you cook, and add salt slowly as needed.

DON'T OVERCOOK: Cheesus is best as a finishing touch for two reasons: First of all, cooking Her for too long or at too high a heat can cause Her fat to separate, making Her tough and stringy. Second, if you mess up your dish halfway through, you can still comfort yourself by eating the saved body of Cheesus.

TRUST YOUR SENSES: Recipes are not gospel, so make adjustments here and there as you cook with the body of Cheesus. Many of the following recipes are meant to be toyed with and adapted as you worship in the kitchen. Trust your senses and palate. If it needs salt, add some. If it needs a splash of acidity, squirt it with lemon. Put a little faith in yourself, and most importantly, enjoy the process.

Baked brie with bourbon-soaked dried figs

GARLIC-HONEY BAKED BRIESUS
WITH ROSEMARY

There's nothing that hits quite like a baked Brie. This hot tub
of silky molten cheese is easy to make, eager to bed an array
of accompaniments, and guaranteed to seduce anyone.

THE CHEESUS

Look for a small format wheel
of Brie, Camembert, or similar
body no more than 6 to 8 oz
(170 to 225 g). I recommend
using a cow's milk body—they
make the best melters! Her
ripeness impacts her baking
time, so keep your eye on Her
as She bakes.

THE INGREDIENTS
Serves 2 to 4

1	8-oz (225 g) wheel of Brie, room temperature
2	small garlic cloves, finely chopped
2 tsp	rosemary, chopped
3 T	high-quality, local honey
pinch	of black pepper
	sliced baguette

THE RITUAL

- Preheat the oven to 350°F (175°C).

- Use a sharp knife to score a crosshatch pattern into the top rind. Don't go all the way to the bottom, though!

- Stuff the garlic into the slits in the cheese and place the wheel in the center of a baking dish.

- Sprinkle the rosemary over the cheese, then drizzle with honey.

- Finish with black pepper.

- Bake for about 15 minutes, until She starts to ooze.

- Let cool for 3 to 5 minutes, then surround with baguette slices and devour.

THE RITES

- **Bring Cheesus to room temperature before baking.** This ensures that She heats evenly and doesn't separate.

- **Keep the heat around 350°F (175°C).** A lot of recipes recommend 400° (205°C), but if you cook Her too hot, the fat will separate and you'll be left with an oily mess.

- **Score the rind with a knife.** This helps the toppings seep in, and makes it easier to dip later. You can also completely take her top off for easy access to dipping decadence. Make sure you keep the wheel contained in a baking dish or even the box it came in.

- **Consume as soon as it cools enough.** Baked Brie doesn't keep.

THE SERVICE

Pair with crunchy carbs and sparkling wine.

THE VARIATIONS

Use the same ritual and swap the toppings for the following suggestions:

- Sliced apples tossed with a pat of melted butter + maple syrup + pinch of cinnamon

- Spoonful of peach preserves + black pepper + chopped almonds

- Handful of ripe berries + honey + chopped pistachios

Garlic-Honey Baked Briesus with Rosemary

EVERYTHING BAGEL
GOAT CHEESE BALL

This cheese ball has all the savory flavors you love in an everything bagel, plus a triple-threat cheese combo. It's time to embrace the glory of the cheese ball.

THE CHEESUS

We've got a holy trinity here: fresh chèvre for fluffiness, mascarpone for creaminess, and cheddar for a snackable tang.

THE INGREDIENTS
Serves 2 to 4

4 oz (115 g) fresh goat cheese, room temperature

4 oz (115 g) mascarpone, room temperature

½ C (55 g) shredded cheddar, room temperature

1 tsp Worcestershire sauce

2 scallions, thinly sliced

½ C (144 g) everything bagel seasoning

THE RITUAL

▶ In a medium bowl, whisk together the goat cheese, mascarpone, cheddar, and Worcestershire sauce until thoroughly combined.

▶ Sprinkle in the scallions and stir until incorporated.

▶ Form into a ball, then cover with plastic wrap and chill in the refrigerator for at least 2 hours.

▶ Pour the seasoning into a large bowl.

▶ Roll the cheese ball in the seasoning, pressing it onto the sides to coat evenly. Serve immediately.

THE RITES

▶ **Look for an everything spice mix** that isn't too heavy on salt, or make your own by combining poppy seeds, sesame seeds, black sesame seeds, minced dried garlic, minced dried onion, and flaked sea salt to taste.

▶ **If you aren't serving your cheese ball immediately, store in an airtight container** in the fridge for up to 3 days. Add the seasoning just before serving.

THE SERVICE

Serve with butter crackers, bagel chips, celery, and a pilsner to scrub your palate clean of stanky garlic breath.

Everything Bagel Goat Cheese Ball

MARINATED CHEESUS

Lubing up the body of Cheesus with flavored oils makes for an easy, sophisticated appetizer. I love using fresh bodies like feta, which take kindly to herbs, spices, and piquant olive oil, but you can also revive any aged bodies that have dried out with this simple technique.

THE CHEESUS

Choose a relatively mild body—something fresh like feta or Halloumi, or hard and dry like Manchego. Avoid anything strong, oozing, or stanky, which can get slimy and overpower the oil.

THE INGREDIENTS
Serves 4 to 6

6 to 8 oz **Cheesus** *(like a feta* (170 to 225 g) *or Manchego)*

2 tsp **herbs or spices** *(see Blessed Flavorings, right)*

2 strips **lemon or orange peel** *(see Blessed Flavorings)*

about ¾ C **extra-virgin olive oil,** (180 ml) **to cover**

¼ cup **grapeseed oil** (60 ml)

THE RITUAL

► Roll soft bodies into ¾-inch (2-cm) balls, slice logs into ½-inch (12-mm) coins, or cut firm bodies into ¼-inch (6-mm) cubes

► Sprinkle one-third of the flavorings into a 12-oz Mason jar, then add one-third of the cheese. Continue layering until both Cheesus and the spices are used up.

► In a small bowl, whisk the olive oil with the grapeseed oil and pour into the jar to cover the Cheesus.

► Screw on the lid and let sit at room temperature for 1 to 2 hours, or overnight in the fridge. Bring to room temperature before serving.

THE RITES

► **Choose any selection of herbs, spices, and citrus peels to complement** the natural flavors of your chosen body of Cheesus.

► **Use a good extra-virgin olive oil** for the best flavor. Grapeseed oil has a neutral flavor and prevents the oil from solidifying in the fridge.

► **Lasts 2 to 3 weeks in a jar**, refrigerated. Once Cheesus is gone, save the oil to use in a salad dressing.

BLESSED FLAVORINGS

► **Fresh herbs:** rosemary, thyme, parsley, oregano, basil, dill, or bay leaf

► **Whole spices:** black pepper, chili flakes, cumin, or coriander

► **Other:** citrus peel, garlic, onions, olives, or sun-dried tomatoes

THE SERVICE

Serve with warm bread and salad greens.

Pair with chilled rosé or Sauvignon Blanc.

THE VARIATIONS

- Fresh chèvre + lemon peel, fennel, dill seed, and thyme

- Feta + oregano, sun-dried tomatoes, black pepper, and olives

- Manchego + orange peel, black pepper, chili flakes, and rosemary

IN A RUSH?

Heat the oil in a saucepan over low heat. Add the herbs and spices, then gently cook for 5 minutes. It should bubble slightly but not sizzle. Let cool, then pour over Cheesus and marinate for 20 minutes before serving.

Marinated Cheesus

PARMIGIANO CRISPS

These delightful little crunchers are essentially a snackable version of the crispy little angel wings that form on the outside of a grilled cheese sandwich. On their own, they're a tantalizing finger food, but they also shine as a halo atop salads and soups.

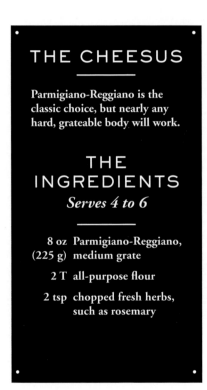

THE CHEESUS

Parmigiano-Reggiano is the classic choice, but nearly any hard, grateable body will work.

THE INGREDIENTS

Serves 4 to 6

8 oz (225 g)	Parmigiano-Reggiano, medium grate
2 T	all-purpose flour
2 tsp	chopped fresh herbs, such as rosemary

THE RITUAL

- Preheat the oven to 400°F (205°C).
- Line a baking sheet with a silicone mat.
- In a small bowl, toss the grated Parmigiano with the flour and seasonings.
- On the baking sheet, form tablespoon-sized circular heaps of the Parmigiano mixture and space at least 2 inches (5 cm) apart. Flatten each with your hand.
- Bake for 6 to 8 minutes, until golden brown.
- Remove from the oven and let cool on the baking sheet for 5 minutes.
- Transfer to paper towels to crisp up.

THE RITES

- **You can add any herbs or spices you like**—avoid anything with too much moisture, lest they sog the crisp.
- **Keeps up to 2 days stored at room temperature** in an airtight bag or container, but make sure to add a dry paper towel to keep them crunchy.

THE SERVICE

Serve with marinated olives.

Pair with a full-bodied wine.

Parmigiano Crisps

WHOLE-MILK RICOTTA

People always ask if I make cheese at home, but I honestly don't really believe in it. There are prophets and disciples who devote their lives to mastering the rituals of cheesemaking, and we're usually better off buying their divine creations than attempting to make them ourselves.

Ricotta is one of the very few exceptions. A lot of store-bought ricotta is grainy and tainted with thickeners and stabilizers that cause the cheese to leak moisture when cooked. Unless you can score some from a trusted creamery, you're better off making it yourself.

High-quality ricotta resembles fresh, creamy clouds with a gentle kiss of sweetness. Ricotta, meaning "recooked" in Italian, is traditionally made with whey leftover from making other bodies, such as mozzarella. You heat it up, add an acid like lemon juice, let it curdle, and then drain it. This recipe uses the same method, except I add whole milk and cream for a sexier texture. It's extremely easy and produces soft, creamy ricotta in as little as an hour.

THE INGREDIENTS

Makes about 4 cups (500 g)

---

1 gallon (3.8 L) **whole milk (not ultra-pasteurized)**

2 C (470 ml) **heavy cream**

1 tsp **salt**

¾ C (175 ml) **lemon juice**

THE RITUAL

- Line a mesh sieve with cheese cloth. Set aside.
- Pour the milk and cream into a saucepan and heat over medium-low.
- Add the salt and continue to heat, whisking regularly, to keep the milk from burning. Do not let the milk come to a simmer.
- As soon as tiny bubbles start to form in the milk, remove from heat, add the lemon juice, and gently stir twice to fully incorporate. Let sit for 10 minutes.
- Gently scoop the curds from the whey, and place in a the prepared sieve to drain. Then pour the rest of the whey through the sieve to capture the remaining curds.
- Drain anywhere from 5 minutes to 2 hours, depending on your desired texture.

THE RITES

➤ **Do not overheat.** The Virgin Milk should quiver a bit, but She should not come to a full simmer.

➤ **Do not overstir the baby curd.** Too much agitation after you add the lemon will result in a tough, rubbery curd. Be gentle while the Virgin Milk gives birth to the baby curd.

➤ **If you don't have cheesecloth,** you can line a mesh sieve with paper towels or stack two mesh sieves together.

➤ **Draining the curd:** The longer you drain the curd, the drier the ricotta. If you want Her soft and creamy, only drain for 5 to 10 minutes. If you want Her crumbly, drain for an hour or more.

➤ **Fresh ricotta is extremely perishable** and won't last more than 3 days in the fridge.

THE VARIATION: PANEER

If you take the process one step further, you can make paneer. I recommend omitting the cream for a bouncier body.

- Perform the first four steps of the Ricotta Ritual.

- Let drain for 10 minutes, then wrap in cheese cloth and squeeze out as much moisture as possible.

- Unwrap the curds, shape into a disc, and place on a plate.

- Put two plates on top of the disc of baby curds.

- Refrigerate for 2 hours and let gravity do its work.

- Remove from the fridge, unwrap, slice into 1-inch (2.5-cm) cubes, and enjoy!

Whole-Milk Ricotta

SEVEN BLESSED TOASTS

Cheesy toast is the morning quickie of breakfast foods. It takes no time to make, yet has the power to keep you pleasured and satisfied until lunchtime. It's also an exciting blank canvas for playing with pairings. Think of that toasted bread as an edible platter for Cheesus.

THE RITES

- **Life's too short for bad bread.** Get something delicious and slice it thick.

- **Don't overtoast it.** Burnt spots have a bitterness that can overwhelm the body of Cheesus, so make sure your bread stays golden and delicious.

- **A sprinkle of black pepper** brings a little heat and helps marry all the flavors. I recommend it for all of the toasts below.

- **Serve immediately.** Soggy toast is sacreligious.

THE RITUALS
Each serves 1

SOURDOUGH + FRESH CHÈVRE + RASPBERRIES + HONEY + FLAKY SALT

Lightly toast the sourdough. While it's still warm, smear on the chèvre so it softens. Evenly space the berries on top, then pop the toast in the oven at 350°F (175°C) for about 3 minutes, until the juices flow out over the chèvre. Drizzle with honey and finish with salt.

BAGUETTE + FUNKY CAMEMBERT + TOASTED NORI + SPICY HONEY + SESAME SEEDS

Slice the baguette lengthwise and lightly toast. Shingle the Camembert over the baguette, then pop it in the oven at 350°F (175°C) for about 3 minutes, until She gets nice and gooey. Crumble the nori over the toast, drizzle with honey, and sprinkle with sesame seeds.

SEEDED BREAD + AVOCADO + LIME + SLICED PICKLED BEETS + CRUMBLED BLUE + CILANTRO

Toast the bread to desired crispness. Let cool for a minute or so, then layer with avocado slices and add a squeeze of lime juice. Place beet slices over the toast, evenly spaced. Sprinkle with the blue, then finish with cilantro.

SOURDOUGH + MASCARPONE + ANCHOVIES + RADISH + PICKLED ONIONS + EXTRA-VIRGIN OLIVE OIL

Toast the bread and spread on the mascarpone. Cut the anchovies into small pieces and lay them over the mascarpone. Thinly slice the radish and place on top. Sprinkle with pickled onions and drizzle with olive oil.

RYE BREAD + TALEGGIO + HEIRLOOM TOMATOES + CHOPPED CHIVES

Lightly toast the bread and layer with Taleggio slices. Pop it in the oven at 350°F (175°C) and toast about 3 minutes, until melty. Top with three ¼-inch-thick (6-mm) slices of heirloom tomato and sprinkle with chives.

WHOLE WHEAT + ONION FIG JAM + GRUYÈRE + SPECK + ROSEMARY

Lightly toast the bread, then spread with onion fig jam. Thinly slice the Gruyère, and shingle with the speck over the toast. Sprinkle with rosemary sprigs. Pop the toast in the oven at 350°F (175°C) for about 3 minutes, until melty.

PULLMAN LOAF + BUTTER + PARMIGIANO + EGG + SALT + HOT SAUCE

Cut 2 teaspoons of butter into thirds. Put one third into a frying pan and heat over medium. Spread another third over one side of the bread, then cut a 2½-inch (6-cm) circle in the center of the bread. Place in the pan, unbuttered side down. Grate Parmigiano over the buttered side until fully coated. Cook for 4 minutes, then flip. Place the remaining butter in the hole, then crack an egg into it. Sprinkle a bit of salt over the egg and cook for 2 minutes. Flip and cook for 1 more minute. Finish with hot sauce and serve.

Clockwise from top: avocado blue toast, tomato Taleggio toast, anchovy mascarpone toast, and Camembert nori toast

SACRED SALADS

Salads are basically just cheese plates on lettuce. Fresh vegetation and zippy dressing create a perfect contrast against rich fat. It's not only healthy, but there's something super romantic about it, too. Cheesus may be vegetation reincarnated through milk, but She lacks fiber and vitamin C. Leafy greens add all of that, and the ample fat content in Cheesus helps you absorb their vitamins and minerals. If you think salads aren't satisfying enough for a meal, you're not adding enough Cheesus. The key is using fresh ingredients and keeping everything simple so that She can be the star.

THREE EASY DRESSINGS
Makes enough for 2 salads

THE CLASSIC

2 tsp lemon juice

2 T extra-virgin olive oil

THE BALSAMIC

2 tsp Balsamic Glaze (page 340)

1 tsp Dijon mustard

2 T extra-virgin olive oil

THE SPICY HONEY

2 tsp apple cider vinegar

1 tsp spicy honey

2 T extra-virgin olive oil

THE RITUAL

▶ **Make the dressing**: Whisk the acid with the other ingredients first, then slowly whisk in the oil until it's incorporated.

▶ **Season all the veg:** Cheesus is already salty, so you don't need to season the whole salad. Just sprinkle all of the fresh fruits and vegetables with a bit of salt so they stand out against the other ingredients.

▶ **Prepare the bed:** Toss the greens with the dressing and salt, then pile them into a wide bed that expands across your plate. Make it comfortable and inviting for the body of Cheesus and Her accompaniments.

▶ **Anoint with Cheesus:** Slice or crumble Her body, and place Her lovingly either in the center or off to the side of the bed of greens. Make sure She's nice and prominent.

▶ **Finish with the toppings:** Top with other vegetables, tucking them in next to Cheesus. Follow with the other accompaniments.

▶ **Baptize with a kiss** of black pepper and any fresh herbs you're using.

▶ **No, you will not toss this salad, honey:** Tossing a beautifully plated salad is sacrilegious. All of the delicate toppings sink to the bottom and the whole thing ends up looking cluttered and messy. Keep everything in separate sections, so you can easily build a perfect bite and play around with different flavor and pairing combinations.

THE VARIATIONS

- Queso fresco + baby kale + The Spicy Honey + sliced grapefruit + diced avocado + lime juice

- Burrata + mesclun mix + The Classic + sliced peaches + sliced tomatoes + basil

- Clothbound cheddar + red leaf lettuce + The Spicy Honey + sliced green apples + dried cherries + chopped pecans

- Blue cheese + butter lettuce + The Balsamic + sliced strawberries + chopped pistachios

- Pecorino + arugula + The Classic + chopped almonds + bacon + slivered dates

SAINTLY SANDWICHES

Cheesus knows how to fill out a sandwich. The following are based on classic pairing combinations, all tucked inside some sexy carbs. I recommended a few different bodies of Cheesus for each variation, so you have lots of room to experiment.

THE RITUAL
Each serves 1

THE VEG

2 slices toasted ciabatta + 2 tablespoons pesto + 2 ounces (55 g) fresh mozzarella + 3 slices roasted red peppers (homemade or store bought) + handful arugula + drizzle Balsamic Glaze (page 340)

Slather the bottom slice of bread with pesto. Layer with mozzarella, peppers, and arugula. Drizzle with balsamic glaze, and close the sandwich.

➡ Try with feta or fresh chèvre!

BBLT: BLUE, BACON, LETTUCE & TOMATO

3 slices tomato + sca salt + black pepper + 2 slices toasted white bread + lots of mayo + 2 leaves crisp lettuce + 1 ounce (28 g) crumbled blue cheese + 3 strips cooked bacon

Season the tomatoes with sea salt and pepper and slather both pieces of bread generously with mayo. Layer the bottom slice with lettuce, then top with the tomatoes and bacon. Sprinkle the blue cheese over the bacon, then close the sandwich.

➡ Try with a smoked blue or something spicy, like Gorgonzola Piccante!

BUTTER, BRIE & PROSCIUTTO

3 cornichons + ⅓ baguette, sliced lengthwise + 1 tablespoon softened butter + whole-grain mustard + 5 slices prosciutto + 1 ounce (28 g) Brie

Cut cornichons in half lengthwise. Swipe the bottom half of the baguette with butter and the top with mustard. Layer the bottom with prosciutto, pickles, and Brie, then close the sandwich.

➡ Try with Camembert, soft-ripened chèvre, or a stinky washed rind like Taleggio!

COMTÉ ET PÂTÉ

1½ ounces (40 g) Comté + 2 ounces (55 g) pâté + baguette, sliced lengthwise + Dijon mustard + pickled shallots

Cut the top and bottom rind off of the Comté and slice thinly. Cut the pâté diagonally, then slice again to form big triangles. Swipe both halves of the bread with mustard, then layer with pâté, pickled shallots, and Comté. Close with the top slice.

➡ Try with Gruyère, Fontina, or even raclette!

THE RITES

➤ **Slice your bread about ½ inch (12 mm) thick.** You'll need a lot of heft to handle these voluptuous fillings.

➤ **Drain any fillings that are pickled, brined, or oiled, lest they sog your sammie.** This includes brined bodies like feta and mozzarella.

➤ **These sandwiches are best when served right away**, but they'll keep a few hours when wrapped tightly and stored in the fridge.

The BBLT

GRILLED CHEESUS

Few pleasures can compare to the simple comfort of a crispy, melty Grilled Cheesus. Behold the sacred principles behind crafting the perfect toastie, followed by four of my favorite variations. Once you know the formula, you are set for a lifetime of pleasure.

THE CHEESUS

For a perfect cheese pull, choose one or more of the Majestic Melters on page 303. You can also try a soft body like Brie or Taleggio, but they're more likely to liquify then stretch.

THE INGREDIENTS
Serves 1

2 slices   bread, ½-inch
           (12mm) thick

2 to 3 oz Cheesus, freshly
(55 to   shredded and
85 g)   room temperature

1 tsp   softened butter or
           mayonaise

THE RITES

➤ **Choose a bread that's sturdy but not too thick.** Pullman has the right amount of heft but the crust doesn't get too hard. I also love sourdough, but make sure it's sliced thin so it's easy to eat.

➤ **A good body of Cheesus is all you need** for a perfect toastie, but it's nice to get kinky with a thin layer of a spread like spicy mustard, pesto, or fruit preserves. You can add vegetables or meat, but don't steal the spotlight away from Cheesus.

➤ **Keep the pan at medium-low, and make sure you set a timer.** If it gets too hot, the bread will burn and Cheesus won't completely melt. If it's too low, the bread won't crisp up and you'll end up with a flaccid toastie.

➤ **Mayo vs. butter:** Butter lends a rich sweetness, while mayo provides a savory note and a perfect golden crunch. They're both great options, but I tend to favor mayo.

➤ **Serve immediately.** You need it hot and fresh.

THE RITUAL

➤ Heat a skillet or nonstick pan over medium-low.

➤ Spread a thin layer of mayo on one side of each slice of bread. Put one slice on the frying pan, mayo side down.

➤ Layer Cheesus on top of the bread, leaving a ¼-inch (6-mm) border to prevent too much from spilling out.

➤ Close the sandwich with the mayo facing up. Set a timer for 5 minutes.

➤ When the timer goes off, use your spatula to press down on the sandwich to help glue all the components together. Then flip and toast on the other side for an additional 4 minutes.

➤ Remove from the pan and let cool for 1 to 2 minutes. Slice in half and devour.

PEPPER JELLY & BACON GRILLED CHEESUS

1 teaspoon finely shredded Parmigiano + 1 teaspoon mayonnaise + 2 slices bread + 2 ounces (55 g) Havarti + 2 slices cooked bacon + 1 teaspoon pepper jelly

Whisk the Parmigiano into the mayo. Spread a thin layer of mayo on one side of each slice of bread, then place one slice in the frying pan mayo side down. Layer with Havarti and bacon. Spread pepper jelly on the inside of the top slice, close the sandwich and prepare according to the ritual.

FRENCH ONION GRILLED CHEESUS

1 teaspoon mayonnaise + 2 slices bread + 2 tablespoons caramelized onions + 3 ounces (85 g) sliced Comté

Spread a thin layer of mayo on one side of each slice of bread, then place one slice in the frying pan mayo side down. Spread the caramelized onions over the bread, then layer with half the Comté. Close the sandwich and continue the ritual as described.

French Onion
Grilled Cheesus

FALL HARVEST GRILLED CHEESUS

crispy sage + 1 teaspoon mayonnaise + 2 slices bread + 2 ounces (55 g) sliced young Gouda + ¼ apple, thinly sliced + 1 ounce (28 g) crumbled blue + 2 teaspoons honey

Make the crispy sage: Heat olive oil in a skillet over medium-high. Add sprigs of fresh sage and cook for 2 minutes. Transfer to a paper towel to drain and cool.

Spread a thin layer of mayo on one side of each slice of bread, then place one slice in the frying pan mayo side down. Layer with Gouda, apple, blue, and a drizzle of honey. Prepare according to the ritual, and serve with crispy sage on top of the sandwich.

GRILLED KIMCHEESUS

1 teaspoon mayonnaise + 2 slices bread + 2 ounces (55 g) shredded young block cheddar + 1 ounce (28 g) shredded low-moisture mozzarella + 2 tablespoons kimchi, chopped and drained

Spread a thin layer of mayo on one side of each slice of bread, then place one slice in the frying pan mayo side down. Toss the cheddar and mozzarella together, then layer half the mixture onto the toasting bread. Sprinkle the kimchi over, then cover with the remaining cheese. Close the sandwich and continue the ritual as described.

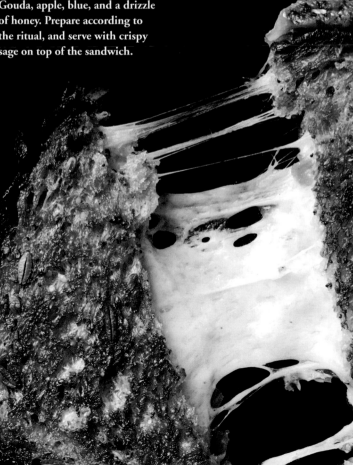

MONGER'S
MAC 'N' CHEESUS

This skanky, slurpy three-cheese mac is one of my all-time favorite recipes.
It's fast, easy, devilishly cheesy, and adaptable enough to satisfy all of your
cravings. It's my favorite way to use up any leftover bits of Cheesus.

THE CHEESUS

You want a 3:1 ratio of melting
cheese to soft-ripened cheese for extra
creaminess. My favorite combination
is a mix of cheddar and Gruyère with
Taleggio for texture.

THE INGREDIENTS
Serves 4 to 6

1 lb (450 g)	shell pasta
	salt, for pasta water
4 T	unsalted butter
2	garlic cloves, grated
1	sprig of rosemary, stemmed and diced
4 T	all-purpose flour
2½ C (600ml)	whole milk, room temperature
½ tsp	nutmeg
1 C (240 ml)	cream, room temperature
16 oz (340 oz)	melting cheese, at room temperature
4 oz (110 g)	soft-ripened cheese, rind removed and chopped

THE RITUAL

➤ Preheat the oven to 350°F (175°C).

➤ Fill a large pot with water, salt heavily, and bring to a boil over high heat.

➤ Add the shells and cook according to the packaging instructions until 2 minutes before al dente, stirring occasionally. They'll cook more in the oven.

➤ Drain the pasta and rinse with cold water to stop the cooking. Transfer to a 9x9-inch (23x23-cm) baking dish.

➤ In a saucepan, melt the butter over medium heat. Stir in the salt, garlic, and rosemary. Cook for 2 minutes, stirring occasionally.

➤ Sprinkle the flour in the pan. Cook while continuing to whisk for about 1 minute, until it forms a sticky paste.

➤ Combine the milk and cream, then slowly add in a little at a time, whisking to incorporate as you pour. After you pour it all in, whisk in the nutmeg.

➤ Bring to a boil, then reduce to a simmer. Cook, whisking occasionally, until thick and smooth, about 6 to 8 minutes.

➤ Toss the cheeses together, then add them to the sauce a handful at a time, whisking until melted after each addition. Reserve a handful for topping.

➤ Cover the pasta in the baking dish with the sauce. Stir until coated.

➤ Cover with the reserved melting cheese and bake for 20 minutes, or until brown and bubbly.

➤ Remove from the oven and let rest for 5 minutes. Devour!

Monger's Mac 'N' Cheesus, left;
Instant Mac with Harbison, below

THE RITES

- **The noodles:** Shells are my favorite because they act like little pasta bowls that hold the sauce, but feel free to swap in elbows, rotini, or cavatappi.

- **Add extra cheese:** It's never a bad idea to layer extra shredded cheese on top.

THE VARIATION: INSTANT MAC WITH A SPRUCE-WRAPPED BODY OF CHEESUS

This one's a private, single-serving kind of indulgence.

Buy yourself a ripe wheel of any spruce-wrapped body, such as the classic Vacherin or Jasper Hill Farm's Harbison. Remove the top with a paring knife, slicing all around the wheel, just inside the outer bark. Gently slide off the top. Pour roughly a cup of hot, freshly cooked shell noodles into the center, and toss with a fork. Light a candle, pour some Pinot, and enjoy with abandon.

THE SERVICE

Pair with a pale ale, fruity red, or crisp cider.

TRANSCENDENT
TARTIFLETTE

Tartiflette is a rustic French dish of bacon lardons, potatoes, onions, and Reblochon, a stinky French washed rind. It's a classic one-skillet meal that'll give you those warm, cuddly feels throughout the cold winter months.

THE CHEESUS

The classic choice is the French washed rind Reblochon, but you can sub in any funky, soft-ripened body, like Taleggio or even a stinkly little Camembert. You can also shred up a classic melter like Fontina or raclette.

THE INGREDIENTS
Serves 2 to 4

¼ tsp   salt

1 lb   thin-skinned potatoes,
(455 g)   such as fingerling,
  Yukon, or red

¼ lb   bacon, cut into 1-inch
(115 g)   (2.5-cm) pieces

1   shallot, sliced

⅓ C   dry white wine
(75 ml)

8 oz   pudgy washed-rind
(225 g)   body, sliced thin

  freshly ground black
  pepper

THE RITUAL

▶ Preheat your oven to 350°F (175°C).

▶ Fill the pot with water and salt heavily. Bring to a boil.

▶ Add the whole potatoes and boil until fork-tender, about 15 to 20 minutes, depending on size.

▶ Drain and let cool until touchable. Cut into 1-inch (2.5-cm) pieces.

▶ Add the bacon to a cold 10-inch (25-cm) skillet and cook over medium heat until browned and crisped. Remove bacon, and set aside. Reserve 1 tablespoon of the fat and drain the rest from the pan.

▶ Cook the shallots in the reserved fat over medium heat until golden and sweetly fragrant, about 5 minutes.

▶ Pour in the wine, and stir with a wooden spoon to scrape up any browned bits. Let cook for 5 minutes, stirring occasionally.

▶ Add the potatoes to the skillet and sprinkle with a pinch of salt. Sautée for 5 minutes to let the flavors mix and mingle.

▶ Turn off the heat and return the bacon to the skillet. Stir to incorporate, then evenly layer Cheesus on top of the potatoes.

▶ Bake in the oven for about 20 minutes, until brown and bubbling.

▶ Remove from the oven and let cool for about 5 minutes. Finish with pepper and serve straight out of the skillet.

THE RITES

▶ **Tartiflette is endlessly adaptable.** You can easily swap out the cheese or sub the potatoes for sautéed kale, steamed cauliflower, roasted cabbage, or broccoli. After all, the best way to get in your daily servings of vegetables is to bless them with Cheesus.

▶ **Store in the fridge** in an airtight container for 3 to 5 days.

THE SERVICE

Pair with a bright red wine, malty beer, or stiff cocktail.

THE VARIATIONS

Replace the veggies and washed-rind body with the following:

· Sauté sliced onions and cabbage in the bacon fat, then cover with 8 ounces (225 g) shredded Gruyère. Bake till bubbly.

· Roast up some broccoli and cover with 8 ounces (225 g) shredded young block cheddar. Bake until bubbly.

Transcendent Tartiflette

FONDUE FANTASY

Fondue is liquid luxury: a simple, silken emulsion of wine and Cheesus. It's one of the most luxurious ways to worship our Lord and savior. Though it may feel decadent, traditionally it was a peasant food meant to use up bits of cheese, stale bread, and leftover wine. It's a meal of necessity that's entirely transcendent. Fondue has very few ingredients, so make sure they all stand on their own before using them (check page 190 for tips on buying great cheese on the cheap).

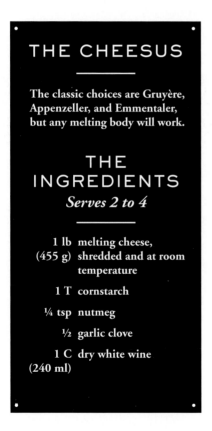

THE CHEESUS

The classic choices are Gruyère, Appenzeller, and Emmentaler, but any melting body will work.

THE INGREDIENTS
Serves 2 to 4

1 lb (455 g)	melting cheese, shredded and at room temperature
1 T	cornstarch
¼ tsp	nutmeg
½	garlic clove
1 C (240 ml)	dry white wine

THE RITUAL

- Toss the tempered cheese with the cornstarch and nutmeg. Set aside.
- Rub the pot with the cut side of the garlic and discard.
- Add the wine to the pot and bring to a simmer over medium-low.
- Gradually whisk in the Cheesus a handful at a time. Wait for Her to fully melt before adding more.
- Once Cheesus has fully melted into silken luxury, move the pot to your heating setup and serve.

THE RITES

- **The wine:** You can use anything bright and not too sweet, like Sauvignon Blanc or Grüner Veltliner. Fondue is a wine-based sauce, but you can substitute cider, beer, or even broth if you'd like to omit the alcohol. This will change the flavor, but it's fun to play around with.

- **The equipment:** A traditional fondue set-up includes a pot, long-stemmed dipping forks, and some sort of heating contraption. If you don't have a fondue set, you can rig one by using a ceramic or cast-iron pot, putting it on a tall trivet, and placing four tea candles underneath. A hot plate also works well.

- **Bring Cheesus to room temperature:** Adding cold cheese to hot liquid results in a drastic temperature fluctuation that will cause your fondue to separate, creating a tough blob in a slick grease puddle.

THE RITES
continued

➧ **Don't skip the cornstarch:** This ingredient is essential for keeping the fondue thick and smooth.

➧ **Respect *la religieuse*.** Meaning "the nun," la religieuse is the Swiss term for the sacred crust of cheese that forms at the bottom of the fondue pot. Break it into pieces and serve at the end of your fondue worship.

➧ **Fondue is best enjoyed immediately,** but you can prolong its life by stirring in a tablespoon of cream cheese before serving. The Swiss would deem this sacrilege, but it helps create a reheatable fondue that lasts up to 5 days in the fridge.

THE SERVICE

Serve with boiled baby potatoes, cubed baguette, baked tater tots, pretzels, sausage, salami, roasted broccoli, roasted Brussels sprouts, pickles, or poached lobster.

Pair with kirschwasser, black tea, or lightly chilled wine or beer. Avoid cold beverages or water—those can cause the cheese to coagulate in your stomach, which is super uncomfortable.

THE VARIATIONS

Sacred stuff to stir in:

- 1 teaspoon Dijon mustard
- A couple spoonfuls of minced caramelized onions
- Sautéed garlic
- Minced herbs
- Dash of Worchestershire sauce
- Dash of kirschwasser or calvados
- Dash of sherry vinegar
- Shaved truffles

Right: A half recipe makes the perfect amount of fondue for one hungry worshipper.

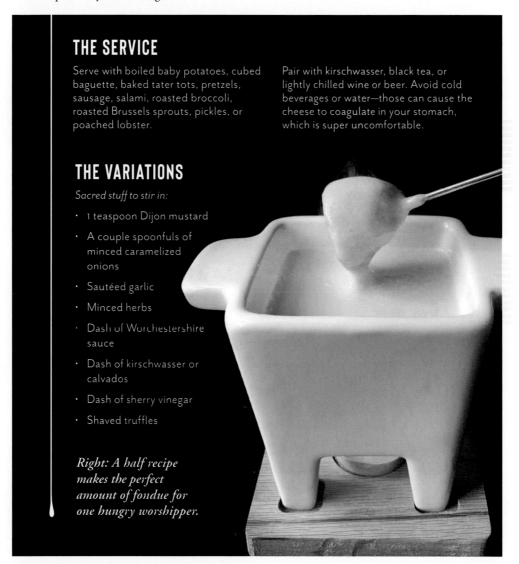

GOAT CHEESE CHEESECAKE

I love cheesecake, but sometimes I crave a real salty, cheesy flavor that transcends the humble cream cheese base. Fresh chèvre brings the complexity that too many cheesecakes lack. It's tangier, lighter, and less sweet, especially when perfumed with lemon zest and vanilla, which highlight that fresh, cheesy flavor.

THE CHEESUS

Use a good chèvre, as the flavor is really prominent. You don't want to ruin the cake with something gamey or chalky.

THE INGREDIENTS
Makes 1 cheesecake

FOR THE CRUST:

9 oz (255 g)	gingersnap cookies
2 T	sugar
¼ tsp	salt
6 T (75 g)	unsalted butter, melted

FOR THE FILLING:

16 oz (340 g)	fresh chèvre, room temperature
8 oz (170 g)	cream cheese
¾ C (100 g)	sugar
¼ tsp	salt
zest of 1	large lemon
2	large eggs, beaten
1 tsp	vanilla extract

THE RITUAL

MAKE THE CRUST:

➤ Preheat the oven to 350°F (175°C).

➤ Place the cookies in the bowl of a food processor and pulse until they resemble sand. Add the sugar and salt and pulse again to combine.

➤ Pour in the melted butter and pulse until the mixture is thoroughly moistened.

➤ Press the mixture into the bottom of a 9-inch (23-cm) springform pan. Use a glass or measuring cup with a flat bottom to ensure the mixture is evenly spread.

➤ Bake for 7 to 9 minutes, until the crust is slightly browned. Let cool.

MAKE THE FILLING:

➤ Preheat the oven to 400°F (205°C).

➤ In the bowl of a standing mixer, whisk together the goat cheese, cream cheese, sugar, salt, and lemon zest until smooth.

➤ In a mixing bowl, whisk together the eggs and vanilla. Pour the egg mixture into the cheese mixture and whisk to combine.

➤ Pour the filling into the crust. Bake 20 to 25 minutes, until the edges are golden but the center is still a little jiggly.

➤ Remove from the oven and cool to room temperature. If storing for later, cool completely (about 3 hours) before transferring to the fridge.

THE RITES

▶ **Use any cookie for the crust.** I like using gingersnaps, but you can use shortbread or chocolate cookies, too. Graham crackers are also great, but they're extra absorbent, so add an extra tablespoon of butter.

▶ **Keeps for 3 to 4 days in the fridge.**

CHEESECAKE: AN ANCIENT FOOD

Cheesecake dates back at least two thousand years. During agricultural holidays, the ancient Greeks would serve cheese-based cakes as bloodless sacrifices to the gods in the hopes of ensuring a fruitful harvest. The first cheesecake recipe was published in *De agri cultura* by the Roman agriculturist Marcus Porcius Cato. The manual also detailed recipes for cheese soufflés, puddings, and luxurious desserts known as placenta cake, which were enormous pastries filled with about 14 pounds (6.4 kg) of cheese and nearly 5 pounds (2kg) of honey.

Above: Goat Cheese Cheesecake

APPLE CAMEMBERT
CLAFOUTIS

Clafoutis is a simple French dessert similar to a giant pancake, served at room temperature and dusted with powdered sugar. It's traditionally made with just cherries, but I like sexing things up with whiskey-spiked apples and stinky Camembert, which creates pools of savory cheese. The French would call this nontraditional take a flaugnarde, but I prefer the ring of clafoutis, so désolée! This custardy goddess of funk is like a cheesed-up love child between a German apple pancake and the classic French recipe.

THE CHEESUS

Use a real Camembert from Normandy, which has an unmatched savory funk, rather than tasting like mild butter. For extra flavor, leave the rind on.

THE INGREDIENTS
Serves 4

FOR THE BATTER:

1 C (240 ml) whole milk

3 eggs

3 T unsalted butter, melted

1 tsp vanilla extract

½ C (80 g) all-purpose or pastry flour

¾ C (135 g) sugar

pinch salt

(continues opposite page)

THE RITUAL

➤ Put a 10-inch (25-cm) pie plate or oven-safe skillet in the oven and preheat to 375°F (190°C).

➤ Make the batter: In a blender, combine the milk, eggs, butter, vanilla, flour, sugar, and salt until smooth. Set aside.

➤ Make the filling: Melt the butter in a separate skillet over medium heat. Add the apples, whiskey, and spices. Stir and cook until the apples are soft and the whiskey is absorbed, about 5 minutes.

➤ Remove the pie plate from the oven and immediately pour in half the batter from the blender.

➤ Evenly spoon the apple slices over the batter. Then pour the remaining batter over the apples.

➤ Arrange slices of Camembert on top of the batter, pushing the slices down a bit so they're partially submerged.

➤ Bake until the clafoutis is golden and set in the center, about 40 minutes.

➤ Remove from the oven and cool for at least 15 minutes. Finish with powdered sugar and serve.

THE RITES

➤ **For a more tender bake,** let the batter rest at least 30 minutes or overnight before baking.

➤ **This is best served the day it's made,** but it keeps up to 3 days when stored in an airtight container in the fridge.

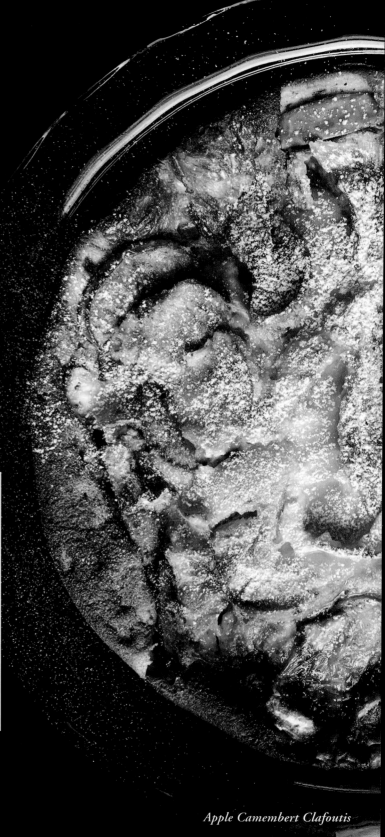

THE
INGREDIENTS
continued

FOR THE FILLING:

1 T	unsalted butter
3 to 4 (about 1 lb)	small, tart apples such as Granny Smith, peeled, cored and sliced
2 T	bourbon or other delicious whiskey
½ tsp	cinnamon
⅛ tsp	nutmeg
⅛ tsp	ground cloves
6 oz (170 g)	Camembert, cut evenly into ¼-inch-thick (6-mm) slices
	powdered sugar, for finishing

THE SERVICE

Pair with a chilled Riesling or sparkling wine.

THE VARIATIONS

Swap out the Camembert and apples for the following. Keep these fruits fresh; they're delicate and don't require sauteeing before they bake.

- Pitted cherries + Brie
- Sliced peaches + blue
- Raspberries + chèvre

Apple Camembert Clafoutis

DARK CHOCOLATE
GOAT CHEESE TRUFFLES

These goat cheese truffles are as luxurious as silk lingerie. They taste just as indulgent as a classic ganache truffle, but with a fluffy, tangy center. This recipe takes little more skill than making a cheese ball. There's only about thirty minutes of real effort involved and zero expertise needed, but you'll feel like a master chocolatier.

THE CHEESUS

Fluffy chèvre makes these truffles much lighter than traditional ganache-based ones.

THE INGREDIENTS

Makes about 12 truffles

6 oz (170 g)	fresh goat cheese, room temperature
2 T	cocoa powder
3 T	honey
½ tsp	salt
1 T	almond butter
½ tsp	cinnamon
1 tsp	cardamom
10 oz (280 g)	dark chocolate chips
	flaky salt, for garnish

THE RITUAL

- In a medium mixing bowl, whisk together the goat cheese, cocoa, salt, honey, almond butter, and spices until thoroughly combined.

- Let chill in the fridge until firm, about 30 minutes.

- Scoop the cheese mixture with a melon baller or a teaspoon and roll in your hands to make evenly sized balls.

- Place onto a baking sheet lined with wax or parchment paper. Chill in the fridge until firm, about 30 more minutes.

- Set up a double boiler: fill a medium saucepan with water one-third of the way and place over medium-low heat. Place a small heat-proof bowl inside.

- Pour the chocolate chips into the small bowl and melt, stirring every so often.

- Turn off the heat and use two spoons to lower the truffles into the melted chocolate, twirl them until they're coated, and place them back onto the wax paper. Repeat with all of the truffles.

- Sprinkle with flaky salt and let sit at room temperature until the shells are hard.

THE RITES

- **The extra fat and sweet, nutty flavor** of nut butter balances the tangy chèvre. Use anything from peanut butter to cashew butter.

- **I'm all for the darkest, richest chocolate,** but you can use whatever suits your fancy.

Dark Chocolate Goat Cheese Truffles

THE SERVICE

Pair with a glass of bubbles.

THE VARIATIONS

- Substitute ½ teaspoon of matcha powder for the cocoa powder, skip the spices, and try it with cashew butter and white chocolate. Finish with black sesame seeds.

- Substitute maple syrup for the honey, and try it with pecan butter. Finish with cinnamon.

- Skip the spices and try it with peanut butter and milk chocolate. Finish with chopped peanuts.

SWEET CHEESUS
7 PERFECT DESSERT BITES

An elaborate dessert may be an impressive, ritualistic end to a meal, but if you've already labored over an appetizer and main course, you might not have it in you to do all that. And that's OK, because Cheesus has your back. Let these composed bites be your no-fuss mistresses of dessert.

The following 7 perfect pairings are as simple as blessing a sweet treat with the salty body of Cheesus. They're classic flavor combinations, each dressed to impress with that wow factor, yet without involving the chore of actually baking something. Use the serving size guide on page 211 to portion, and when in doubt, make extra. No one can resist one more bite of sweet Cheesus.

THE RITES

- ► **Use a base strong and sturdy enough** to support the toppings.
- ► **Assemble just before serving** so they don't get soggy.

THE RITUAL

PISTACHIOS + SHORTBREAD + RICOTTA + HONEY + ROSE PETALS

Roughly chop the pistachios. Spread the ricotta over the shortbread and top with pistachios, honey, and rose petals.

RICE CRISPY TREATS + PURPLE HAZE GOAT CHEESE + DRIED CALENDULA PETALS

Slice the rice crispy treats in half horizontally. Spread with the Purple Haze, then top with calendula petals.

LEMON COOKIES + BLUEBERRY JAM + TRIPLE-CREAM BRIE + FRESH THYME

Dollop each cookie with blueberry jam and lay thinly sliced Brie on top. Finish with a few thyme leaves.

AGED GOUDA + CHOCOLATE CRINKLE COOKIES + SEA SALT

Chip crumbles off the Gouda, and gently push into the center of the cookie. Garnish with sea salt.

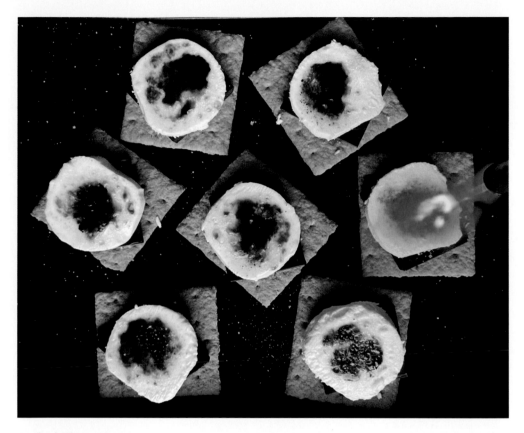

Brûléed Chèvre S'mores

GORGONZOLA DOLCE + ALMOND COOKIES + PEAR PRESERVES + ROSEMARY

Spread the Gorgonzola onto the cookies. Dollop with pear preserves and garnish with two rosemary leaves.

LUXARDO CHERRIES + SMOKED BLUE CHEESE + GINGERSNAPS

Cut the cherries in half. Thinly slice the blue, letting it crumble at will. Layer cheese atop the gingersnap and top with a cherry half.

BRÛLÉED CHÈVRE S'MORES: GRAHAM CRACKERS + DARK CHOCOLATE + FRESH CHÈVRE + SUGAR

Top each graham cracker piece with a chocolate square and set aside. Slice the chèvre log into 8 coins. Place one coin on top of each chocolate square. Sprinkle each coin with sugar, making sure to fully coat the top. Use a brûlée torch to sear each coin until the top bubbles and crisps. Serve and enjoy.

A HOLY TRINITY OF
SAUCY SAVIORS

There's a dizzying variety of jams, sauces, and spreads out there, and some are so delicious it's damn near sinful. I usually prefer to buy an artisanal accompaniment because they're often better than what I can make at home, but this threesome is the exception. They bring a sizzle of flavor to anything they touch, whether they're blessing a recipe or lubing up a body of Cheesus. Of course, you can buy a premade version of these, but it's hard to compare to the sensual pleasures of making them yourself.

FIG & ONION JAM *Makes 1 cup (240 ml)*

I've never met a body of Cheesus that didn't get down with a fig and onion jam. The perfect mix of savory and sweet, it soothes and enhances the symphony of salty flavors within any body of Cheesus. It's truly my ride-or-die condiment, and it's as simple as mixing caramelized onions into fig jam. Seriously.

1 tsp olive oil + 1 medium Spanish onion, sliced razor thin + pinch of salt + ¾ cup (180 ml) fig jam

Make the onions: In a skillet, heat the olive oil over medium-low. Add the onion and sprinkle with a pinch of salt. Toss to combine. Cook the onions, stirring occasionally, until deep brown and caramelized, about 20 minutes. Let cool.

Roughly chop the onions, then add to the fig jam. Stir to combine and enjoy.

- ▶ Keeps for about 1 week in the fridge.
- ▶ Pair with blue cheese on a pizza, Gruyère on a grilled cheese, or spoon over Brie and bake until bubbly.

BALSAMIC GLAZE *Makes 1 cup (240 ml)*

Thick, sweet, and deeply tangy, balsamic glaze is eager to add a syrupy zip to platters, sandwiches, pizza—honestly, pretty much anything. This gal is one of those accompaniments that deserves a permanent spot in your pantry. You can always buy it premade, but why bother when it's so easy to make yourself?

16 oz good balsamic vinegar + good honey (optional)

In a saucepan, bring the vinegar to a simmer over medium heat. Let it reduce by half, about 10 to 15 minutes, depending on the vinegar. It should still look a little watery because it will continue to thicken. Turn off the heat and let cool completely. Give it a taste. If it's too tangy, stir in a little honey to even it out. Transfer to a squeeze bottle or a jar with a tight-fitting lid.

- ▶ Store in a cool dark place. If you use real balsamic, it should last months in your pantry or years in your fridge.
- ▶ Pair with Parmigiano-Reggiano or drizzle over a salad of tomatoes, arugula, and mozzarella.

KATH'S FAMOUS PESTO *Makes 2 cups (480 ml)*

Pesto is one of those essential condiments that belongs everywhere. Not only is it amazing alongside cheese, it's also made with cheese. This is my mom's version, and it's a little different than the classic, but it's hands down the best pesto I've ever eaten.

½ cup pine nuts + 2 to 3 garlic cloves + 2 cups (80 g) tightly packed basil leaves + 1 cup (50 g) tightly packed parsley leaves + 1 cup (85 g) Parmigiano, grated + 1½ tsp kosher salt + 1 tsp freshly ground black pepper + 1 cup (240ml) extra-virgin olive oil

Heat a medium skillet over medium-low. Add the pine nuts and toast, stirring occasionally, until browned, about 5 minutes.

In the bowl of a food processor, combine the toasted nuts and the garlic. Pulse until smooth.

Add the basil, parsley, Parmigiano, salt, and pepper. Pulse to combine.

Pour the olive oil in slowly, pulsing as you go.

Taste and add extra salt to taste.

▶ Keeps for about 1 week in the fridge, or 6 months in the freezer.

▶ Serve on pasta, sandwiches, baked Brie, etc.

Clockwise from top left: Balsamic Glaze with Manchego; Kath's Famous Pesto; Fig and Onion Jam on a cracker with Alpha Toleman and a fried onion

Epilogue

I hope this tome not only helps you worship our savior, Cheesus, but also awakens a new appreciation for the history and labors of love that have come together to bring Her to your altar. By allowing Cheesus to pleasure your palate and bless your bod, you are participating in this grand economy and long-standing tradition. Every wedge or wheel purchased is an offerring to the Church of Cheesus.

This is only the beginning of your journey. *A Bible for the Cheese Obsesssed* merely scratches the surface of the many forms of Cheesus and the ways to worship Them. These pages are limited to the bodies I know, the pairings and recipes I love, and the rituals I employ. Find yourself a trusted cheesemonger and let them guide you toward new and exciting bodies of Cheesus and ways to worship. When you travel, explore the local cheese offerings. While this book focuses on easily found cheeses from North America and Europe, there are bodies to be discovered across the globe. It's up to you to continue your education from here, and spread the holy curd word far and wide. Try all the cheese, get wild with pairings, share it all with your loved ones, and never stop worshipping.

May Cheesus bless your bod,
forever and always. Amen.

ACKNOWLEDGMENTS

First and foremost, thank you to my design genius, generous hype girl, and bible godmother, Jen Quinn. You are the reason why this book exists. You pushed me to write it, brought me into the Indelible Editions family, and made it look so damn fierce! You've fully understood my vision from day one, and I deeply value the talent and time you've poured into this book.

Thank you to the whole team at Indelible Editions. Dinah, you pulled this whole project along, secured the publishing house of my dreams, made me feel like a superstar even when I was panicking, and made it all look so seamless. A special shout-out to Carol and Andrea for providing your expertise and input. I know all of you worked so hard to bring out the best in this book. I'm so excited to see what we create together next.

Thank you to everyone at Abrams for taking a chance on my dark and slutty little cheese book. You leaned into my weirdness, and even pushed me to further indulge in the gothic glamour. Laura, Glenn, and everyone who edited, proofread, and edited again, thank you so much for bringing out the best possible version of this book. You're the best!

This book is for the cheesemakers, dairy farmers, mongers, distributors, delivery drivers, and worshippers who spend their time, labor, and money on the miracle that is Cheesus. Thank you to anyone who has bought my merch, double-tapped my posts, or bought tickets to my events. Thank you to my cheese fam for understanding my mission, encouraging me, and telling your customers about my blog. A special thank you to Andy Hatch for letting me visit Uplands during a pandemic, and to both Mateo Kehler and Pat Polowsky for letting me steal your precious time and invaluable expertise.

Thank you to the many, many incredible prophets and disciples who have shaped our industry. I hope this book excites a whole new wave of cheese sluts who fall hopelessly in love like the rest of us have. There are no people like cheese people. May our reign be long and prosperous.

I would never have written this book if it weren't for all the people who started my cheese career, especially Tenaya Darlington, a.k.a. Madame Fromage. Your writings led me to buy my first cheese book, apply to work at my local cheese shop, and start my own cheese blog. Thank you to the folks at Pastoral for giving me the foundational knowledge that set my career on this track. To my favorite boss, Matt Whalen, you're the one who said, "Food is my religion, and cheese is my church." I can never properly thank you for what that meant to me.

My greatest blessing is my circle of family and friends. Thank you to my mom for teaching me the importance of great food, especially when homecooked, and for patiently testing my recipes. Thank you for letting me publish your sacred pesto recipe, too. Thank you to my dad for teaching me everything I know about wine, and helping me with the beverage pairings in this book. You've both always supported my creativity, even when it was weird. Thank you to my whole family for leaning into my cheese preaching and greeting my platters with such enthusiasm. I'm so lucky to have you.

To my chosen family, thank you for your honest feedback, endless support, and incredible taste. Writing this book during a pandemic was intense, and all of my friends kept me going, especially my pod people, Danielle, Adrienne, and Sophia. I love you all so much and I don't know how I'll ever repay you. Special shout-out to my cat, Chandler, who took the brunt of my emotional neediness. You're the cutest of all the cheese sluts.

Finally, to my loving partner, Jacob, the Jeffrey to my Ina. Thank you for everything: coming up with the original concept for Cheese Sex Death, editing my blog posts and many parts of this book, taste-testing every pairing and recipe, constantly reassuring me, taking care of me, drying my tears, rubbing my back, and believing in me unconditionally, especially when I was ready to give up on all of it. Don't tell Cheesus, but you're the true love of my life.

RESOURCES

The Art of the Cheese Plate by Tia Keenan

The Book of Cheese by Liz Thorpe

Cheddar: A Journey to the Heart of America's Most Iconic Cheese by Gordon Edgar

Cheese and Culture by Paul Kindstedt

The Cheese Plate by Max McCalman and David Gibbons

Cheese Primer by Steven Jenkins

Cheese Science Toolkit (cheesescience.org) from Pat Polowsky

Cheese Slices hosted by Will Studd

The Complete Encyclopedia of French Cheese by Pierre Androuët

Cooked by Michael Pollan

DiBruno Bros. House of Cheese by Tenaya Darlington

Mastering Cheese by Max McCalman and David Gibbons

The Oxford Companion to Cheese edited by Catherine Donnelly

CREDITS

Boaz Walker/Good Pepper, 15, 133, 220, 221

John Jennings, 10, 11

Shutterstock.com: Alexander_P, 51, 52, 225; AllNikArt, 82, 83; Alyona Bekleshova, 44; Annie Dove, 142; ArtMari, 20; Artur Balytskyi, 126; AVA Bitter, 20, 39, 42; AVIcon, 275; AZ Outdoor Photography, 70; Bildagentur Zoonar GmbH, 68; Bodor Tivadar, 39; Brum, 71; bsd, 202; Cameron Watson, 66; cgterminal, 127, 190, 212; chempina, 50; DianaFinch, 278; Dn Br, 40; Drawlab19, 142; Elena Pimonova, 109, 127, 190, 191, 143; EngravingFactory, 20; Everilda, 46; Evgenia.B, 51; Fischer Fotostudio, 37, 45; Flipser, 177; frescomovie, 138; FrimuFilms, 42, 43, 192; funnybear36, 300; Galina Sorokina, 86, 87; Hein Nouwens, 16, 17; howcolour, 275; ilonitta, 20; intueri, 39; Johnny14, 127, 215; Kallayanee Naloka, 55; Kamieshkova, 180; Kazakova Maryia, 55; Komleva, 43; Lubov Chipurko, 60, 61, 109, 184; m2art, 48; Maisei Raman, 50; mamita, 20, 39; Mary Volvach, 145, 216; monkographic, 236; MoreVector, 37; Morphart Creation, 27, 29, 41, 43, 57, 73, 98, 115, 130, 142, 164; Nadiinko, 18, 19, 275; Nadya_Art, 221; Natalya Levish, 45, 302; NikWB, 178; Oxima, 122; Palau, 208; Pinchuk Oleksandra, 276; provector, 234; RIMM_Art, 45; Robyn Mackenzie, 154; RP designs, 55; SAXANA-art, 165; Sebastian Knight, 44; Skeleton Icon, 174, 175, 178; Sketch Master, 51, 57; soniazhel, 165; sweet marshmallow, 53; the Proicon, 17; T VECTOR ICONS, 275; valrylar, 56; Vectorgoods studio, 32, 51, 90, 91, 143, 190, 191, 210, 212, 215; Vera Petruk, 40; Very_Very, 37; Victoria Sergeeva, 91; Vonts, 218; Voropaev Vasiliy, 40; Vorobiov Oleksii 8, 41; WinWin artlab, 138; Yaroslava D, 109, 127, 165, 212; Yevheniia Lytvynovych, 56; Yuravector, 272

Index

About the Author

Erika Kubick is a monger-turned-preacher and founder of Cheese Sex Death, where she advocates for the good curd word through sultry cheese porn, educational church services, and more. She lives in Chicago with her partner, Jacob, and her cat, Chandler. This is her first book. Visit CheeseSexDeath.com and follow @CheeseSexDeath to take yourself to Cheese Church.